A Century of Controversy

A Century of Controversy
Constitutional Reform in Alabama

EDITED BY BAILEY THOMSON

THE UNIVERSITY OF ALABAMA PRESS
Tuscaloosa and London

Typeface is Minion

∞

The paper on which this book is printed meets the minimum
requirements of American National Standard for Information
Science–Permanence of Paper for Printed Library Materials, ANSI
Z39.48-1984.

Library of Congress Cataloging-in-Publication Data

Thomson, Bailey, 1949–
  A century of controversy : constitutional reform in Alabama /
edited by Bailey Thomson
     p. cm. —
  ISBN 0-8173-1218-8 (pbk. : alk. paper)
1. Constitutional history—Alabama. 2. Law reform—Alabama
History. I. Thomson, Bailey, 1949–. II. Title.
KFA401.5 .C46 2002
342.761/029 21
2002004775

British Library Cataloguing-in-Publication Data available

Contents

Introduction

Bailey Thomson

ALABAMA'S VOTERS elected James E. Folsom in 1946 as a new kind of governor—one who did not have close ties to powerful interest groups such as the Farm Bureau. Big Jim, who stood six feet, eight inches tall, campaigned with a string band called the Strawberry Pickers, which would warm up the crowds in school auditoriums or courthouse squares. Then Folsom would take the microphone and hold up a corn-shuck mop, promising to clean out Montgomery. He liked to talk about letting a "cool, green breeze" blow through the capitol. Rural folks understood him. In their lifetime, nobody in Montgomery had paid much attention to their needs. In his plain, rustic speech, Big Jim articulated what his supporters wanted. He promised to build new roads and provide better schools. Old people would have small pensions, and teachers would earn adequate pay. Above all, Folsom maintained that citizens should rule, not the plantation owners and industrialists who traditionally ran things in Montgomery. He believed in the common people of Alabama, and for a while at least, they believed in him.

Big Jim didn't make excuses for the state. And more important, he didn't appeal to racial prejudice to win votes—something many politicians did in the South. Rather, Folsom tried to explain to people that Alabama—under the rule of the planters and Birmingham's "Big Mules"—had inflicted much of its backwardness upon itself. The state's biggest impediment to progress, he said, was the 1901 Alabama Constitution—the source of the ruling elite's power. This document tied the hands of elected leaders, especially at the local level, and its stingy tax system starved services such as public schools.

Just a few weeks after taking office in 1947, Big Jim called the legislature into special session to demand it approve a constitutional convention. He knew that Alabama could not fulfill its potential without a modern set of fundamental laws to guide the state. His powerful opponents laughed at his request. They controlled the legislature and had no intention of replacing a constitution that had served their interests well since 1901.

Still, Folsom kept pitching for reform. He made some of his best arguments in a radio address on April 3, 1949. The main purpose of the 1901 constitution, he told his listeners, was to deny the ballot to Alabama's black citizens. But the document's many voting restrictions, especially a punitive poll tax, had disfranchised poor whites as well. Thus the 1901 constitution was profoundly racist and antidemocratic, and contrary to the values that Americans had just fought to protect in World War II.

Next, Folsom decried how the state's constitution made no provision for allowing local people to govern themselves. Instead, legislators passed local laws for counties, often swapping favors among themselves to promote pet legislation. Indeed, the constitution so distrusted government at all levels that it impeded progress and the creation of good jobs. For example, it forbade the state from engaging in internal improvements. Counties could not lend their credit to any industrial prospects. To get around such restrictions, voters had approved seventy-four amendments, Folsom said. Remember, he was speaking in 1949.

Finally, the governor said, the constitution enshrined an unfair tax system that afforded certain groups special privileges while denying the state adequate revenues. This practice violated the principle that each should pay according to his means. Big Jim concluded: "I believe that the progress we have made in the past 50 years will be many times surpassed during the half century ahead if we do not remain hide-bound by old-fashioned laws. And certainly the greatest single need toward that progress is a new constitution."[1]

More than fifty years after Folsom made those remarks, Alabamians still labor under the restrictions and legacy of the 1901 constitution. The progress they have made toward correcting the document's worst features has often come through federal action. For example, the courts finally forced the legislature to reapportion itself in the early 1970s, thereby giving urban areas fair representation. After a long and bloody struggle, blacks finally regained their franchise in Alabama through the federal Voting Rights Act of 1965.

Unfortunately, other problems that Folsom identified remain embedded within the state's fundamental law. And as Alabama's population grows and global competition increases, the debilitating weaknesses of the 1901 constitution become more acute. Alabama, for example, still denies its counties the power to write their own laws. In fact, Alabama is the only southeastern state that fails to grant counties planning authority.

Meanwhile, the 1901 constitution has ballooned to 315,000 words—the longest in the nation by far, and probably the most difficult to read and understand. This document has *706* amendments—nearly ten times the number of amendments that Big Jim Folsom complained about in 1949.

As Alabamians look outward to the world in the twenty-first century, they face the intense challenges of global competition, where knowledge is the most valuable asset. And as they look inward at their communities, they often see the consequences of poor or non-existent planning. In truth, they are passing the costs of sprawl, pollution, and similar hazards to their children. What great corporation would dare go forward under a mission statement that looked back to a time that will never come again? What great company would tie the hands of its leaders just as crises loom on the horizon?

But there is hope. Just as Big Jim Folsom wanted Alabamians to do, citizens have begun to contemplate a new state constitution—one that would allow them to throw off the shackles of a shameful and mean-spirited past and encourage economic growth, good education, and government close to the people. Today, a reform movement is gathering momentum. And its leaders fully understand the need to generate support both at the top, beginning with the governor, *and* at the grass roots, where the citizens are.

In fact, this bottom-up approach is the great difference between the current reform effort and the failed attempts of a long line of Alabama governors, including Folsom. Constitutional reform has become an important issue in Alabama precisely because a large number of citizens want a voice in shaping their state's future. Groups such as civic clubs and chambers of commerce have a key role to play in this process. Far more than any special interest, they represent the heartbeat of Alabama.

The authors of the essays in this volume wish to share with citizens the knowledge and insights they have gained from investigating issues related to Alabama's antiquated constitution. No one expects a citizen to acquire a specialist's grasp of state constitutional issues. The functioning of democracy does not require such scholarly expertise. But citizens do need to understand how their constitution came about and the consequences it has produced. They also need to know the choices they have in writing a modern replacement.

My own epiphany about the 1901 constitution occurred more than thirty years ago when I was an undergraduate at the University of Alabama. As a history student, I was taking my first class with an African-American instructor. And I was studying the violent period leading up the disfranchisement of Alabama's black citizens. I wrote a paper on the state's Sayre Election Law, which was a precursor to the 1901 constitution's assault on voting rights. With the help of books and articles by historians such as Auburn University's Malcolm McMillan, I grasped the enormity of what the constitution's framers perpetrated on my native state as they sought to consolidate their elite rule. Those lessons never left me. When I returned to Alabama in 1992 as a journalist with the *Mobile Register,* I resumed my interest in Alabama's history and saw connections to present difficulties that beset the state, such as poorly funded schools, a tyrannical tax system, and unchecked urban sprawl. And always at the center of any such investigation loomed the 1901 constitution, still in force.

I think it's time to quit making excuses for Alabama. Big Jim Folsom had his agenda right when he called for a new state constitution to put this state on the right course. With a new constitution, Alabama can make amends for past injustices while inviting its citizens to look over the mountain to a better future. Thus I commend these essays in hopes that each reader will sense the potential that lies within this state. Yes, any attempt to write a new constitution will meet with many obstacles and much cynicism—particularly from those who benefit unfairly from the current system. But I am reminded of an old proverb which says that for any great undertaking, the first step is always the most difficult.

Notes

1. "Radio Address on the Need for a Constitutional Convention, April 3, 1949," in *Speeches of Gov. James E. Folsom, 1947–1950* (Wetumpka, Ala.: Wetumpka Printing Co., n.d.), 132.

A Century of Controversy

1

The Populist Revolt in Alabama

Prelude to Disfranchisement

Samuel L. Webb

THE CONSERVATIVE DEMOCRATS who wrote and supported the ratification of the 1901 Alabama Constitution were not trying merely to "restrict" voting rights. Since the end of Reconstruction, they had been faced with one political revolt after another against their party. Each time, the Democrats won by limiting the political rights of their opponents. In the 1890s, however, the opposition became so intense, and white men were so divided, that Democrats decided to take a more extreme step: they sought in 1901, through a new state constitution, to end democracy itself in Alabama by eliminating their opponents.

Only by taking a step backward into the 1890s, by examining that turbulent time and the nature of the opposition, can Alabamians in the twenty-first century understand what led conservative Democrats to make this decision. Events of the 1890s, often called the "Populist Revolt," also reveal how close Alabama came to actual revolution.

On the first Tuesday in August 1894, for example, Alabama voters were supposed to choose their state and local officials in the first of two general elections. In many parts of the state, however, there was such extraordinary tension that violence lurked just beneath the surface. Two years earlier, the state's ruling Democratic Party, in a desperate effort to hold onto the governorship and other state offices, had engaged in widespread ballot box fraud and outright theft in deflecting a serious challenge from a coalition of three opposition parties.

In Conecuh County, one of the few southern Alabama counties where the anti-Democratic opposition controlled the county government, the sheriff and the probate judge were taking no chances in 1894. Guards armed with shotguns and Winchester rifles surrounded the county courthouse at Evergreen to protect local ballot boxes from state Democratic officials until local election supervisors could publicly announce the results. Armed men guarded returning officers from various precincts as they brought ballot boxes into the courthouse, and ballots were locked in the county jail. Opposition candidates won in Conecuh County, but Democratic candidates for governor and other state offices triumphed again. Opposition leaders argued that another state election had been stolen by Democrats, and strong evidence backed up their assertions. In Black Belt counties, where African Americans made up more than three-quarters of the total voting population, Democrats had stolen the votes of black citizens to win the election. Some members of the opposition parties vowed to participate in a "Winchester" revolution to restore democracy to Alabama.[1]

On November 6, 1894, the day of Alabama's general election to choose federal officials, a shooting war broke out when Democratic Party officials at Shelby County's Harpersville precinct refused to allow the Populist Party to have an official observe the counting of ballots. Each side charged the other with starting the carnage, but Democratic voting officials were firing out of the polling place while Populists shot into it. When the battle ended, one man lay dead and several others severely wounded. Populist Party leaders John W. Pitts and his son John Singleton Pitts, members of one of the most respected and politically active families in the county, were charged with murder.[2]

Only a month after the Shelby County fracas, the state faced the possibility that the revolution might actually occur. Minutes before William C. Oates, a former congressman and Confederate hero, was scheduled to take the oath of office as governor of Alabama on the capitol steps in Montgomery, about two hundred men, all leaders of the Populist or other parties that had jointly opposed Oates's election, marched up Dexter Avenue toward the capitol. Outgoing governor Thomas Goode Jones, standing with Oates, watched the procession with growing anxiety. The marchers knew that Oates had been illegally elected and that the candidate of their coalition, Reuben F. Kolb, should be the next governor. In fact, they had already visited a justice of the peace who had administered the oath of office to Kolb. The marchers knew that the election of 1892 had also been stolen from Kolb by the Democrats and that Jones should never have been inaugurated either. A Populist newspaper editor expressed the attitude of thousands of Alabamians when he wrote that the state's people were "but slaves to a despotism of fraud and political serfdom as intolerable as were the chains that bound the black man to the slave auction block." As the angry men began their ascent up the slope toward the inaugural ceremony, they found members of the Alabama state militia waiting on them, and Kolb was refused permission to address the inaugural crowd. Outmanned and outgunned, the protesters went over to a side street, where Kolb climbed on a mule-drawn wagon and spoke to his supporters, encouraging them not to pay their state taxes as a way to protest the denial of the right to cast a fair ballot. Oates went on to serve as governor, but the revolt against the Democrats that led to the march was far from over.[3]

In November 1894 a coalition of candidates from the Populist, Jeffersonian Democratic, and Republican Parties had rallied to defeat the ruling Democratic Party in several congressional elections despite the corrupt practices of the latter. Milford Howard, a Populist candidate, was elected to the U.S. Congress by polling an astounding two-thirds of the vote in the Seventh Congressional District. Meanwhile, a candidate of the Jeffersonian Democratic Party was sent to Washington from the Fifth District. Several months later, Congress overturned an ostensible victory by the Democratic Party in the Sixth District by declaring that the election there was stolen from the Republican candidate.

Alabama's Democrats were in trouble, and they knew it. Their blatant efforts to stifle the opposition parties had not entirely succeeded. November's elections made it clear that they would have to sully their precious honor in future elections, and they knew that more vote stealing was likely to lead to more violence.[4]

This uprising in the 1890s against the Democrats was part of the last true grassroots political movement in United States history. By no means confined to Alabama, the movement was led by southern and western farmers suffering from a combination of low prices and the inability to obtain credit on reasonable terms. This agrarian distress was intensified in Alabama both by smoldering anger over how Democratic Party leaders had unfairly controlled the state's political processes since the end of Reconstruction and by sectional rivalries that had existed almost since the beginning of statehood. Thus economic, political, and sectional disharmony all shaped Alabama's post-Reconstruction political atmosphere. Still, if farmers had been able to make a living in the late nineteenth century, a revolt would have been unlikely.

Prior to the Civil War, most southern farmers had been a self-sufficient group who worked small plots of land with family members, raised food crops and stock that fed the family, and, unlike their large planter neighbors, rarely sold anything at the marketplace. After the war, finding their farms and homes in dilapidated condition and needing an infusion of cash to get started again, farmers throughout the South jumped into the business of growing cotton. The low cost of starting a cotton farm, a rise in cotton prices in the late 1860s, and the growth of new railroads to haul the crop led many into the marketplace. Cotton prices began to fall in the early 1870s, however, and with little interruption they fell for the next twenty years. Increasingly dependent upon credit for survival, farmers borrowed supplies and money from merchants or large landowners at high interest rates. When prices did not rebound, the farmers had to sell their land, mortgage it, or give liens on their crops as collateral. Former landowners soon became tenant farmers, paying cash or a share of their crops to rent the land they had worked so hard to make productive. Heirs to the Jeffersonian ideal that the only truly free citizens in a republic were independent landowners, many viewed this form of existence as a form of servitude.[5]

As the economic walls closed in on these rural southerners, many of them despaired. For them farming was not merely a business, but a way of life that created a culture that had nourished their families for generations. The prospect of giving up their farms to work in textile or lumber mills, or perhaps to become coal miners, meant relinquishing their traditional ways and entering a precarious existence where employers would control their lives even more than merchants and landlords did. Looking to restore their independence and protect their culture, they joined farm organizations that promised them hope. The most important of these was the Southern Farmers' Alliance.[6]

The Alliance began in Texas and achieved successes there by the mid-1880s. The Texans sent lecturers across the South and West to form new Alliance chapters and train additional lecturers to appeal to even more farmers. Alliance leaders hoped to break the hold that a "system of finance capitalism," concentrated in "eastern commercial banks," had on the agricultural economy. After the Civil War there was little money in the South. Instead, money was concentrated outside the region in New York, Boston, Philadelphia, and Baltimore banks. Southern landlords and supply merchants borrowed heavily from northeastern bankers, who controlled the nation's credit system and dictated the interest rates charged in all parts of the country. Capitalist forces in the Northeast used their political clout in the national government to maximize their growing economic advantages over other regions. Farmers' Alliance leaders hoped to reform and decentralize the nation's credit system, and they asked their members to join cooperative ventures that would free them from dependence on loans from people who were financed by northeastern bankers. Lecturers called on farmers to pool their resources, create their own mercantile stores, start credit agencies that would lend them money at low interest rates, and even manufacture the products they needed.[7]

Alliance lecturers also aimed their rhetorical fire at merchants who charged usurious interest rates, at the system that demanded that farmers give liens on their crops, at the power of monopoly corporations, and at the railroads' unreasonable warehouse and freight charges. The Alliance supported strong antitrust laws and government ownership of the railroads and telegraph lines, but its most insistent demands concerned the nation's currency and credit system. Calling on the federal government to print and distribute greenback dollars without regard to whether this paper money was backed by gold, Alliance leaders charged that using the nation's gold supply as a standard for measuring the amount of money allowed into the economy starved the country of badly needed currency, drove interest rates too high, and made it impossible for farmers to obtain credit. The Alliance's program included a call for both the coining of silver and the increased mining of silver to expand the money supply.[8]

The centerpiece of the Farmers' Alliance program was the subtreasury plan, which called for the creation of federal crop warehouses in every county that yielded more than $500,000 worth of agricultural produce. Farmers could store nonperishable crops such as cotton, tobacco, rice, wheat, and oats in these subtreasuries, wait up to a year for the price to reach a higher level before selling, and receive a subtreasury certificate of deposit allowing them to borrow up to 80 percent of the local market price of their product upon storage. This program would allow farmers to circumvent creditors in the South who were controlled by banks in the Northeast. Some referred to the Alliance movement and its hope for a more flexible currency and credit system as the "revolt against the East." By 1889, more than 125,000 farmers in Alabama had joined.[9]

Southern Alliance proposals seemed dangerously radical to the men who dominated the state's economic system. These merchants and landlords were active in local and state affairs of the Democratic Party, and if the Alliance hoped to accomplish its goals it would have to enter politics and exercise power in that party or take control of it. Since the end of Reconstruction the Democrats' statewide leaders had been a group of wealthy, elite men known popularly as the "Bourbons." Whether they were large Black Belt planters, directors of railroads, corporation lawyers, or leaders of Alabama's growing iron and steel industry, Bourbons had one common interest: they wanted to control the tenant farmers, sharecroppers, farm laborers, textile workers, lumber millhands, coal and iron ore miners, and workers in iron and steel mills who produced the wealth for the state's upper classes. Thus Bourbon Democrats served the state's economic hierarchy. They knew that if they lost control of state government laws governing landlord-tenant and master-servant relationships, agricultural liens, mortgages, interest rates, banking, and other important economic matters might be changed to their disadvantage by the state's laboring classes. They could not let that happen.[10]

Even more important to Bourbons was the maintenance of the racial system of white supremacy. Most of Alabama's workers on farms, in the homes of whites, or in the mines and iron factories were black men and women. Controlling them and keeping them in a subordinate position was absolutely essential, and convincing the state's middle- and lower-class whites that blacks should be kept separate from and beneath them was necessary to achieve this goal. When the Southern Farmers' Alliance affiliated with and sometimes invited to its meetings members of the Colored Farmers' Alliance, the threat to the Bourbons' political and economic power became palpable. An opposition political movement that included small farmers and workers of both races might affect the Democrats.

Democrats believed that they had seen all of this before, and they knew how to deal with it.[11] From 1868 to 1870, and again from 1872 to 1874, during Reconstruction, the Republican Party controlled Alabama's state government. The great majority of newly freed blacks had become Republicans during Reconstruction because of the support that the party of Abraham Lincoln had given to their civil rights. Running as Republicans, black politicians were elected to Congress, the state legislature, and many local offices. They were joined in the Republican Party by a small group of whites, and this biracial group defeated the Democrats in a number of elections. Democrats developed an elaborate myth that portrayed Reconstruction Republican officeholders as corrupt, incompetent, and venal. In truth, the Republicans had been no more corrupt or incompetent than had most state governments of the era. But in 1874 the Democrats determined that they would take total control of Alabama's government again and that any means they used in doing so would be justified. Most whites in every region of the state agreed, and in the 1874 elections the Democrats used force, fraud, intimidation, and trickery at the polls to win. Barbour County's white Democrats literally stood with shotguns and stopped Republicans of both races from voting. Having "redeemed" the state in that famous election with the support of the great mass of Alabama's whites, Democratic Party leaders no doubt felt that they would be equally justified in using the same tactics if white supremacy or the rule of their party was ever endangered again.[12]

Democrats equated loyalty to their party with loyalty to the white race, and hence disloyalty meant racial treason. Democratic newspapers and orators warned that any break with the party, however slight, could divide white men and lead to a Republican victory and the return of biracial government.

Those who broke with their party, wrote one editor, were "enemies to the cause of good government and social order ... occupying a position false to themselves, to their country and to their God." But Democratic leaders were not just content to force white people within the confines of one political party. Because so many different groups of people would be under the party roof, there had to be unity within the party as well, and these efforts to enforce unity also helped to create the uprising of the 1890s. Bourbon Democrats created a system of nominating candidates calculated to control dissidents within their party's ranks.[13]

Only nominees of conventions authorized by the state Democratic Executive Committee could receive the party's blessing, and conventions were governed by rules that allowed elite groups to ensure that only safe candidates would be chosen. Those dissatisfied with the nominees had little choice but to vote Democratic, since otherwise they would be censured by their communities as traitors to the party of white supremacy. State conventions that nominated candidates for statewide office were completely under the Bourbons' control, and state party leaders also found ways to control conventions at the county level. The county conventions were "mass meetings" called by members of the local Democratic committee, who had few scruples about setting the date and time of the sessions so that their friends were available but it was inconvenient for backcountry farmers to come to town and attend. Town men, particularly lawyers and merchants, were nearly always in attendance. From the early 1870s to the 1890s, convention nominations rarely represented the sentiments of the great mass of citizens. A "few spirits work the wires and make up the conventions," wrote one dissident editor, and the people were asked to support candidates nominated by "intrigue." Since most whites felt compelled to vote for Democrats in the general election, the nomination system "bound them hand and foot," leaving them little choice in naming their leaders.[14]

Many Democrats were irritated by these practices. Too many men who wanted a chance to participate as candidates felt shut out of the political process, and there were too many issues over which Democrats disagreed for this kind of artificially enforced unity to prevail. In the late 1870s and throughout the 1880s, there were a variety of local revolts against Democratic rule. In a few counties, men who disagreed with the policies of the national and state Democratic Parties on credit and currency issues joined the Greenback-Labor Party, ran against the ruling Democrats, and achieved surprising successes. The most common kind of revolt, however, occurred at the county level, when men furious about the voting processes in local Democratic conventions decided to run in the general election as independents. These local uprisings occurred in every part of the state and were usually unsuccessful, but in the Hill Country of northern Alabama they were more numerous and victorious than in other areas. From 1876 through 1886, seventeen northern Alabama counties sent Greenback, independent, or Republican state legislators to Montgomery. In some counties in the Hill Country, Democrats were driven out of the courthouses, and independents or other parties controlled all local offices. Independent candidates often accepted the support of the Republican Party. Thus well before the 1890s, deeply held anger and resentment built up against Democratic Party leaders in the Hill Country, and it spilled over into the great revolt of that decade.

The Hill Country had chafed under Democratic rule ever since the Civil War, but differences between that region and the powerful Black Belt in southern Alabama had existed long before secession. This sectional division had more to do with socioeconomic differences than with mere geography. The Black Belt was blessed with rich soil, flat land, staple crop agriculture, and water transportation routes to economic marketplaces. The Hill Country was mountainous, rocky, more subject to soil erosion, and more isolated from market centers. These differences led to disparities between the two regions in the value of farmland, the economic and social class of the farming population, and the percentage of black population. In the antebellum period the Black Belt became the center of Alabama's plantation region, dominated by large landholders. Black slaves constituted the majority of the region's population. Most self-sufficient small farmers lived in the predominantly white Hill Country of northern Alabama or in the much smaller Wiregrass region in the southeastern corner of the state, where large plantations were rare.[15]

Political differences between the state's regions surfaced well before the Civil War when the Whig Party found its greatest support in the Black Belt and most Hill Country voters were staunch Jacksonian Democrats. Their "Jacksonianism" referred in part to their devotion to Andrew Jackson but more broadly to an ideology that became fixed in the popular mind of the Hill Country even before Jackson's presidency. The white yeoman farmers of northern Alabama were attracted to Jacksonian ideas because of their self-sufficient and individualistic view of the world and also because of their distrust of the lowland planters to their south. The Jacksonian ethos held that yeoman farmers were in a perpetual battle with elites who sought from the government special privileges that were unavailable to average people. Often operating secretly, these elites threatened the independence of small farmers by tempting politicians to pass laws that benefited wealthy private interests and corporations.[16]

The principle of "equal rights for all and special privileges to none" was the central tenet of Jacksonian thought. Protection against elites' privileges lay in the ballot box, and Jacksonians "campaigned for the abolition of all property qualifications for voting and officeholding." Subjected to frequent elections, public officials were turned out of office with regularity in the Hill Country, where the feisty voters made incumbency a disadvantage. Jacksonian Democrats hoped that a broader electorate would use government to restrict the power of corporations, which the government gave artificial privileges not held by ordinary people. "Class hatred and fear of corporate wealth was a continuing theme" in antebellum Alabama's politics, where Hill Country people believed that the Democratic Party should be a "trade union" of the electorate that functioned as a counterweight to wealth and special privilege. Colorful politicians from the hills practiced a unique Jacksonian political style in which their oratory pitted the masses against the upper classes. This politics of class against class was often just demagoguery, but the common people responded to it, and the view of the world described in this oratory continued to flourish long after the Civil War. In the antebellum period, small farmers in the Hill Country and in the Wiregrass section of southeastern Alabama often voted together against the planters of the Black Belt and their allies in the plantation sections of the Tennessee Valley.[17]

The strongest opposition to secession had also come from the Hill Country, where the institution of slavery had not been as critical to the economy of small farmers. Disloyalty to the Confederacy was greater in this area than in any other section of the state, and several thousand soldiers from counties in northern Alabama actually fought in the Union army. After the war, mutual suspicions between the sections grew when a substantial minority of Hill Country whites supported the Republican Party and backed Radical Reconstruction. Even those who remained Democrats were angry about the Black Belt's power in the Democratic Party.[18]

Many Hill Country people believed that since the late 1870s the wealthy Black Belt planters had been manipulating state government to the detriment of small farmers. These Black Belters, along with rising industrialists in the state's cities who were their allies in controlling the state's laboring classes, constituted the Bourbon elite that ran the Democratic Party. Because the Bourbons' attitudes were the antithesis of the Jacksonian view, many Hill Country farmers concluded that the post–Civil War Democratic Party in Alabama had betrayed its antebellum principles and no longer represented the common man. Hill people expressed this view repeatedly in their many revolts against the party in the period before the 1890s, but these local movements had not been part of a unified statewide effort until the arrival of the

Southern Farmers' Alliance. By 1890 the Alliance had brought together thousands of farmers angry about their economic condition. Joining them were people who were angry about elites' control of the Democratic Party and about the Black Belt's power in state government.[19] The Alliance also made enormous headway in the Wiregrass and among small farmers in the valley of the Tennessee River. It was ready for a full-scale assault on the Bourbons.

In 1890 the Alliance supported Reuben F. Kolb for governor. Kolb was a Barbour County farmer and state commissioner of agriculture. Alliance members also sought other state offices and seats in the legislature. They were trying to take control of the Democratic Party, return it to the Jacksonian principles of their fathers, build support for the currency and credit reforms they favored, and place into power men who were friendly to small landowners, tenants, and sharecroppers. They called on black farmers to help them. The Black Belt planters and their industrialist allies were horrified, and they resolved to use the same tactics they had employed to defeat the Republicans during Reconstruction.[20]

County conventions across northern Alabama and the Wiregrass heavily supported Kolb's candidacy and sent delegates to the state Democratic nominating convention committed to him. Indeed, any fair count of the delegates found a plurality for the Alliance's candidate, but party officials would not abide by this result. When the Democrats convened, state party officials adopted rules that barred a number of pro-Kolb delegates from the meeting, and on the thirty-fourth ballot Thomas Goode Jones, an attorney for the Louisville and Nashville Railroad, won the nomination with 269 votes to Kolb's 256. The Alliance's candidate had been defeated by the "unjust rulings" of the convention chairman, observed one delegate, who said that the Bourbons had resorted to "every strategy and device" to deprive Kolb of the nomination. Alliance leaders agreed to accept defeat and loyally supported Jones in the general election, but they were determined to prevail two years later.[21]

In 1892 Kolb again sought the Democratic gubernatorial nomination, but when the campaign got under way many Alliance leaders asked Alabama's farmers to leave the Democratic Party and join a new third party. The National People's party had been formed in 1891 by midwestern Alliance members at a meeting in Cincinnati, Ohio, and the new organization was already being called the Populist Party. Some of the most economically radical Alliance members in Alabama aligned with the new party, whose platform was essentially a restatement of the currency and credit programs of the Southern Alliance. Reuben Kolb, however, wanted to remain a Democrat. When he realized that he would probably be denied the Democratic nomination again, he decided to form yet another party within Alabama, and his supporters called it the Jeffersonian Democratic Party. They would not become Populists, and Kolb never fully supported the most radical Populist ideas, but he needed the support of the thousands of Alabama farmers who had joined the new national party. The two dissident organizations met together and nominated a common slate of candidates. Kolb was quickly selected as their candidate for governor, and the most exciting political campaign in Alabama's history began. Despite the separate names of the two new parties and the fact that there were probably more Jeffersonians than Populists, historians have since referred to the uprising against the Democrats as the "Populist Revolt."[22]

Kolb and his supporters made a strong plea for the votes of African Americans and criticized Democrats for adopting another "white supremacy" platform. One Populist orator, speaking at Opelika, called on "the colored man" to "stand up for his race and vote for a free ballot and civil liberty." A vote for Kolb, contended Populists and Jeffersonians, was a vote for economic and political reform that would lift the poor of both races. Kolb's coalition also accepted the endorsement of the state's Republican Party, whose voters were primarily black but which had many supporters in northern Alabama among the families of the old Unionists and anti-secessionists. Democrats raised the specter of domination by African Americans if a biracial movement triumphed, and they called on voters to stand by whites in the Black Belt, where "the necessity for Caucasion [sic] supremacy is most keenly felt." In the end, the Black Belt was where the election was decided.[23]

When the voting was over, the Democratic secretary of state in charge of giving the official count declared Jones the victor by 126,959 votes to Kolb's 115,524. Kolb had swept the Hill Country and the Wiregrass, winning a huge majority of the white vote in Alabama. In addition to the votes of farmers, the dissident leader won strong support from Birmingham's rising labor force, carrying precincts in Jefferson County where coal miners lived. Returns from the Black Belt, however, where blacks constituted three-quarters of the population, told a very different story. In fifteen Black Belt counties, Jones's majority exceeded 30,000. In most of these counties the Democrats received in excess of 80 percent of the vote. In order to believe that the outcome of the election was fair and accurate, historians must accept that blacks went to the polls in overwhelming numbers to vote for the self-proclaimed "party of white supremacy." Evidence of voter fraud was spectacular, and the parties who opposed the Democrats called on the legislature to overturn the false returns. Democrats who controlled the body, however, turned a deaf ear to such complaints.[24]

The election had been too close for the Democrats' comfort, and despite their victory they made plans to stop the opposition juggernaut before the 1894 elections. In the 1892–93 legislative session they rushed through a new election law that would put balloting more firmly under state control. Over the opposition of Populists and Jeffersonians, the Democrats passed the Sayre Election Law, with provisions aimed at restricting the voting rights of illiterate or semi-literate citizens. In previous elections, ballots had been distributed by the parties, and illiterate voters could see by the color of the ballots or symbols on them what they needed to know. Under the new law, however, the state would print ballots that would list candidates for office in alphabetical order, without party or office symbols. Voters had to cast their ballots within five minutes after receiving them, and they could ask for help only from one of the official poll watchers appointed by the Democratic governor. Other complex provisions of the law required voters to register in front of Democratic officials in May and to bring a certificate proving that they had done so to the polling place.[25]

The Sayre law badly damaged the Populist-Jeffersonian cause in the 1894 election, as the turnout of voters in areas sympathetic to this movement fell significantly. The election was essentially a replay of the events of 1892. While Kolb was defeated by a wider margin, few people doubted that he had actually won this election also. Again, Black Belt votes spoke loudest. William C. Oates, the Democratic candidate, won the election by 28,583 votes, but fifteen Black Belt counties gave him a lead of 29,722 votes over Kolb. In Dallas County more than 80 percent of the registered voters were black, but Oates won by 6,517 votes there to Kolb's 167. These obviously doctored or controlled returns were absurd, but aside from the opposition's protest on the day of Oates's inauguration, little could be done. Returns from the congressional elections in November were encouraging, and opposition leaders prepared for the 1896 election.[26]

The events surrounding the 1896 state and presidential election are some of the most confusing in Alabama's political history, as the state's Populists found themselves aligned with Republicans in the state election and with Democrats in the national election. The events of that year decimated the Populists, and they were never again a threat to the Democratic Party's rule in Alabama. Their first problem came from the emergence of a state Democratic Party leader who sounded like a Populist and called for third-party voters to return to the party of their fathers. Joseph Forney Johnston had once been a typical Bourbon, but in 1895 he suddenly styled himself a reformer, bought a newspaper to trumpet his ideas, called for currency reform and the coinage of silver, and announced his candidacy for governor. He blasted reactionaries of the status quo who controlled the party, and he pledged the return of honest elections. His rhetoric was appealing, and many who had been part of the opposition were won over. But Johnston's victory was assured by events at the 1896 Democratic and Populist national conventions, which met before Alabama's state elections.[27]

The Democrats nominated a young Nebraska congressman named William Jennings Bryan for president. He jettisoned the conservative economic policies that had previously dominated the party's platforms, endorsed the coinage of silver, and called for an end to the gold standard. Populists, meeting in convention two weeks later, faced a dilemma: they could either nominate Bryan also, or they could choose another candidate who would split the reform vote. If they nominated Bryan, they would incur the wrath of committed Alliance and Populist leaders who believed that the Democratic Party was a desiccated institution heavily influenced by Bourbon Democrats. These "Mid-Road" Populists pointed out that Bryan did not support the subtreasury and other radical demands of the Alliance. In short, if Populists fused with Democrats they risked dissolution of their party. After a brutal floor fight the party agreed to nominate Bryan, causing many Populists to go home in disgust. Some never again gave their full loyalty to their party's cause, and thousands of southern Populists, including Reuben Kolb, returned to the Democratic Party. Populism as a national movement was dead, and the third-party movement in individual states was not far behind.[28]

Alabama's Populist Party, without its former leader Reuben Kolb, insisted on nominating candidates for state and local office again in 1896, 1898, and 1900, and in each successive election the party's share of the total vote dwindled until the party was no longer a threat to Democrats. Milford Howard was elected to Congress again from the Hill Country's Seventh Congressional District in 1896, and Populists continued to roll up large votes in a few Hill Country and Wiregrass counties, but even in these areas the reform movement lost much of its clout. Nevertheless, Democrats still had much to worry about despite this rapid decline of the third-party cause.[29]

Although whites in the Black Belt maintained a precarious hold on the votes of blacks, many black voters cast their ballots freely in other parts of the state. A biracial political movement was still a possibility, and stealing votes was the only way to defeat such an uprising. Stunning proof developed that another revolt might occur when William McKinley, the Republican presidential candidate, won fourteen white hill counties in the 1900 presidential election. McKinley's support presaged a sizable movement of Hill

Country Populists into the Republican Party. These angry ex-Populists had refused to return to the Democratic Party, which they viewed as an engine of corruption. Despite the Democrats' efforts to stamp out dissent, the Populist Party had seemingly reappeared under the Republican banner. Election returns from white counties, wrote one Democratic editor, "point very clearly to a future coalition between many of the white Populists and negro republicans."

A movement among conservative Democrats for a constitutional convention to disfranchise blacks and poor white farmers had been aborted by Governor Johnston in 1899, but within only days after the 1900 general election it gained new life. Restricting or stealing the votes of dissenters was either insufficient or had become unseemly. The opposition had to be eliminated, and a new state constitution was the ideal means to achieve this goal.[30]

Notes

1. William Warren Rogers, *The One-Gallused Rebellion: Agrarianism in Alabama, 1865–1896* (Baton Rouge: Louisiana State University Press, 1970), 271–92, 285.

2. Samuel L. Webb, *Two-Party Politics in the One-Party South: Alabama's Hill Country, 1874–1920* (Tuscaloosa: University of Alabama Press, 1997), 137–38; *Columbiana People's Advocate*, November 25, 1894; *Columbiana Shelby Chronicle*, November 15, 1894.

3. Rogers, *One-Gallused Rebellion*, 291–92, 286 (quote).

4. Ibid., 287–89; Webb, *Two-Party Politics*, 138–39.

5. Lawrence Goodwyn, *Democratic Promise: The Populist Moment in America* (New York: Oxford University Press, 1976), 11–33; Steven Hahn, *The Roots of Southern Populism: Yeoman Farmers and the Transformation of the Georgia Upcountry, 1850–1890* (New York: Oxford University Press, 1983), 137–69.

6. Hahn, *Roots of Southern Populism*, 137–69; Rogers, *One-Gallused Rebellion*, 1–30 and 121–46.

7. Goodwyn, *Democratic Promise*, xvii (quotes), 11–21; Richard Franklin Bensel, *Yankee Leviathan: The Origins of Central State Authority in America* (Cambridge: Cambridge University Press, 1990), 416–36; Robert McMath, *American Populism: A Social History, 1877–1898* (New York: Hill and Wang, 1993), 83–107.

8. McMath, *American Populism*, 66–107; Bruce Palmer, *"Man Over Money": The Southern Populist Critique of American Capitalism* (Chapel Hill: University of North Carolina Press, 1980), 96–104.

9. Goodwyn, *Democratic Promise*, 166–68; Palmer, *"Man Over Money,"* 104–10; Rogers, *One-Gallused Rebellion*, 138.

10. William Warren Rogers, Robert David Ward, Leah Rawls Atkins and Wayne Flynt, *Alabama: The History of a Deep South State* (Tuscaloosa: University of Alabama Press, 1994), 259–74.

11. Edward L. Ayers, *The Promise of the New South: Life after Reconstruction* (Oxford and New York: Oxford University Press, 1992), 234–37.

12. Rogers et al., *History of a Deep South State,* 259–74; Dan T. Carter, *The Politics of Rage: George Wallace, the Origins of the New Conservatism, and the Transformation of American Politics* (New York: Simon and Schuster, 1995), 36–37.

13. Webb, *Two-Party Politics,* 32–33.

14. Ibid., 32–33 (quotes); Allen Johnston Going, *Bourbon Democracy in Alabama* (University: University of Alabama Press, 1951), 30–31.

15. Webb, *Two-Party Politics,* 59–85, 2–10.

16. J. Mills Thornton, *Politics and Power in a Slave Society: Alabama, 1800–1860* (Baton Rouge: Louisiana State University Press, 1978), xviii, 5–8, 50–52, 323–42; Harry L. Watson, *Liberty and Power: The Politics of Jacksonian America* (New York: Noonday Press, 1990), 61–65; J. Mills Thornton, "Jacksonian Democracy," in *Encyclopedia of Southern Culture,* ed. Charles Reagan Wilson and William Ferris (Chapel Hill: University of North Carolina Press, 1989), 630.

17. McMath, *American Populism,* 52 (first quote); Thornton, "Jacksonian Democracy," 630 (second and fourth quotes); Thornton, *Politics and Power,* 50 (third quote), 74–76, 151–55.

18. Allen W. Trelease, "Who Were the Scalawags?" *Journal of Southern History* 29 (November 1963): 445–68; Michael W. Fitzgerald, "Radical Republicanism and the White Yeomanry during Alabama Reconstruction, 1865–1868," *Journal of Southern History* 54 (November 1988): 565–96.

19. Webb, *Two-Party Politics,* 59–85, 124–27.

20. Rogers, *One-Gallused Rebellion,* 165–87.

21. Ibid., 180–83; Webb, *Two-Party Politics,* 99 (quote).

22. Palmer, *"Man Over Money,"* 154–57; Rogers, *One-Gallused Rebellion,* 213–22.

23. Rogers, *One-Gallused Rebellion,* 218–22 (all quotes).

24. Ibid., 222–28, 238–39.

25. Ibid., 236–43.

26. J. Morgan Kousser, *The Shaping of Southern Politics: Suffrage Restriction and the Establishment of the One-Party South, 1880–1910* (New Haven: Yale University Press, 1974), 134–38; Rogers, *One-Gallused Rebellion,* 271–92, 283.

27. Webb, *Two-Party Politics,* 142–44, 147–50, 155, 162; Michael Perman, "Joseph F. Johnston, 1896–1900," in *Alabama Governors: A Political History of the State,* ed. Samuel L. Webb and Margaret E. Armbrester (Tuscaloosa: University of Alabama Press, 2001), 127–29.

28. Ayers, *Promise of the New South*, 295–98.
29. Rogers, *One-Gallused Rebellion*, 308–35.
30. Webb, *Two-Party Politics*, 167–68 (quote).

2
White Supremacy Triumphant

Democracy Undone

Harvey H. Jackson III

Following the end of Reconstruction in Alabama, victorious conservative Democrats, often referred to as Bourbons, wanted to disfranchise black voters in 1875. But the Fifteenth Amendment to the U.S. Constitution, which made it illegal to deny or abridge the franchise "on account of race, color, or previous condition of servitude," was too fresh on the books, and memories of federal intervention were too vivid. Instead, these conservatives wrote a constitution that year to "fix things," according to the *Montgomery Advertiser,* "so the Republicans could do little harm if they should return to power." By limiting taxation for the general welfare, prohibiting state aid for internal improvements, restricting local government, and outlawing a host of Radical Republican innovations, conservatives believed "they cured many of the evils of the carpetbag regime." But they just "could not make those provisions as to suffrage which [they felt were] so necessary for the future well-being of the State." That action would have to wait for another day.[1]

During the next decade, many Bourbons were glad they stopped short of disfranchisement. By 1880, planters in the Black Belt, a region across the center of the state with large African American majorities, had brought the landless black electorate under their control and were once again running their counties. Bourbons found that they had at their disposal thousands of votes they could present to candidates of their choice, which they did with frequency and skill to defeat Populist challengers from the mostly white counties in the Hill Country of northern Alabama and the southeast corner of the state, known as the Wiregrass.

Delivering majorities where no majority existed, stuffing ballot boxes, voting "in" and counting "out" at will, Black Belt Bourbons, in the words of a Perry County planter, "piloted the old Democratic ship from among the breakers . . . and saved her from wreckage." Thus, he continued, Black Belt Bourbons turned fraud into "an art . . . an achievement of faith with the evidence not seen . . . Christianity, but not orthodox . . . wrong but right . . . justice but injustice . . . life instead of death." Allies outside the region praised "the Democrats of the Black Belt [who] stood their post, [who went into] the ballot box and counted out the Negro in order to preserve the political welfare of the whole state of Alabama." But those who practiced this "art" knew it was "fraught with danger," and many would have preferred not to be so frequently forced "to crimes of larceny," if they could find another way to hold power at home and in Montgomery.[2]

For Bourbons, preserving the "political welfare" of Alabama consisted of two things. First, they had to maintain white supremacy, and they did not hesitate to admit that "the justification for whatever manipulation of the ballot that has occurred in this State has been the menace of Negro domination." Yet there was a second objective. The Populist insurgency of the 1890s left Bourbons badly shaken, and the core of that protest's constituency was poor farmers from the northern Alabama hills and from the Wiregrass. Those farmers were white. As long as they had the vote, Bourbon control could never be secure, and Bourbons knew it. So when conservatives spoke of constitutional reform to "rid the state . . . of the corrupt and ignorant among its electorate," white supremacy was not their only motive.[3]

Of course, matters other than suffrage caused Alabamians to believe that a new constitution was needed. Between 1875 and 1900, the state's population doubled. Most of the increase was in the northern mineral belt, where, despite constitutional limitations written in 1875, Birmingham, Anniston, and a score of lesser towns emerged as industrial centers. These and other municipalities struggled to fund services and cursed the constitution that restricted them. Meanwhile, commerce lagged for lack of infrastructure, and underfunded education limped along. Because the constitution required most town and county issues to pass through Montgomery, the "evils of local legislation" tied up government while backroom deals were cut. Voter fraud was not the only corruption loose on the land.[4]

Yet there were many Democrats who were happy with the 1875 constitution. Planters felt that the state should not spend their tax money on roads, bridges, and other pet projects. They approved of the document's anti-industrial, anti-urban bias and were convinced that "too much" education only "ruined a good field hand." Meanwhile, though businessmen might wish for internal improvements and a bit more home rule, they were pleased that under the 1875 constitution the state could do little to regulate corporations. Small farmers, for their part, liked the constitutional limits on property taxes as much as any planter or industrialist did. Moreover, restraints on legislative power in Montgomery satisfied their political sensibilities, which reflected the influence of Andrew Jackson.

What each of these groups wanted was to control the forces that governed their lives. If suffrage restriction helped accomplish this goal, they were for it. Thus the constitution of 1875 was hardly a decade old before efforts were under way to nullify the black vote. Districts were gerrymandered, more offices became appointive, and election laws imposed such complicated restrictions as to make education all but a requirement. But few conservatives were satisfied with this piecemeal approach. When news arrived that federal courts were allowing Mississippi and other southern states to disfranchise the "ignorant, vicious and incompetent" voter, Bourbons took heart. Poll taxes, property ownership and literacy requirements, and the like offered a way to relieve the state "of the burden of the black man" and get rid of many poor white voters in the process. The question, of course, was how to have such a state constitution written and, once written, ratified.[5]

In 1890, Governor Thomas Seay took note of Mississippi's success and suggested that a constitutional convention might be in order for Alabama. But concerns that the issue would divide white voters and give blacks more clout doomed the attempt. Two years later, as the Populist movement gained momentum, conservatives blocked efforts to add a call for a convention to the Democratic Party's platform for fear that reformers would dominate the gathering and write their agenda into law. Instead, they adopted a plank calling for changes that would "better secure the government of the state in the hands of the intelligent and virtuous." Next, conservatives passed the Sayre Election Law, an insidious bit of legislation that eliminated many voters through complicated and discriminatory registration and voting rules. Though the Sayre law was, as a leading state senator explained, "the best and cheapest method of swindling [that] the white people have ever devised for the maintenance of white supremacy," it also cut deeply into the ranks of Populist supporters, which was just what conservatives intended.[6]

By 1896 the conservatives had defeated Populism, and most of the movement's adherents had returned to the Democratic fold. Finally, Black Belt Bourbons and northern Alabama industrialists were ready to draft a constitution that would define an electorate dominated by men like themselves—white, propertied, and socially and fiscally conservative. So when the newly elected governor, Joseph F. Johnston, asked the legislature to approve a constitutional convention, conservatives quickly endorsed the plan. But up in the hills and down in the Wiregrass, the farm folks—many of them former Populists—feared that the conservatives' intention to disfranchise many voters would fall as heavily on poor whites as on blacks. These farmers bitterly opposed the plan. Thus the battle line was drawn and the campaign begun.[7]

Meanwhile, Governor Johnston was having second thoughts. Considered a "half-way Populist" by many, he watched the anti-convention movement grow among voters upon whom his political future depended. Realizing the folly of disfranchising a loyal constituency, the governor reversed himself, and in his 1898 message to the legislature he opposed a convention. Despite the governor's change of heart, conservatives quickly pushed through the Senate a bill calling for a popular vote on the convention question. In the House, representatives for the mainly white counties, after failing to add a provision pledging that "the right to vote should be kept inviolate," decided that when the bill reached the floor they would "slip out and prevent a quorum." But legislative leaders got wind of the scheme. They rounded up the strays and, with the doors locked to prevent defections, passed the bill. Governor Johnston, with his eye on a seat in the U.S. Senate, signed the measure just before Christmas.[8]

Before the question was put to a popular vote, supporters presented it to the Democratic Party, which met in convention in March 1899. Desperate for official endorsement and fearing that opposition in northern Alabama would divide Democrats and doom the plan at the polls, conservatives pledged that a new constitution would not "deprive any white man in Alabama of the right to vote." They also agreed that the document would be submitted to the people for their approval. For many opponents, however, such promises still were not enough. A bitter, protracted debate followed at the party's convention, and the measure's endorsement won approval by just 10 votes—257 to 247. Meanwhile, Governor Johnston, finding that a majority in both houses now opposed a constitutional convention, announced a special session to repeal the legislature's call. Chaos reigned. A Democratic governor backed by a legislative majority was defying the state Democratic Executive Committee and the Democratic Party's convention. Rumors of a Populist revival spread. The Bourbons were worried.[9]

As the anti-convention forces rallied around Governor Johnston, former governors Thomas G. Jones and William C. Oates, along with the state's entire congressional delegation and most of the major newspapers, opposed repealing the call for a constitutional convention. On April 22, 1899, the Democratic Executive Committee met and condemned Governor Johnston, and on May 2, the night before the special session was scheduled to convene, conservatives held a rally in Montgomery to press their cause upon the legislators—but to no avail. The session opened as expected, and after four days of debate a coalition of Democrats and Populists from the state's mostly white counties repealed the convention call.[10]

Conservatives quickly began a campaign to recapture the legislature and repeal the repeal. To accomplish this goal, they urged voters to select legislators who would reelect popular U.S. senator John Tyler Morgan and reject his challenger, Joseph Johnston, the now-former governor and anti-convention leader. The point, of course, was that legislators committed to Morgan would pass a new convention bill, and the movement for what the *Wilcox Progressive* called "white supremacy and purer politics" would be back on track.

The conservatives' line of argument was clear. Disfranchising blacks would secure white supremacy and end the corruption that had marked so many elections. By taking from black voters what whites had been stealing, whites would no longer be forced to commit "crimes of larceny and perjury," and elections would, once again, be honest. This argument presented an interesting leap of logic, but one which whites, even those who opposed a convention, found reasonable. The pro-convention campaign worked. Morgan's supporters carried the day. In December 1900 the legislature met, reelected the senator, and passed a new bill calling for a convention. The new bill asked voters to go to the polls on April 23, 1901, and decide whether they wanted a convention and, if so, whom they wanted to serve as delegates. Meanwhile, the Democratic Executive Committee met on January 15, 1901, and recommended that the Democratic Party endorse the convention. Six weeks later, Democrats gathered in Montgomery for their annual state convention. There they declared that "after an experience of thirty years . . . it has been demonstrated that as a race [the Negro] . . . is incapable of self-government," and called for a new constitution to disfranchise him.[11]

Speakers covered the state and followed a simple strategy: focus on white supremacy, and if other questions are raised, remind audiences that the Democratic Party would honor previous pledges, including the promise to disfranchise only blacks. Still, a majority of voters in northern Alabama could not be swayed. So once again, conservative Democrats turned to the Black Belt for fraudulent votes, and once again the Black Belt's political masters were ready. Meeting privately less than three weeks before the election, the state Democratic Executive Committee heard how black votes would be manipulated and stolen. "All we want," a Black Belt leader confidently told the group, "is a small vote and a large count." They got it. On April 23, Alabamians went to the polls, or were sent to the polls, and cast their votes, or had their votes cast for them. The call for a constitutional convention had 70,305 votes counted in favor and 45,505 against. Most of the 24,800 votes that gave supporters their majority came from the Black Belt. In Dallas County, for example, where blacks outnumbered whites by more than four to one, 5,668 votes were recorded in favor of a convention and only 200 against. In Lowndes County, where the ratio of blacks to whites was even greater, the vote was 3,226 in favor to 338 against. Other Black Belt counties registered similar majorities. From such reported results, one might have concluded—and some did argue—that black Alabamians willingly put their political fate in the hands of white Democrats whom they knew and trusted. However, most Alabamians, white and black, knew the truth. Once again, the Black Belt's "magnificent system" had carried the day.[12]

Less than a month later, the 155 delegates chosen in the election met in Montgomery. Most were elected from House and Senate districts around the state. Each congressional district elected two delegates, and four delegates were elected from the state at large. All but fourteen of the delegates were regular Democrats. Many were or had been legislators. Two of the delegates, William Oates and Thomas Jones, had been governors, and a majority of the others had held some political office. Some of the delegates were planters; others were businessmen. Ninety-six were lawyers. Not many came from what might be called the middle class. There were no poor whites and no blacks. Max Bennett Trasher, correspondent for the *New York Evening News*, reported that "at least a third of the delegates [were] gray heads," and noted, in a classic understatement, that it was "in the main, a conservative body of men."

The delegates chose John B. Knox of Anniston as their president. Some had expected Oates to lead the group, but when, in a letter to the *Montgomery Advertiser* published just before the convention, the former governor had suggested that "the disfranchisement of the whole Negro race would be unwise and unjust," delegates turned to Knox, who harbored no such reservations. Described by the *Mobile Register* as "a lawyer of distinguished ability," Knox had much to recommend him to the convention. He had support from the economic interests in the state's mineral district around Birmingham, Gadsden, and Anniston. These interests wanted to control both black labor and Populist whites. Knox also was uniquely suited to advance the alliance already forming between industrialists from northern Alabama and planters from southern Alabama, especially in the Black Belt. Not counted among the "gray heads" and unprejudiced by prior political experience, Knox was heralded as the symbol of a new era, one in which the state would be "in the hands of its young men—men to whom the Civil War is history—men full of faith in the possibilities and resources of Alabama."[13]

In his opening address, Knox made it clear that before the delegates could consider the future, they first had to deal with the past. To justify and explain what they were about to do, he repeated the conservatives' refrain of how during Reconstruction, "by force of Federal bayonets, the negro was placed in control . . . [and] inspired and aided by unscrupulous white men, he wasted money, created debts, increased taxes until it threatened to amount to confiscation of our property." Faced with this situation, Knox continued, brave Alabamians had no choice but to manipulate the ballot "as an act of necessity for self-preservation." Conveniently ignoring how the ballot was also manipulated to defeat the Populists, Knox remained focused on the "Negro issue" and expressed sympathy for those who stole votes rather than for those from whom votes were stolen. He challenged the convention to establish white supremacy "by law—not by force or fraud." Other states had shown the way, he explained, and at last it was recognized that suffrage limitations were "justified in law and in morals, because . . . the negro is not being discriminated against on account of his race, but on account of his intellectual and moral condition." White supremacy could at last be constitutionally established, Knox declared, and that was what the delegates were assembled to do.[14]

But how? One way, Knox suggested, was an "education requirement," something delegates from the mostly white counties bitterly opposed, since so many of their constituents were illiterate. Meeting this opposition head-on, Knox advised opponents that the Democratic Party's pledge not to deprive any white man of his vote "does not extend . . . beyond the right of voters now living." Arguing that education was "a necessary and essential part of any just and wise scheme for the regulation of the right of suffrage, and for the purification of the ballot," Knox contended that the state should require it of its voters. Besides, he noted, since "learning to read and write are [sic] within reach and easy to obtain," literacy would be no restriction for those who really wanted to vote. The rest of the citizens, he implied, had no right to the ballot.[15]

While Knox's speech reveals the position conservatives would take on the question of suffrage, one has only to look at the committee chairmen he appointed to infer what else would and would not be done by the convention. A corporate lawyer chaired the Committee on Corporations, a railroad attorney led the Committee on the Judiciary, and a Black Belt attorney pledged to preserving his region's strength in the legislature guided the Committee on Representation. To head the Committee on Taxation, on which the hopes of so many progressive Alabamians rested, Knox appointed a Talladega lawyer and legislator who would honor the Democratic Party's pledges not to increase levies. Although a superintendent of schools chaired the Committee on Education, fourteen of its nineteen members came from counties with black majorities and where adequate schooling was hardly a priority. Clearly, reforms other than suffrage were not high on President Knox's agenda.[16]

The composition of the Committee on Suffrage and Elections also revealed the conservatives' intentions. Judge Thomas W. Coleman of Greene County was appointed chairman. A Princeton graduate, prewar lawyer-planter, former slaveholder, and veteran, Coleman came home from the Civil War to serve in the convention that wrote the 1865 constitution. Later he became an associate justice of the Alabama Supreme Court. Of the twenty-five members of his committee, nine were also from the Black Belt, and a majority of the rest represented urban and industrial interests. Later, some delegates would charge that Knox had "stacked" the suffrage committee. The membership of the committee and what it accomplished suggest those critics had a point.[17]

Events in the weeks that followed made it apparent that black disfranchisement was a common goal of the convention's majority. Yet there was considerable disagreement over the details. Although most delegates accepted the argument that "honest elections" were impossible as long as blacks voted, many from the mostly white counties hoped that the Black Belt's influence would decline once the "fictitious Negro vote" was abolished. Fearing this outcome, delegates from the Black Belt insisted that even after blacks were disfranchised, representation for their counties still would be based on their entire populations—and not just on the number of people who actually voted. Such representation would leave those counties with black majorities as strong as before—and their white minorities even stronger. Northern Alabama's industrialists indicated that they might accept this outcome if in return the Black Belt's planters would agree to disfranchise "corrupt and ignorant" whites along with "ignorant, vicious, and incompetent" blacks. This agreement, of course, was just what the delegates from the white counties suspected. By limiting the franchise to the "intelligent and the virtuous" voters, conservatives in fact intended to create an electorate in their own image, and delegates from the white counties rallied to oppose this scheme.[18]

The Committee on Suffrage and Elections faced what seemed to be an enormous task. Yet other southern states already had demonstrated how to disfranchise blacks. Some used residency requirements; others denied the vote to people convicted of specific crimes. Some states used literacy tests as a requirement for voting, and many imposed poll taxes as a prerequisite to voting. All of these methods, however, could and did disfranchise whites—a result that Alabama's convention delegates had pledged to avoid. In fact, they could not threaten to disfranchise whites without jeopardizing ratification of their new document. Mississippi had slipped many whites through rigid voting requirements by resorting to an "understanding clause." It allowed registrars to certify voters if they "understood" the duties of citizenship—something blacks seldom could do to the satisfaction of white election officials. Louisiana had added a "grandfather clause." It gave the vote to descendants of people who voted before 1867, another qualification beyond the reach of blacks. But all of these schemes, in one way or another, aroused suspicions among various delegates; so the committee debated, in secret, and the convention waited.[19]

On June 30, the Committee on Suffrage and Election made its report. Actually, there were two reports. The majority recommended that a man, twenty-one years of age or older, be allowed to vote if he met a residency requirement, paid a poll tax of $1.50 a year, could read or write in English, and had been in a lawful business for the last twelve months or owned $300 worth of property (or forty acres of land). No one could register, however, if he had been convicted of one of more than thirty crimes that ranged from treason to vagrancy—a list heavily weighted toward crimes of which blacks were most often accused. But because any or all of these requirements might also disfranchise whites, the committee added a temporary measure that would allow anyone who met the age, poll tax, and residency requirements to register until January 1, 1903, provided he had served in any American war, was a descendant of such a veteran, or was a man "of good character" who understood the duties of citizenship. Thus the committee's plan would write blacks out of the electorate but would give illiterate whites a loophole, thereby honoring the "no disfranchisement" pledge. The committee's members, however, were not unanimously behind this plan. Four members, two of them former governors and all of them Confederate veterans, issued a minority report. It objected to the descendants clause as not only a violation of the U.S. Constitution but also as an innovation that established an "undemocratic . . . un-American . . . heredity, governing class." The dissenters had no reservations about disfranchising blacks, but they felt this exemption was an unnecessary subterfuge that insulted whites by "requiring . . . a lower standard of capacity and intelligence than that required of the Negro." With that disagreement, the issue went to the floor.[20]

The gallery was full on July 23 when debate began, and the local press reported that "over in the south-east corner quite a large group of negroes sat." In the eleven days that followed, this audience heard some of the most open and frank discussion of political corruption, racial attitudes, and class distinctions ever recorded in Alabama. Repeatedly, delegates admitted that elections had been stolen not only in the Black Belt region of the state, but also in the industrial districts and even in the mostly white counties. Expressing no regret, they praised the "courageous men who decided that the negro should no longer be a factor in Alabama affairs," admitting only that "the time has come when we are tired of it." Thomas H. Watts of Montgomery declared, "We want the day of honest elections to dawn in this fair state." Everyone assembled, even those "over in the south-east corner," knew how that new day would be accomplished. Black votes would be stolen again, only this time the theft would be constitutional and permanent.[21]

Addressing the minority report, those in the majority admitted that the temporary plan with its "fighting grandfather clause" was "a child of necessity" required to persuade unqualified whites to accept the other restrictions and vote for ratification. But the plan was also fair, its supporters argued, for "it was the illiterate and uneducated white man that fought the battle of the Confederacy." And it was the sons of these Confederate soldiers, another added, "who supported their widowed mothers and schooled their sisters . . . and were themselves denied an education." Besides, they claimed, veterans and their descendants knew "the traditions and principles of free government . . . [while] the negro . . . has no traditions of liberty, no pride of ancestry, no environments which fit him to intelligently discharge the great duties of citizenship." So it made sense to exempt veterans and the first generation of their descendants whose lives had been altered by the conflict. However, that was as far as conservatives were willing to go. After those exemptions, a Black Belt delegate told the group, "the book closes and the state of Alabama says to all of her people . . . you must come up on the question of intelligence and industry . . . in order to take part in the conduct of this great government. . . . We have made no guarantee to unborn ages of the ballot."[22]

Still, members of the convention understood that the poll tax, collected in February when cash from the previous year's crop was running low, would nullify most features of the temporary plan. Conservatives believed, as President Knox later admitted, that the only way the convention could "place the power of government in the hands of the intelligent and the virtuous" was to disfranchise "not only a large mass of Negro voters, but quite a number of white voters" as well. In this effort, the federal government became the conservatives' ally. The Fifteenth Amendment, which the conservatives claimed forced them to write restrictions that did not discriminate against "the negro race ... [but] against its characteristics and ... offenses," allowed them also to discriminate against "weak and vicious white men." For Black Belt Bourbons and their industrialist allies, the irony must have been sweet.[23]

For others, however, this development was a bitter turn of events. Napoleon Bonaparte Spears, an unrepentant Populist-Republican from predominantly white St. Clair County, denounced disfranchisement of either race, praised the Reconstruction amendments to the U.S. Constitution as the greatest ever "pinned to the beautiful Goddess of Liberty," and castigated the conservatives as enemies of democracy. Outraged, committee chairman Coleman rose and declared that "if there were no other reason for calling this Convention here, and no other reason for ratifying this Constitution, it would be sufficient for me ... that so many of [Spears's] constituents might be eliminated from the suffrage plank as to retire the gentleman" from office.[24]

Other delegates, including most of the convention's veterans, supported suffrage reform but opposed the temporary plan as an "unconstitutional subterfuge" that gave special privileges to many who did not deserve them and denied the same privileges to many who did. "I am for eliminating from the right to vote all those who are unfit and unqualified," declared William C. Oates, the former governor and Confederate hero, "and if the rule strikes a white man as well as the negro, let him go." Some delegates agreed with Oates. One from northern Alabama, recalling how many from his region had deserted the cause, declared that it was an insult to those who served faithfully to give the vote to the disloyal or to a descendant of a "dodging granddaddy." "Some of the sorriest men I ever knew," he concluded, "wore the grey."[25]

Delegates listened patiently while opponents had their say, but no argument could sway the majority from the task. As a Tallapoosa County delegate explained with guileless simplicity, he liked the temporary plan "because it practically permits all white men to vote, and it practically denies all negroes to vote." Most other members agreed. Warnings from the minority that the course the majority had chosen would "teach the negro to feel the state of Alabama is his enemy ... [and make him] look to Washington and not to Montgomery for protection" fell on deaf ears. The issue had been decided long before it was debated, and when the vote was taken, the temporary plan, including the grandfather clause, passed, 104 to 14.[26]

Opposition to the permanent plan met the same fate. The majority paid scant attention to fears that registrars authorized to determine who was or was not qualified might allow political prejudice to play a role. Nor did supporters spend much time defending property and education requirements. As a Black Belt delegate put it, "men who have come into control of property are more conservative and intelligent as a class," which was the sort of voter he wanted. "The young man who has put forth energy and skill sufficient to have a capacity to read and write," he added, "has the sense of responsibility which will ensure a reasonable exercise of the elective franchise." As for the poll tax, everyone understood that it would disfranchise many poor whites, but few spoke against it. Some delegates seemed content that since it was a "voluntary" tax, people would be disfranchising themselves. Because receipts were to go to public schools, others might have seen the poll tax as an education measure rather than a prerequisite for voting. But whatever the reason, delegates debated the requirement less than one might have expected before they added it to the plan.[27]

Black Alabamians were aware of how such provisions might affect them. Early in the deliberations, blacks sent four petitions to the convention. The most famous of these, whose signers included Booker T. Washington at Tuskegee Institute, requested that since members of their race paid taxes and performed the other duties of a citizen, they should be allowed "some humble share" in deciding who should rule over them. Although each petition approached the problem from a different perspective, together they argued that if the Negro was denied an education and the possibility of voting, "there will be [a] danger that he will become a beast, revelling in crime and a body of death around the neck of the State." In short, if Alabama was to advance, the black man must be allowed to advance with it.[28]

Some delegates, especially those who were not yet "gray heads," were insulted that blacks would dare question what they were doing, and they wanted to reject the petitions outright. Having come of age after the Civil War, they had few if any of the paternalistic notions of those who looked on themselves as "custodians" of a weaker race. "We of the younger generation," a member from Marengo County told the convention, "have known but one slavery . . . [we have been] slaves to the negro vote." And as future U.S. senator J. Thomas Heflin put it, since "God Almighty intended the negro to be the servant of the white man," the junior delegates were determined that blacks should be given nothing, including an education, that might fit them for any other role. At this juncture, however, the old paternalists won the day. The petitions were accepted, read into the record, and then ignored. After a few adjustments in residency requirements and a declaration that if one part of the plan were found unconstitutional the rest would remain in force, the matter was put to a vote and passed, 95 to 19.[29]

The suffrage plan, however, came with conditions. As delegate Reuben Chapman of Sumter County explained, "The Black Belt has come to this

Convention bearing a gift, an unusual gift . . . the power it has heretofore held and heretofore used." By agreeing to this disfranchisement, Black Belt patricians were turning over majorities ranging from 25,000 to 50,000 votes that had kept the Democrats in power and the white man supreme. But the gift was not free. In return, the convention had to agree that the whole population would be the basis for representation and that the agreement could not be amended later. Although the deal included five extra representatives and two new senators for the mostly white counties, southern Alabama would still dominate the legislature. Delegates from the white counties and critics in the press grumbled, but to no avail. Upstate industrial interests accepted the arrangement. The suffrage plan was approved, and the stage was set for the state to reverse one of its oldest political traditions. Since Alabama was admitted to the Union, it had been recognized for the minimal requirements it imposed on male citizens to cast a ballot. Now, if voters approved this new constitution, the state would have one of the most intricate systems of disfranchisement in the nation. Democracy in Alabama would be a thing of the past.[30]

As for the rest of the constitution, the status quo prevailed. To no one's surprise, the Committee on Corporations, dominated by corporate lawyers, lived up to the Democratic Party's pledge that "restrictions in the [1875] state constitution as to corporations shall remain unchanged." Other hopes for reform met the same fate. Questions of child labor and convict leasing were ignored. Municipalities got little relief from the restrictions that inhibited their self-government, and the state was still prohibited from supporting internal improvements. The judiciary remained essentially as it was. As for the limitations on taxation, which many Alabamians believed impeded progress more than any other constitutional provision, the convention concluded that the current levy was actually too high. Therefore, delegates lowered the tax rate on property from 7.5 mills to 6.5, with the provision that a county could add an additional mill if it chose. Then they earmarked the revenues so that 3.0 mills went to schools, 1.0 mill to support of Confederate veterans, and 2.5 mills to administration of the state, which seemed more than enough, considering how little the state could actually do. Finally, the delegates concluded that in "view of the prohibitions to be placed on the legislative power there will be hereafter neither a demand or a need for biennial sessions"; so they confined meetings to fifty days every four years.[31]

Now came the hard part—ratification. Pledged to submit the constitution to the voters, supporters set up headquarters in Birmingham and rallied behind a campaign committee headed by future U.S. senator Oscar W.

Underwood, whose ties to northern Alabama's industrialists were considered critical to getting votes in that region. The state Democratic Executive Committee, sensitive to opposition within the party, avoided a divisive endorsement and simply commended "the new constitution to the impartial consideration of the voters." Meanwhile, Underwood and his committee—under the slogan "White supremacy! Honest elections! And the New Constitution! One and inseparable!"—set out to rally supporters, especially those in the Black Belt, whom they counted on to "roll up one of those old-time Democratic majorities" for the cause.[32]

The campaign was spirited, made even more so because many on both sides were laying foundations upon which to build future political careers. Opponents from northern Alabama played on poor whites' fears of disfranchisement while confirming a commitment to Jacksonian principles of low taxes and limited government, which at times made it seem that they were for, rather than against, ratification. Meanwhile, advocates in southern Alabama underscored their determination to maintain white supremacy, reform the suffrage, and (though they never came right out and said so) keep power in the hands of people like themselves. Blacks' protests, though vigorous, went largely ignored outside their own communities, where leaders were preparing to challenge the proposed new constitution in court. As the date for the vote drew near, opponents could see what was about to happen. "Are we in the white counties," one of them wrote the *Birmingham Age-Herald*, "to understand as white men that we are to have a constitution forced upon us by the Negro vote in the black counties?" The question was rhetorical. The writer knew the answer.[33]

On November 11, Alabama voters went to the polls. Or at least they did in most of the state. In the Black Belt, however, black voters did not have to make the trip. White officials handled the matter for them. If a black voter did appear to cast a ballot, he was allowed to vote as he wanted, since supporters of the proposed new constitution knew his vote would be counted the way they wanted. Throughout the state, 190,347 votes were cast, and 108,613 were tallied in support of the new constitution. The rest, 81,734, were cast against ratification. Twelve Black Belt counties gave the constitution more than 30,000 votes. Take the Black Belt's votes out of the equation, and the constitution would have failed.

For years, historians have played with the figures, calculated and recalculated to determine if the constitution of 1901 was legally ratified. The answer has always been the same. The "art" that Black Belt leaders had perfected over the years and which other Democrats had readily endorsed was practiced once more so that it would never need to be practiced again. In this fashion, Alabama got a new constitution.[34]

Notes

1. *Montgomery Advertiser*, July 7, September 4, 1901. The most complete account of the 1901 constitutional convention is in Malcolm Cook McMillan, *Constitutional Development in Alabama, 1798–1901: A Study in Politics, the Negro, and Sectionalism* (Chapel Hill: University of North Carolina Press, 1955). Much of the information in this paper is based on chapters 15 through 20 of this work, and it will be the source unless otherwise cited. For additional information on the events leading up to the convention, see Sheldon Hackney, *Populism to Progressivism in Alabama* (Princeton: Princeton University Press, 1969); William Warren Rogers, *The One-Gallused Rebellion: Agrarianism in Alabama, 1865–1896* (Baton Rouge: Louisiana State University Press, 1970); William Warren Rogers, Robert David Ward, Leah Rawls Atkins, and Wayne Flynt, *Alabama: The History of a Deep South State* (Tuscaloosa: University of Alabama Press, 1994); and Samuel L. Webb, *Two-Party Politics in the One-Party South: Alabama's Hill Country, 1874–1920* (Tuscaloosa: University of Alabama Press, 1997).

2. *Official Proceedings of the Constitutional Convention of the State of Alabama, May 21, 1901 to September 3, 1901* (Montgomery: Brown Printing Company, 1901), reprinted in 4 volumes (Wetumpka, Ala.: Wetumpka Printing Company, 1940), 3:2982, 3079; *Mobile Register*, January 20, 1900.

3. *Official Proceedings*, 1:10; *Montgomery Advertiser*, September 25, 1901. Both Rogers, *One-Gallused Rebellion*, and Webb, *Two-Party Politics*, cover the Populist movement.

4. McMillan, *Constitutional Development in Alabama*, 233–36, 242–43.

5. The *Official Proceedings* are full of references to ways in which the franchise restrictions would apply regardless of race, especially in volume 3, which covers the debate of the suffrage report. Newspapers, especially the *Montgomery Advertiser*, also recorded these attitudes.

6. Webb, *Two-Party Politics*, 132–36; *Mobile Register*, April 23, 1901.

7. Rogers, *One-Gallused Rebellion*, has a good account of the Populists' defeat. See Michael Perman, "Joseph F. Johnston, 1896–1900," in *Alabama Governors: A Political History of the State*, ed. Samuel L. Webb and Margaret E. Armbrester (Tuscaloosa: University of Alabama Press, 2001), 127–33.

8. Albert Burton Moore, *History of Alabama* (University, Ala.: University Supply Store, 1934), 632; Rogers et al., *Alabama*, 343–45; *Mobile Register*, December 11, 14, 1898.

9. McMillan, *Constitutional Development in Alabama*, 255 n. 45.

10. *Montgomery Advertiser*, April 26, 28, May 2, 3, 5, 1899.

11. *Wilcox Progressive* quoted in the *Montgomery Advertiser*, May 13, 1899; *Mobile Register*, January 20, 1900; Minutes of the Democratic state convention quoted in McMillan, *Constitutional Development in Alabama*, 258, 259 n. 76.

12. McMillan, *Constitutional Development in Alabama*, 260– 62. See especially page 261, note 93 for the minutes of the state Democratic Executive Committee, April 3, 1901.

13. Trasher's "special correspondence" was reprinted in the *Montgomery Advertiser*, June 16, 1901. Oates's letter is in the May 15, 1901, issue of the *Advertiser*. For other accounts of events in and around the opening of the convention see the *Mobile Register*, April 7, 1901, and the *Birmingham Age-Herald*, May 22, 1901.

14. *Official Proceedings*, 1:9–12.

15. Ibid., 9–16.

16. Ibid., 101–3.

17. Ibid., 101, 3:3121. Biographical sketches of leading delegates were published in the *Montgomery Advertiser*, June 16, 1901.

18. Rogers et al., *Alabama*, 346–47. Phrases such as these were used often in the *Official Proceedings*.

19. McMillan, *Constitutional Development in Alabama*, 271–80; Rogers et al., *Alabama*, 346–47. Among the proposals put before the convention were plans calling for giving women the vote to balance and negate black voting strength. None, however, were seriously considered. *Birmingham Age-Herald*, May 16, 1901.

20. The majority report is in the *Official Proceedings*, 1:1257–64; the minority report is in 1264–66.

21. *Montgomery Advertiser*, July 24, 1901; *Mobile Register*, April 23, 1901; *Official Proceedings*, 3:2875, 2982, 3035, 3079, 3225, 3233, 3280, 3372, 3396.

22. *Official Proceedings*, 3:2785–86, 2848, 3039, 3207.

23. John B. Knox, "Reduction of Representation in the South," *Outlook* 79 (1905): 171; *Official Proceedings*, 3:2990.

24. *Official Proceedings*, 3:2971, 3097.

25. Ibid., 2:2720, 3:2789, 2797, 2886.

26. Ibid., 3:2979, 3083.

27. Ibid., 3:3018, 3172, 3267, 3374, 3376, 3381, 3386, 3389, 3390. The poll tax was particularly oppressive because it was cumulative. If a voter failed to pay one year, he had to pay for the missed year (or years) before he could register. For newspaper commentary see the *Birmingham Age-Herald*, May 5, 8, 11, 19, June 6, 1901, and *Montgomery Advertiser*, June 5, 1901.

28. *Official Proceedings*, 1:188–92.

29. Ibid., 3:2836, 2840–41, 4:4303. According to Trasher of the *New York Evening News*, the petitions backfired and "had the effect of making many of the delegates more conservative as regards the Negroes." *Montgomery Advertiser*, June 16, 1901.

30. *Official Proceedings*, 2:2343–53, 3:3442, 3907–25.

31. McMillan, *Constitutional Development in Alabama*, 310–339; *Official Proceedings*, 1:1119.

32. *Birmingham Age-Herald*, September 5, 1901; *Montgomery Advertiser*, August 22, 1901.

33. *Birmingham Age-Herald*, October 4, 1901.

34. McMillan, *Constitutional Development in Alabama*, 349–59. Each of the studies mentioned in note 1 assessed the outcome and reached the same conclusion—the election was stolen.

3
A Tragic Century

The Aftermath of the 1901 Constitution

Wayne Flynt

THE MOST DRAMATIC consequence of the 1901 Alabama Constitution was the one most desired by its drafters, the sudden and precipitous decline in voting. In 1900 approximately 181,000 African American voters had been eligible under the old 1875 constitution. By January 1, 1903, only 2,980 had been permitted to register under the new document. Particularly dramatic was the decline in the Black Belt, where registration of African Americans in fourteen counties declined from 79,311 to 1,081. Among white voters the decline was less dramatic but still substantial. In 1900 the state had 232,800 eligible white voters; three years later only 191,500 white males were registered, a decline of 41,300 despite increasing population. Some 25,000 to 50,000 who registered did not pay their poll tax during the first year, hence becoming ineligible to vote.[1]

As decades passed, the effect of the poll tax became more punitive and exclusionary because of the accumulative feature that required voters to pay it every year from age twenty-one to age forty-five whether or not there was an election (a feature found elsewhere only in the Georgia Constitution). When the Alabama Policy Institute studied voter participation in 1941–42, it estimated that some 600,000 whites and 520,000 blacks were disfranchised by various provisions of the 1901 constitution.[2] In most counties, more whites were disfranchised than were registered, limiting the vote to a select elite. African Americans remained shut out of participation in their own government despite the fact that some of them were at that very moment fighting in the armed services to protect it.

Consequently, the restriction of suffrage led to a decline in voting. By the middle of the century, Alabamians would grouse about the low turnout for elections, yet that condition was precisely both the intent and the effect of the 1901 constitution. In 1900, 153,300 citizens cast ballots in the gubernatorial election. Six years later, only 94,700 voted in the highly contentious 1906 governor's race, a decline of nearly 40 percent despite a population increase. In presidential elections Alabama's turnout declined from 34 percent in 1900 to 21 percent in 1904 and to 14 percent in 1924. In the decade before 1900 as many as 80 percent of eligible Alabamians, white and black, voted; in 1940 only a third of adults were even registered.[3]

The suffrage provisions of 1901 become even more significant when compared with those of the 1819 Alabama Constitution, the state's first charter. Otherwise one might assume that the operative principle in Alabama public policy had always been anti-democratic. Actually, the opposite was true. The 1819 constitution, which ushered Alabama into the Union, was a projection of the towering presence of Thomas Jefferson and the democratic aspirations of the American Revolution. Delegates to the 1819 convention had pointedly refused to restrict suffrage based on literacy, ownership of property, or even church affiliation. Any white male twenty-one years of age or older could vote, whether or not he could read or write and whether or not he owned property, belonged to a church, or believed in God. But then the democratic assumptions of that first gathering of founding fathers at Huntsville in July 1819 were not shared by their successors when they met in Montgomery in May 1901.

Nor was the democratic assumption of Alabama's own past the only principle violated by the framers in 1901. So was the dominant democratic thrust of the twentieth century both in America and throughout the world. It was the federal government and not the state of Alabama that enfranchised women in 1919. It was the U.S. Supreme Court in 1962 that demanded that every vote count the same by compelling reapportionment after the Alabama Legislature refused to do so for six decades. It was Congress in the 1965 Voting Rights Act that finally enfranchised Alabama's blacks. And it was the U.S. Supreme Court in 1966 that ensured the right to vote for all the state's poor of whatever color when it struck down the poll tax.

If the century-long wail for states' rights by Alabama's white elite struck many Americans as hollow and hypocritical, perhaps it was because that otherwise noble ideal for restricting tyranny was so often employed in Alabama on behalf of tyranny. For in Alabama the 1901 constitution did not empower the people; it empowered the legislature. Without recall, initiative, referendum, or home rule, power was vested in government, not in citizens. And democracy was forfeited to the U.S. Congress and to the federal courts.

White power was the central, though not the only, consequence of the constitution that the framers drafted in 1901. The Alabama Democratic Campaign Committee urged party members to ratify the new constitution with a curious modification of America's motto *e pluribus unum* ("of many, one"). Printed on each envelope soliciting a vote to ratify the new constitution was the motto "White Supremacy, Honest Elections, and the New Constitution One and Inseparable."[4]

Living in a nation newly engaged in building an American empire, colonizing dark-skinned people, and rationalizing white supremacy from Darwinian science, the architects of the 1901 constitution were not surprised when the U.S. Supreme Court upheld their handiwork. After all, their racial ideology had taken root in the most elite American universities, in government offices in the nation's capital, and in popular culture. Why not in the chambers of the Supreme Court as well?

So the constitutional fathers of 1901 operated with immunity for their racial assumptions. The generation that had written the 1875 constitution had sought the same racist ends but was restrained by uncertainty regarding federal reaction. No such qualms prevailed in 1901. What had been merely implicit in 1875—that African Americans must expect far less in government services—became explicit in 1901: blacks could not vote; they could not marry whites.

Black anger focused on these matters. But greater long-term damage was wrought by the cap on taxes. As the state's poorest citizens, African Americans had most to gain from public services. Free public schools, universal public health programs, humane prisons, and mental hospitals all would disproportionately favor them. But after 1901 there was neither the will nor the money to provide such services.

Some delegates to the 1901 convention, such as future U.S. senator Thomas J. Heflin, sought to deny rights because they envisioned a future race war and feared that education would better equip blacks to win it. Others, like John B. Knox, the convention's president, were paternalists who discriminated according to class rather than race. In their view, all poor and uneducated people should be denied the full rights of citizenship; there was no reason to set blacks apart for special discrimination. But whether a framer was a racist from the Alabama Hill Country like Heflin or an urbane, well-educated paternalist like Knox, the effect was the same. Blacks would attend inferior schools, die more frequently of most diseases, experience worse health, and be overrepresented in the convict lease system. Striking down overtly racist sections of Alabama's constitution became, in retrospect, a relatively easy task of the civil rights movement. The less obvious and more profound discrimination was deeply embedded in provisions dealing with tax policy, education, and home rule.

Tax policy was central because taxes funded virtually all public services. As we will see, Alabama ranked throughout the twentieth century at or near the bottom among all states in three interrelated categories: property taxes, public services, and quality of life. This circumstance was no accident. It was the intent of the 1901 framers that government have a difficult or impossible task in taxing property. Even some people with little property, black and white, joined with those who had much in support of low tax rates.

Virtually all of Alabama's twentieth-century problems were related to the state's tax structure. The Brookings Institution concluded in 1932 that the taxing authority of the 1901 constitution "warped and distorted" revenue production and created a "gravely defective" budgetary system. With property taxes capped by the constitution, officials struggled to locate alternative sources of revenue to fund state services: license and privilege taxes, sales and occupational taxes, personal and corporate income taxes—a hopeless "conglomeration," as the Brookings experts phrased the situation. By 1940 more than 75 percent of the state's tax revenue came from sales or other direct taxes on individuals.

And as sales taxes increased, property taxes as a proportion of state revenues declined. In 1920 property taxes provided 63 percent of state tax revenue. In 1978 the figure was 3.6 percent. By 1992 it was less than 2 percent. The next lowest state's property taxes were 30 percent higher than Alabama's, and the national average was 375 percent higher.[5]

Reliance on sales taxes also shifted the tax burden from those best able to pay to those least able. By century's end, Alabama had the nation's most regressive and unfair tax system. The wealthiest 1 percent of Alabamians paid some 3 percent of their income in state and local taxes, while the poorest fifth of the population paid 12 percent of their income.[6] In 1933 Birmingham spent less money on vital city services than sixty-seven of sixty-eight American cities of 120,000 population or more.[7]

Even sales taxes were applied differently to various businesses, which hired lobbyists to win individual exemptions. Tobacco distributors purchased tax stamps from the state that granted them discounts (a tax exemption that amounted to $5.5 million in lost revenue in 1990). Farm interests were particularly adept at winning exemptions. Sales of food and milk carried sales taxes; sales of fertilizer and chicken litter did not.

Because local governments could levy sales taxes without legislative approval, these taxes steadily increased after they were first permitted in the late 1930s. The original state sales tax was 2 percent, but by 1963 the rate had doubled. In 1969 local governments gained the authority to add taxes on retail sales, and the combined sales tax for the city, county, and state some-times reached 11 percent, with 8 percent being common statewide.

Although Alabama had the nation's lowest property taxes, some special interests—notably the forest products industry and the Alabama Farmers' Federation (ALFA)—demanded still greater protection. At their urging, Governor George Wallace and the legislature passed Amendment 373 in 1978, placing yet another cap on the amount of taxes that could be collected. The amendment also changed the way land was assessed. This legislation applied value to land based on its "current use" rather than its actual market value. The state set a single standard for farmland and timberland statewide and determined the value of each category—$443 per acre for farmland and $275 per acre for timberland, often well below market value. Tax assessors were responsible for determining current use and enforcing payment of taxes. But they were locally elected and feared lawsuits challenging their assessments. So the easy way to do business was simply to grant all applications for current use.

The result was incredible abuse of the system and chronic underfunding of schools, which otherwise would have received the money. Newspaper reports uncovered the following examples:

• In 2000 a parcel of land in Montgomery County was taxed at $1.84 an acre based on its current use to grow trees; later it sold for $200,000, meaning it could have been assessed at its actual value of $35,000 per acre.

• In Fairhope, the owner of a house and a half-acre lot valued at $41,000 paid twenty-five times more in property taxes than owners of a prime piece of Gulf Shores waterfront property valued at $95,000 but taxed under current use for its timber value.

• In 1994 three dozen subdivisions in Baldwin County contained lots whose current use was listed as timber.

• In Mobile, Buchanan Lumber Company, which owned thirteen acres near the state docks in 1999, paid $5,876 in taxes on an assessed value of $570,500. Meanwhile, CG Investment Venture in the same city and during the same year paid taxes of $38 (on assessed value of $387 per acre) on a nineteen-acre timber-covered tract in a choice Mobile suburb. When CG Venture sold the property in June 2000, the buyer paid $912,871, or $48,046 per acre.

• For Mobile County as a whole, half the property in 2000 enjoyed current-use protection and produced 1 percent of the county's property taxes. Taxed at its real market value, that property would have generated $2.4 million in taxes; taxed under current use, it yielded $1.3 million.[8]

Current use gave Alabama a tax advantage over all other southern states. A state homeowner in 1984 with a house valued at $100,000 paid $352 in ad valorem taxes compared to $1,069 in Georgia, $1,090 in Florida, and $1,410 in Mississippi. Businesses valued at $500,000 paid $4,160 in Alabama compared to $5,600, $7,250, and $3,750 in the other states. Timber and farm owners with property worth $500,000 market value paid $1,475 in Alabama compared to $3,150, $7,250, and $5,625 in the three neighboring states.[9]

This advantage in property taxes for Alabama's landowners, however, translated into an equally huge disadvantage in comparisons of per-pupil expenditures for education. As each new funding crisis struck Alabama, public officials desperately sought another bandage to stop the bleeding.

After the state's entire school system closed in December 1932 for lack of funding, educators lobbied legislators to allocate specific new taxes exclusively for education. As a consequence of this practice, called "earmarking," Alabama by 1993 earmarked 87 percent of its revenue, compared with the national average of 24 percent. Ideally, a state constitution omits reference to specific rates of taxation, leaving such policies to legislative bodies. Not Alabama. For example, the constitution dedicates most of the state income tax to paying teacher salaries, and it dedicates nearly half of the state's property tax revenues to education. Gas taxes and state motor vehicle registration fees are earmarked, mostly for expenses related to public highways.

Inadequate revenue and excessive earmarking tied the hands of legislators, who were restricted from moving revenue from one category to a more critical one during financial crises. As a result, the state was frequently sued for violations of the constitutional rights of state prisoners, the physically and mentally handicapped, juveniles in protective custody, and children in foster care programs or public schools. One mental health suit took thirty years to resolve. A case challenging the child welfare system remained active into the new century, as did another involving equitable spending on students in poor school districts. For lack of revenue, legislators could not resolve these cases, but they could and did allocate tens of millions of dollars in legal fees to litigate the cases.

Another palliative that legislators tried unsuccessfully was to tax out-of-state corporations at rates higher than in-state businesses. Section 232 of the constitution required companies incorporated outside Alabama to establish in-state headquarters and pay a special franchise tax. In 1989 Reynolds Metal Company sued the state, charging that these "foreign" corporations should not be made to pay higher taxes than their "native" competitors paid. ALFA, which by this time had developed its own insurance business, helped sponsor discriminatory legislation that favored in-state companies, and it advertised how it charged lower rates than did competing companies. Of course, the reason ALFA could charge lower rates was obvious. It forced competitors to pay higher taxes, which had to be added to their operating costs. As a result of Section 232, 18,556 companies based out-of-state in 1994 paid a total of $90 million in state taxes. Meanwhile, 63,777 Alabama-based companies paid a total of $10 million.[10]

As almost all tax experts predicted, the U.S. Supreme Court in 1999 declared that Section 232 violated the U.S. Constitution, throwing the state into yet another financial dilemma. At least by then the state had nearly a century's experience dealing with financial crises generated by the flawed tax structure created by the 1901 constitution.

The primary state function crippled by insufficient tax revenues was education. The problems were fourfold: citizens' historic resistance to taxation, their lack of commitment to education, inadequate funding, and an unpredictable and unreliable funding source. The first two problems were rooted in the culture. The last two were rooted in the 1901 constitution.

Because property taxes were so constitutionally difficult to increase, school systems and other governmental units relied ever more heavily on revenue from sales and income taxes. By 2000, for instance, the city of Mobile derived $524 (56 percent of total revenue) per person from its local sales taxes, but generated only $41 per capita from property taxes.[11] This distribution not only taxed the city's poorest citizens unfairly but also created a volatile budgetary system. During economic good times, revenue from retail sales and income taxes flooded into state coffers, encouraging wasteful and duplicative expansion of community colleges and state universities. During recessions, sudden and precipitous declines in sales and income taxes required prorating education budgets. By contrast, property taxes virtually never declined; they moved slowly, predictably higher as property values were reassessed every three years or so.

The result of overreliance on sales and income taxes was painfully obvious. On average about every three or four years the state education budget had to be prorated in midyear because of unanticipated declines in state tax revenues. Most other states escaped such severe disruptions by obtaining a much larger share of their education funding from property taxes. Furthermore, when proration occurred in Alabama, it tended to place public schools at loggerheads with higher education as each group battled to minimize its proration at the expense of its "rival."

Complicating the problem still further was the constitutional restriction on local education funding, which was set extraordinarily low. A local community or county had to generate only ten mills in taxes (which produced less than $200 per student in some school districts). As a result, Alabama ranked ninth in the percentage of school revenue provided by the state government.

Compounding the lack of local revenues were differing land values across the state. The ten mills of required local effort produced sharp variations in revenues depending on the value of local property. If one lived in Huntsville, Hoover, Homewood, Vestavia Hills, or Mountain Brook, where property values were high, local millage rates produced a great deal of money. And well-educated citizens in those communities, who both valued education and were committed to excellent public schools, raised their local property taxes from three to five times above the state minimum.

The situation was quite different in rural Coosa County, where parents cared less about education and had fewer resources. Acres of timber outnumbered people in the county by thirty-two to one. But the 360,000 acres of timberland generated insufficient revenue to balance the education budget, and the state had to bail out the county. The top four county landowners together controlled 130,000 acres in 1994 but paid only $98,000 in property taxes, averaging less than a dollar an acre. When the school system was unable to balance its books, the superintendent proposed a twelve-mill increase in property taxes. The increase would have boosted taxes by $58 a year on a house valued at $48,600. Angry voters, however, defeated the referendum three to one. Coosa County's commissioners were not prohibited by the constitution from raising sales taxes, but such an act would have required more political courage than most commissioners had. Moreover, the rural county had only one grocery store and one hardware store and *no* Wal-Mart. Thus sales taxes were not a realistic option.

The solution, as so often happened with education in Alabama, was to rely on charity. Kimberly-Clark Lumber Company, headquartered in Texas, objected to higher property taxes but consented to a tax-deductible, charitable contribution of $660,000, and county parents helped raise $100,000 more in matching funds. One of the major projects funded with the contributions was a new football stadium for the consolidated Coosa County High School. Other money went for books and computers, although the schools could not afford professional improvement days for teachers to become proficient in using the new technology. Nor could schools afford to hire teachers' assistants to help children learn to use computers.[12]

Coosa Countians' defeat of a local increase in property taxes to improve schools was not unusual. Nearly two-thirds of all such tax referenda failed in Alabama. And the places where they passed—in affluent suburbs—were the ones that needed them least and wanted them most. The result was a public school system in shambles. Schools asked parents to donate paper, pencils, even cleanser and toilet tissue. Public schools increasingly charged most students what amounted to tuition (though the fees were called "recommended donations"). Foreign languages, advanced placement classes, art, music, and honors classes disappeared from curricula.

Rapidly growing schools such as Castlen Elementary in southern Mobile County operated portable classrooms (constructed to serve 350 children in 1968, Castlen enrolled three times that many in 2000, housing them in twenty-seven portable units served by two portable rest rooms). Mobile County voters rejected the higher taxes necessary to build a new school three times before finally approving new tax revenues in 2001. In other schools around the state, elementary children took recesses on playgrounds standing in raw sewage backed up from antiquated plumbing systems. Children rode to school on aging buses declared unsafe for use.[13]

Faced with similar conditions at home, DeWayne Key, superintendent of Lawrence County schools, organized poor systems into the Alabama Coalition for Equity and sued the state. Hundreds of pages of evidence and testimony demonstrated conclusively to Montgomery Circuit Judge Eugene Reese that the quality of education a child received in Alabama depended substantially on where he or she lived. In his written opinion, which revealed compassion as well as literary skill, Reese declared in 1993 that the state's support for public schools was inadequate and inequitable. Ironically, he cited a provision in the 1901 constitution that required the state to provide for a "liberal" system of public schools. Unfortunately, a succession of Alabama governors refused to implement the ruling, legislators rejected it (claiming that separation of powers prohibited the judiciary from compelling the legislature to levy new taxes), and the elected Alabama Supreme Court was too timid to enforce it. At the end of the century, the school equity suit remained unresolved. Meanwhile, another generation of students had completed their education in school systems that the courts agreed were inadequate and unfairly funded.

If one consequence of the 1901 constitution seemed the greatest anomaly, it was the denial of home rule. The state's motto, "We Dare Defend Our Rights," had been played out often in its long history. Localism, devotion to community, states' rights, antipathy to outsiders (especially self-righteous ones), resistance to external threats, and opposition to centralized authority—all these attributes inclined even the casual observer to predict that Alabamians would fiercely resist any attempt to infringe upon their capacity to govern themselves or to remove that power far from them. Yet that is precisely what the 1901 constitution did.

Neither towns nor counties initially had much control over their own affairs, although subsequent actions loosened the legislative grip over cities. Counties were not so fortunate. Although residents elected county commissioners, these officials had little authority. Only the legislature could write local laws for unincorporated areas, which meant that the county's legislative delegation functioned as its de facto government. And a single senator in the delegation could veto any proposal merely by exercising what the legislature referred to as "local courtesy." In fact, Alabama was the only state in the Southeast that denied its counties even minimal authority to plan for land use.

The results became more painfully apparent as the century progressed. In the early 1990s, 87 percent of Cullman County's citizens voted to elect their school board members. But they had no authority to do so. Instead, the county's legislative delegation had to introduce an amendment to the state's constitution. The legislature had to approve the proposed amendment. If a legislator objected, the amendment had to be passed in a statewide referendum as well as in the county where it originated. Two years after Cullman County's voters expressed their overwhelming desire for change, the state finally granted them permission to elect their school board members.

The Cullman case, though silly and time-consuming, was successful, but not all cases ended so well. Where conflicting interests collided, especially when one of the interests was that of ordinary citizens and the other of powerful groups, the outcomes were not so obvious. In Mobile County, for example, real estate developers opposed efforts to require paved roads or sewer systems in new subdivisions. As a consequence, during one twelve-month period in the late 1990s developers constructed sixty-eight substandard dirt roads for forty-one private subdivisions. Nor were the developers required to grade, drain, or repair the roads.[14]

In DeKalb County, a commercial hog farm with four thousand animals was located next to rural houses. For Brenda Ivey it was like the end of the world. She tried everything to remedy the problem of odor from the hogs' wastes. She hung sheets in front of air vents, emptied cans of air freshener, stuffed towels in door cracks, wore a mask while mowing her lawn, held her breath on the way to her car, and complained to her county commissioners. Local officials sympathized but had no zoning authority and could not help her. To protect the hog farms, ALFA sponsored legislation guaranteeing the right of an owner in rural areas to use land any way he or she desired without regard to the rights of neighbors. Brenda Ivey may have expressed more insight than frustration when she told a reporter for the *Birmingham News*, "I don't feel like we live in America."[15]

Her problems were serious but not unique. The Jefferson County Department of Revenue had to ask legislative permission to allow residents to renew car, boat, and mobile home registrations over the Internet in order to avoid long lines at the county courthouse. Fayette County officials tried to save $5,000 a year by repealing a provision involving beaver tails. At one time the county had requested a local act to allow payment of a $10-per-tail bounty because beaver dams were causing flooding. But when the danger of flooding passed, trappers continued to bring in beaver tails, demanding their bounty. Because beaver tails did not identify themselves as coming from Fayette County, local commissioners became suspicious that "ringers" were trapping the beavers in other counties and claiming the reward. But, of course, repealing the bounty required the same lawmaking process as had enacting the original bounty.[16]

Over and over, citizens ran into the same kind of lunacy. One frustrated journalist/professor perfectly captured conditions. Bailey Thomson wrote: "Our situation is like asking Moses to tack a few hundred amendments onto the Ten Commandments, including one to legalize camel racing for the tribe of Judah. Local matters just don't belong in the fundamental law."[17]

The fact that purely local matters had to be enacted by the legislature meant that lawmakers, not renowned for their abilities to resolve complex problems anyway, spent approximately half their time passing purely local legislation. That is, they passed such bills if they proved noncontroversial; if any powerful special interest opposed a local bill, its fate was pretty well sealed.

As a consequence, by the end of the century Alabama's constitution was the longest and probably also the most idiotic in the world, with 315,000 words. It had more than 700 amendments and was 40 times longer than the U.S. Constitution, which had been amended only 27 times in more than two centuries. Moreover, as life became more complex, the constitution had to be changed more and more frequently: 326 times between 1901 and 1974, 246 times between 1974 and 1994, and more than 140 times between 1994 and 2001. And well over half the amendments dealt with a single county or municipality. By contrast, from 1819 to 1901, under the state's first five constitutions, the people ratified only six amendments.

One result of the lack of home rule was a dysfunctional, inefficient state government. Decades of judicial and congressional intervention clearly proved that legislators were far better at governing counties than at governing the state. Several national surveys by *Governing* magazine and other nonpartisan professional groups rated Alabama's legislature the least effective in the nation (see Anne Permaloff's chapter later in this volume). Most of these evaluations did not refer to the character or ability of legislators. Instead, they criticized the planning process, the size and quality of staffs, and access to an independent legislative research agency. It was not that part-time legislators failed to understand the need for such resources. They simply lacked the money to pay for them.

That deficiency, in turn, made legislators largely dependent on lobbyists for data and information. In 1972 several dozen lobbyists operated in Montgomery. By 2001 there were 550, nearly four for every lawmaker. Legislators complained that sometimes they could not walk the halls from their offices to legislative chambers because of the mass of lobbyists blocking their way. With power vested in the statehouse rather than in the sixty-seven counties, Montgomery was a magnet for special interests. A lobbyist who could control eight votes on the House Rules Committee could shut down a legislative session. The result was government of, by, and for special interests. The citizens of Alabama did not control their government. Trial lawyers, the Business Council of Alabama, ALFA, the Alabama Education Association, and other special interests held the reins of power.

Alabama's weak ethics rules further diminished the quality of state government during the last century. Lobbyists could contribute "campaign funds" to legislators while bills they favored were being considered by the same lawmakers. There were no limits on contributions by individuals or political action committees. The latter could transfer money among themselves, making it virtually impossible to trace contributions to specific sources. Lobbyists could spend up to $250 a day entertaining lawmakers without even reporting the expenses. In one session filled with gallows humor, the legislature passed a "reform" requiring that lobbyists wishing to contribute to legislators while bills they favored were being considered had to do so in their offices rather than in the halls, thus avoiding traffic congestion and the appearance of impropriety.

Other than its failure to assure home rule, the 1901 constitution's most obvious problem was the death grip it often imposed on economic development. For a century, officials sought to attract business and industry to Alabama by nearly any means. Yet in even this endeavor the constitution failed, as almost any impartial analysis of the state's economy during the century demonstrated. Section 93 of the 1901 document prohibited the state from building roads and other public works. Of course, 1901 was part of the horse-and-buggy era. But by 1912 the state had 3,385 automobiles; by 1920, 75,000; and by 1930, 277,000. Everyone wanted a car, and every driver wanted a hard-surfaced road on which to drive it. Businessmen realized that if roads did not improve, other states would take away their markets. Farmers realized that if they could not transport crops to market more efficiently, competitors from other states would capture their share. Lawmakers hastily amended the constitution in 1920 to allow bonds to be sold to build and pave roads. And a state that spent $1 million on roads in 1921 spent twenty times as much in 1928.[18] What followed was more than forty amendments to evade or change the language of Section 93 in order to ensure modern life in Alabama.

The constitution hindered economic development in other ways as well. For example, local governments could not enter into partnerships with industrial prospects or lend them money, an original prohibition altered by fifty amendments by 2001.

For ten years after 1984, Calhoun County commissioners and the Anniston Chamber of Commerce cooperated on an Economic Development Council to recruit industry for the county's ailing economy. In 1993 the chamber asked the county to formalize the legal status of their arrangement. County commissioners concurred and contacted their legislators. The legislators agreed to sponsor an amendment in the legislature. The legislature passed the amendment, which required a statewide vote. But Calhoun County's proposed change, along with seventeen other local amendments, was put on hold while a federal judge impounded some two thousand absentee ballots in a disputed race for Alabama's chief justice. As a result, what Calhoun County business and political leaders could have done in a matter of minutes required many months to complete.

By the century's end, the 1901 constitution crippled economic development in more substantive ways. The advent of the North American Free Trade Association and the General Agreement on Trade and Tariffs led to a transfer of low-wage, low-skill jobs from America to developing countries. But free trade also created millions of high-wage, high-skill jobs in this country. The problem was that recruiting manufacturing industries, particularly high-tech companies, required economic incentive packages. Meeting this need required frequent amending of the 1901 constitution, which slowed the state's response or required it to innovate in finding spare millions (the Retirement Systems of Alabama and the Oil and Gas Trust Fund were typical sources). Sometimes the governor had to pry funds out of hard-strapped local governments.

Some companies attracted by state incentive packages and low taxes located elsewhere because of Alabama's crumbling roads and bridges. Or they fled from a state constitution filled with amendments establishing specific local taxes, providing tax exemptions, and creating special tax districts, a procedure so complicated that just listing all the exemptions to sales taxes required many pages. And the best and most advanced American businesses avoided the state because of its chronically underfunded schools and colleges, its poorly educated workforce, its high rates of poverty and illiteracy, and its paucity of cultural attractions. The 1901 constitution set Alabama's course as a low-tax, low-service state that did not have even enough money for essential state services, much less enough left over for adequate state parks, theaters, museums, and other cultural amenities.

Nor did Alabamians have to wait for historians to tell them all this. As Professor William H. Stewart demonstrates in the following chapter, visionary political leaders throughout the twentieth century insisted that the 1901 constitution be revised or replaced. Their efforts, however, met resistance from special interests or indifference from citizens and thus failed to achieve results, except for the replacement in 1973 of the judicial article.

In this new century, Bailey Thomson, a journalist and professor at the University of Alabama, who had written perceptively about the problems created by the constitution, joined Samford University president Thomas E. Corts, former governor Albert Brewer, former U.S. representative Jack Edwards, and many other modernizers and reformers to organize Alabama Citizens for Constitutional Reform. At first ignored by Governor Don Siegelman and ridiculed by special interests as a bunch of naive "do-gooders," this new generation of reformers gained traction when an economic downturn and proration of the education budget propelled the state into another of its periodic crises. Polls indicated that citizens who had previously ignored the issue now ranked constitutional reform as one of their highest priorities. Numerous legislators of both parties endorsed reform, though disagreeing on how best to accomplish it. Even many special interests were forced to concede the need for some changes, although they often used delaying tactics to find some way to blunt the reform movement.

Perhaps the most hopeful sign as a new century began was the inability of opponents of reform to find a high-profile leader to champion their cause. Eunie Smith, president of the ultra-conservative Alabama Eagle Forum, and ALFA spokesmen complained that constitutional reform was merely a cover for tax increases. And a new addition to Alabama fringe politics, the Association for Judeo-Christian Values (with ties to Ten Commandments judge and

Alabama Supreme Court chief justice Roy Moore), incomprehensively extolled Alabama's constitution as one of the nation's finest. The association's director, Sandra Lane Smith, claimed that attempts by some reformers to redefine shifting state borders were actually a move to eradicate state boundaries and substitute regional planning groups run by the United Nations. She added that rewriting the constitution threatened its preamble that acknowledged God and advanced a radical anti-family feminist agenda by substituting the words "All men and women are created equal" for the 1901 wording, "All men are created equal."[19] As zany as such allegations were, reformers had to take them seriously because oftentimes more powerful opponents hid behind and supported such groups.

A century of failed efforts at constitutional reform made one thing certain: replacing the flawed 1901 document would be no walk in the park. Inadequate as it was, at least the architects of the 1901 constitution frankly stated the arguments of class privilege and racism that were paramount in their deliberations. By 2001, arguments against reform were couched in appeals to biblical origins and American virtue, neither of which had played much of a role in the morally flawed document that had governed Alabama for a century.

Notes

1. Malcolm C. McMillan, *Constitutional Development in Alabama, 1798–1901* (Chapel Hill: University of North Carolina Press, 1955), 352–53.

2. Ibid., 354.

3. Ibid., 354–55.

4. Quoted in Harvey H. Jackson III, "'White Supremacy' 1901 Battle Cry," "Sin of the Fathers," Special Section, *Mobile Register*, December 11, 1994.

5. There is a rich literature on the injustice and inadequacy of Alabama tax policy from which I drew my analysis. For a brief summary of this argument, see Wayne Flynt and Keith Ward, "Taxes, Taxes, Taxes: Alabama's Unresolved Dilemma," *Alabama Heritage* 24 (Spring 1992): 6–21. For more detailed analysis, see Michael Kieschnick, *Taxes and Growth: Business Incentives and Economic Development*, vol. 11, *Studies in Development Policy*, ed. Michael Baker (Washington, D.C.: Council of State Planning Agencies, 1981); Guthrie J. Smith, "Trends in the Tax System in Alabama" (M.A. thesis, University of Virginia, 1936); *The Alabama Revenue System: Report of the Revenue Survey Committee, An Interim Committee of the 1954 Legislature* (Montgomery: January 1947); *Current Tax Problems of Alabama: A Report of the Committee on the Revision of the Tax Laws* (Montgomery: June 1957); *Report of the Joint*

Continuing Committee to Study the Tax Structure of the State of Alabama and the Distribution of Taxes (Montgomery: The 1981 Legislature, January 1981); *A Legislator's Guide to Alabama Taxes: A Summary of the Major Revenue Sources of the State of Alabama* (Montgomery: Legislative Fiscal Office, January 1991). Three major editorial reform series in Alabama newspapers focus on how the 1901 constitution hamstrung and distorted the tax system: "Sin of the Fathers," *Mobile Register*, December 11, 1994; Bailey Thomson, "Century of Shame: Alabama's 1901 Constitution," *Mobile Register*, October 15–22, 2000; "A New Century, A New Constitution," *Birmingham News*, January 30–February 4, 2001. See also *Proceedings and Selected Papers from the Symposium on the Alabama Constitution*, December 13–15, 1995, published by the Center for Governmental Services, Auburn University, 1996.

6. The negative effect of Alabama's regressive tax structure on the poor has been well documented by Alabama Arise, the state's advocacy organization for the poor, in a continuing series of research reports.

7. For the calamitous effect of lack of tax revenue on social services in Alabama's largest city, see Edward L. LaMonte, *Politics and Welfare in Birmingham, 1900–1975* (Tuscaloosa: University of Alabama Press, 1995).

8. All these examples are taken from a remarkable series combining excellent historical research and graceful prose: Thomson, "Century of Shame," *Mobile Register*, October 15–22, 2000.

9. Data from Center for Government Services, Auburn University; see Flynt and Ward, "Taxes, Taxes, Taxes."

10. Carol B. McPhail, "Reynolds Almost Defeated Alabama's Franchise Tax," "Sin of the Fathers," *Mobile Register*, December 11, 1994.

11. Bailey Thomson, "Faces from the Future," Mobile Register, October 18, 2000.

12. Carol B. McPhail, "Outdated System Has Coosa Schools Struggling for Life," "Sin of the Fathers," *Mobile Register*, December 11, 1994.

13. Thomson, "Faces from the Future," "Century of Shame," *Mobile Register*, October 18, 2000.

14. Thomson, "The Beast in the Garden,'"Century of Shame," *Mobile Register*, October 16, 2000.

15. Editorial, "Hogtied, Handcuffed," *Birmingham News*, February 2, 2001.

16. Ibid.

17. Thomson, "Absurd in Alabama," "Century of Shame," *Mobile Register*, October 20, 2000.

18. William Warren Rogers, Robert David Ward, Leah Rawls Atkins, and Wayne Flynt, *Alabama: The History of a Deep South State* (Tuscaloosa: University of Alabama, 1994), 429.

19. *Birmingham News*, May 14, 2001, February 8, 2002.

4
Failure of Reform

Attempts to Rewrite the 1901 Constitution

William H. Stewart

I n this essay we will examine efforts dating back to 1915 to comprehensively reform the 1901 Alabama Constitution. Many of the concerns of the reformers, past and present, are repeated in successive revision campaigns.

Governor O'Neal's Appeal

Governor Emmet O'Neal was the first major figure in the state in the twentieth century to petition for a new constitution. In a written address delivered to the legislature on January 15, 1915, as he was leaving office, the governor indicted the 1901 constitution, saying, "Many of the provisions of our present antiquated fundamental law constitute insuperable barriers to most of the important reforms necessary to meet modern conditions and to secure economy and efficiency in the administration of every department of state government." O'Neal was in step with the thinking of his era on the place of African Americans in the Alabama political system, and he endorsed the provisions of the 1901 convention that discouraged blacks from voting. However, he felt that "no real or permanent progress is possible until the present fundamental law is thoroughly revised and adapted [in other respects] to meet present conditions."[1]

Two of the reforms Governor O'Neal desired in a new constitution were authorizing the state to engage in internal improvements (especially to construct improved roads) and stimulating more local support for public education. He was convinced that "no permanently successful system of elementary education [could] be maintained that relies entirely upon state aid and not upon local taxation, initiative, and effort." Just as now, the more the state must do for primary and secondary schools, the less money is available for higher education. O'Neal's ideal constitution would be much more succinct. For example, "no other court except the supreme court [would] be specifically provided by the constitution." He wanted "the legislature [to] be free to remodel and readjust." The ballot would be short, and "the election of so many officers by the people" would be limited. The governor summed up his generally ignored plea by contending that the defects of the present constitution, though it had been in effect scarcely more than a decade, "are so numerous and radical, and so intermingled in the different sections," that trying to fix the document through amendments would be practically impossible. What should be done was to elect delegates to a constitutional convention to "take into consideration the entire subject and remodel the entire constitution so that it might make a harmonious whole."[2]

Governor Kilby's Commission

Governor Thomas E. Kilby also made his call for scrapping the 1901 constitution as he was about to leave office. In a written message on January 9, 1923, Kilby reflected that his term as chief executive had demonstrated to him that "much progressive legislation, badly needed and greatly desired, has been restrained because of some constitutional limitation or inhibition." While constitutional amendments helped with this problem somewhat, "the result [was] that we now have much confusion and a great lack of co-ordination in the fundamental law of the State." What was especially noteworthy about Kilby's appeal was that, in addition to a constitutional convention, he also advocated "the creation of a commission composed of, for example, thirty-five citizens of the State, drawn from the worthy members of such groups of our people as the farmers, the business men, the educators, the bankers, the doctors, the bench and bar, the press and organized labor." The task of this constitutional commission would be to make the work of the convention more efficient by drafting in advance suggested changes for the assembly's consideration. This gubernatorial plea was also ignored.[3]

The Brookings Report

On January 30, 1931, at the behest of Governor B. M. Miller, the legislature authorized a comprehensive study of Alabama state government by the Brookings Institution. Its five-volume report did not deal primarily with constitutional problems. However, W. F. Willoughby, one of the main figures in early-twentieth-century public administration in the United States, asserted that "no adequate reorganization of the government of Alabama is possible without amendment of a considerable number of the provisions of the present

Constitution." The Brookings study quoted approvingly and at length the preferences of Governors O'Neal and Kilby for a constitutional convention and wholesale revision to piecemeal amendment. Willoughby's conclusion was the same one that constitutional critics continue to advance—that "the existence of inflexible and unchangeable provisions, essentially statutory, in the Constitution has made it difficult or impossible for the state government to adjust itself to new needs."[4]

The Alabama Policy Committee

Starting in the mid-1930s, a group known as the Alabama Policy Committee (APC) began regularly to urge the drafting of a new constitution. Participants in APC meetings included academics, business leaders, journalists, educators, church activists, and a few elected officials. As examples of the kinds of constitutional changes the group advocated, the APC's model constitution, presented to the public early in 1939, called for a House of Representatives composed of one member from each of the sixty-seven counties and a Senate with a minimum of two members from each congressional district. This would have provided a modicum of reapportionment in the upper house of the legislature. APC members believed that Alabama had gone to the extreme in trying to prevent any black political participation. Thus the new constitution would abolish the poll tax as a prerequisite for voting. The APC dissolved in the mid-1940s, however, without achieving any success against what it described as "reactionary forces."[5]

Folsom's Special Sessions

The only governor up to the middle of the twentieth century to do much more than simply call for comprehensive constitutional revision was James E. Folsom, Sr. He fought vigorously for a new constitution, although his prospects for winning were never any more likely than those of his predecessors O'Neal and Kilby.

Soon after taking office as the result of an election that had shocked the political establishment, Governor Folsom on March 1, 1947, convened a special session of the legislature, asking it to call a constitutional convention. Folsom and his union allies were especially desirous of seeing the poll tax abolished and the legislature reapportioned. Folsom had no honeymoon with the legislature, and the special session quickly adjourned without giving serious consideration to his call for a constitutional convention.

Even though Folsom routinely asked legislators to join him in advocating a new state constitution, he deferred until 1950, the last full year of his first administration, before making seemingly bizarre appeals for a constitutional convention. Newspapers, which were generally unfriendly, interpreted Folsom's actions as mere political ploys to show voters in 1954 how vigorously he had fought for change when he ran again for governor. More special sessions were called during 1950 than in any other year before or since.[6]

At the first special session, in June 1950, Folsom proposed a "reapportionment" amendment that would create a sixty-seven-member upper chamber, reflecting the number of Alabama counties. But the legislature declined to approve this proposal, which scholars warned would have actually made malapportionment *worse* in the state's most populous areas. What Folsom proposed was not representation based on one person, one vote. Nor would the legislature heed his repeated call for a constitutional convention. Folsom called second, third, and fourth failed sessions in July before the fifth and final special session for 1950 was summoned to begin on August 9. In issuing his last call, he threatened that "if the legislature continues to adjourn before the Constitution is properly complied with [particularly with respect to reapportionment], I expect to use whatever power [is] in my command to keep the legislature in session until the woods have been properly and brilliantly persimmoned." For the benefit of those unfamiliar with the fruit-bearing habits of persimmon trees, a reporter pointed out that "Persimmons usually don't ripen until after the first big frost in the Fall."[7] However, the legislature retained the upper hand, and although it remained theoretically "in session" until late October, during no part of this time was a constitutional convention seriously considered.

Only a few months after taking office for a second time, following a landslide victory in the spring Democratic primary in 1954, Governor Folsom summoned a special legislative session to begin on April 13, 1955. However, even though the legislature seemed more susceptible to gubernatorial influence in other areas, it was no more sympathetic at this time to Folsom's calls for a constitutional convention than it had been in the previous decade.[8]

In the year after the U.S. Supreme Court's historic decision that outlawed segregated public schools, the racial climate was even more hostile to such ideas as abolishing the poll tax and otherwise liberalizing provisions on race relations than was the case during Folsom's first term. Folsom tried to be somewhat more politically pragmatic by promising to limit the constitutional convention to the consideration of just legislative reapportionment. However, during a long recess taken by a still unsympathetic legislature, the Alabama Supreme Court ruled that it would not be permissible to assemble a limited constitutional convention. The supreme court also made it difficult for reformers by advising at the same time that it would be unconstitutional to set up a board of reapportionment to perform the reshuffling function, since this act would amount to an impermissible delegation of a legislative power to an administrative agency.[9]

The next year, 1956, Governor Folsom again challenged the legislature to submit the question of calling a constitutional convention to the people. And once more he tried to calm legislative fears by reemphasizing that he was preoccupied with legislative reapportionment and no other issue. "I am not trying to cram a personalized version of the Constitution down the throats of our people," the governor stressed. When the legislature adjourned on February 14, 1956, again turning a deaf hear to Folsom, this was the last time for more than a decade that consideration would be given to constitutional reform at the highest levels of state government.[10]

Revived Interest in Constitutional Reform

Interest in constitutional reform began to be noticeable once again in the mid-1960s. In 1967 the legislature was asked by several members to consider a number of plans for modernizing the state constitution. While Governor Lurleen Wallace and her husband, George C. Wallace, did not concern themselves with constitutional reform, majorities in the House and Senate did agree to set up a joint Constitutional Revision Committee in April 1967. When this committee reported, it suggested "a relatively small constitutional convention [as] the best means for an effective general revision of the Alabama Constitution." Even more noteworthy, however, was the committee's advocacy of "a small representative Constitutional Revision Commission," whose expected role would be to support the contemplated convention with research and advice.

Executive-legislative cooperation that was most likely to lead to constitutional change started in 1968, when Albert P. Brewer became governor upon the death of Governor Lurleen Wallace. During the same year he became governor, Brewer said that "at the proper time" he would call for a study that could possibly result in a major overhauling of the 1901 constitution.

In 1969 Governor Brewer recommended a constitutional commission to propose revisions to the 1901 constitution. This was the first time a constitutional commission had been suggested apart from its supportive role in connection with a constitutional convention. After much wrangling between House and Senate, and with no great enthusiasm on the part of most members for wholesale constitutional change, both houses approved a conference committee report setting up a twenty-one-member commission, which would include fourteen appointees of the governor, the Senate president, the speaker of the House, three designees of the speaker, and two designees of the Senate president.[11]

That this commission would not enjoy much success was determined early on. In one of the bitterest Democratic primaries in Alabama history, former governor George Wallace ousted Governor Brewer in a Democratic primary runoff in May 1970. Thus constitutional reform's inspiration, Albert Brewer, left office in January 1971.

Even so, the commission continued to do the work it was mandated to do. Given insufficient staff, apathy on the part of some committee members, and the unwieldiness of its work focus, the Alabama Constitution of 1901, the commission could not meet the statutory target of a final report by 1971. However, there was enough legislative support to give the commission a two-year lease on life. The price of the extension was an increase from seven to eleven legislators as members, clearly indicative of general legislative distrust of the work of the Constitutional Commission.

In an interim report in May 1971, the commission suggested several changes, the most publicized of which was its call for annual sessions of the legislature.[12] On the last day of the regular session of 1971, the legislature approved for submission to the voters in the general election of 1972 an amendment to the constitution providing both for annual legislative sessions and annual salaries to be paid to legislators. While President Richard Nixon was carrying Alabama lopsidedly in his reelection campaign, voters rejected annual sessions for a generally unpopular state legislature by a margin of 56 to 44 percent.

Despite the rejection of its principal recommendations, the commission continued to meet regularly. Its final report was submitted on May 1, 1973. This document concluded that "the 1901 constitution, with its [then] 327 amendments, is obsolete and should be replaced by a constitution that is more adequate for the citizens of the state and for their government, both state and local."[13]

The commission's entire constitution was introduced for legislative consideration and referred to the House Constitution and Elections Committee, where it still languished when the legislature adjourned sine die almost four months later. However, leadership was available to push for a modernized court system through amendment of the constitution's judicial article.

Judicial Reform

Despite the fact that judicial structures and procedures create little interest in most people, and although even proposals for comprehensive change do not arouse the instantaneous opposition that novel approaches advanced for other areas do, success for judicial reform efforts was not a foregone conclusion. Instead, judicial reform required much political skill on the part of proponents, particularly Chief Justice Howell Heflin of the Alabama Supreme Court. Throughout the 1973 regular session, Heflin and others worked to secure legislative support for an amended judicial article, recognizing the necessity of compromise on such matters as merit judicial selection, unyielding advocacy of which would doom reform.

In its most important aspects, the reformed judicial article that cleared the legislature provided for a unified court system headed by the supreme court under the leadership of the chief justice; established a system of district courts in place of a confusing array of inferior courts (although municipalities were allowed to keep their own courts if they wished); required all judges except probate judges to be lawyers; limited the range of political activities permissible for sitting judges; made it easier for judicial salaries to be increased; specified that judges could not run for reelection after reaching the age of seventy; and established strengthened mechanisms for disciplining erring judges. Judges would continue to be selected by popular vote on partisan ballots.

Typically in Alabama a smaller turnout has been more beneficial for proponents of constitutional change, and this was again true when the judicial article was approved on December 18, 1973, by a margin of 63 percent in favor and only 37 percent opposed. Meanwhile, the proposal for annual legislative sessions was placed on the ballot again in a special referendum in June 1975, and this time, with a low-key campaign and a small turnout, the measure was adopted.

Governor James and Constitutional Reform

Forrest "Fob" James succeeded George Wallace at the end of the latter's third term in January 1979. Shortly after he was elected, James named a committee to consider constitutional reform and make recommendations for revising the 1901 constitution. He especially wanted to change the requirement that even local amendments, a major source of clutter in the constitution, had to be approved statewide. What the new governor's "working group" offered had similarities with the constitution proposed by the Constitutional Commission six years earlier. However, the newer document stressed subjects in which Governor James was most interested—in particular, popular democracy (as through the initiative and the recall), and low property taxes.

For the first time ever a proposed new constitution passed one house of the legislature, the Senate, but the document expired in the House. Postmortem analyses of the fate of the constitution focused most attention on such disputed provisions as the recall, the removal of provisions that earmark tax revenues for education and other categories, and home rule for local governments.[14]

The Baxley-DeGraffenried Initiative

During his winning 1982 campaign for lieutenant governor, Bill Baxley had stressed the need for constitutional reform, and once in office he moved to make good on his pledge to work for it. George Wallace, now serving his fourth and final term, remained uninterested. However, Baxley found an effective ally in Ryan deGraffenried, a state senator from Tuscaloosa.[15]

Baxley named a special committee to draft a new constitution. This group focused on "cleaning up" the cluttered 1901 document by eliminating obsolete and duplicative provisions, the end result of which would be a constitution shorter by two-thirds and more understandable as well. For the first time, a "new" constitution did pass both houses of the legislature in 1983. The Baxley-deGraffenried initiative came to naught, however, only a little more than a week before the scheduled referendum on the proposed new version. The Alabama Supreme Court ruled six to three that the Alabama Constitution did not permit the legislature to put before the voters a new constitution in the guise of a single amendment to the present document.[16]

Incremental Changes

In early May 1993, the Alabama Senate on a voice vote passed a resolution that would have allowed Alabama voters to determine if they wanted a constitutional convention to convene in 1995. However, the speaker of the House, Representative James Clark, believed that any convention might be dominated by the trial lawyers, a group to which he was opposed, and he blocked its approval in the lower chamber.

In 1994 voters did vote for a constitutional amendment setting out a new procedure for consideration of purely local amendments to the Alabama Constitution. It retained the commission, created in 1982 by a previous constitutional amendment, that decides whether or not an amendment is local or statewide, but it removed the veto power of any one member to prevent the submission of an amendment for popular approval. The U.S. Justice Department had concerns that this individual veto was working to the detriment of amendments favored by African American legislators. This change was of no help in the cause of constitutional reform, however. Glut in the constitution of 1901 increased even more when the requirement for a statewide instead of a merely local vote on a proposed amendment was dropped. Logically, purely local concerns should not be the subjects of constitutional amendments.

In 1995 the legislature drafted and the voters subsequently approved an amendment that updated the old Article VIII of the 1901 constitution dealing with voting and elections. Three brief paragraphs replaced twenty sections from the old constitution, much of it invalid because of its unconstitutionally racist nature. However, since the new voting-elections article was ratified, no other constitutional articles have been approved by the legislature.[17]

Approaching the Constitution's Centennial

In 2000 two more replacement parts for the 1901 constitution passed the House but did not reach the floor in the Alabama Senate. One would have updated the Declaration of Rights by, for example, adding an equal protection clause and eliminating seemingly male-only language. The second would have clarified state boundaries that now no longer are in dispute. In 2001 the House again approved a "modern" version of the declaration, including the equal protection provision, and also authorized six-person juries. Male-oriented language was replaced with gender-neutral wording. Lastly, state and county boundary descriptions were updated in a new Article II for the constitution.[18]

The previous year, in 2000, a new organization was formed to champion reform in Alabama. The Alabama Citizens for Constitutional Reform (ACCR) gave itself the mission of leading the charge for change. ACCR's president is Dr. Thomas E. Corts, president of Samford University. The group's first event was a rally held on April 7 on the old capitol grounds in Tuscaloosa. No statewide leader except for Secretary of State Jim Bennett, a Republican, attended. Albert Brewer, the former governor, moderated the event.[19]

A poll sponsored by the Alabama Education Association early in 2001 found that 75 percent of its respondents believed that "it's somewhat or very important for the state to have a new constitution." However, 58 percent also said that they had a favorable impression of the current constitution. A survey in April 2001 found that voters did endorse the concept of a new constitution for Alabama but had some anxieties that it could lead to their paying higher taxes.[20]

Bill Smith, development director for ACCR, said his organization's "biggest challenge [was] educating the people on the need for constitutional reform." Somehow his group and others needed "to raise awareness and convince people that [the constitution] does have an effect on their lives." Another ACCR leader, former U.S. congressman Jack Edwards of Mobile, said the old constitution should be viewed as "the root of all the primary ills of the state."[21]

Legislative Initiatives

Within the legislature, several strategies for constitutional reform continued sporadically and simultaneously. An Associated Press survey of Alabama legislators found that 61 percent of the House members and 62 percent of those in the Senate approved in principle the idea of the assembly's rewriting a small number of articles of the old constitution annually. This action would amount to a modest, generally cosmetic approach to constitutional reform. In the Senate, Roger Bedford, a Democrat, sought to revive the Baxley-deGraffenried strategy of the 1980s by proposing a constitutional amendment that would reverse the Alabama Supreme Court's decision prohibiting voters from voting on a new constitution in the form of a single amendment to the old one. In the House, another Democrat, Ken Guin, proposed that the governor call the legislature into session to function as a constitutional convention itself, an approach that has limited public or official support.

Showing the relevance of partisanship as a new and significant variable in the complex equation of constitutional reform in Alabama, Republicans as a group were mostly responsible for the defeat of Democrat Bedford's constitutional reform efforts. One Republican senator, Larry Dixon, said: "I don't want the trial lawyers, the unions and the people who keep putting Roger Bedford in office in charge of the constitution." Another Democratic legislator, Senator Ted Little, introduced a bill in the upper chamber calling for a permanent constitutional revision commission. This was similar to the approach advocated by Secretary of State Bennett, who proposed a thirty-one-member bipartisan revision commission. It would conduct public hearings and attempt to mobilize support for the new constitution that it would write based on ideas and suggestions it received.[22] Bennett later embraced ACCR's plan for a citizens committee to do preparatory work for a convention but not produce the proposed constitution itself. He became the new commission's chairman.

Gubernatorial Leadership

As early as 1976, Don Siegelman was on record as favoring constitutional reform. While serving as Alabama's secretary of state in 1983, he continued to advocate a new constitution and sought to generate support for it in public meetings. He also published an essay entitled "A New Constitution—What Does It Mean to You?" In Secretary Siegelman's view, "the [1901] Constitution hinders democratic values . . . it produces inefficiency. A document of this length and detail greatly exceeds the statement of basic principles and structure of government a constitution is supposed to be." The 1901 constitution put "both the legislature and local governments in a constitutional straightjacket." The fundamental problem, Siegelman continued, was "not the number of amendments or the length of the document," but rather "a framework that is archaic and illogical in the context of today."[23]

At the beginning of the most recent movement for constitutional reform in Alabama, however, Governor Siegelman's reported opinion was that "there is no grass-roots support for reforming the constitution, and until there is, he won't spend any time thinking about it." In late March 2001, however, Siegelman began to signal a shift in his stance on the urgency of constitutional reform. In a position paper published in the *Birmingham News,* the governor wrote, "We need to change the way we do business [in Alabama]. The only meaningful way to do this is to look at reforming Alabama's antiquated constitution."[24]

In an address to a constitutional reform rally in Montgomery on April 4, 2001, Governor Siegelman stressed education (just ordered into proration due to revenue shortfalls) almost to the exclusion of all other considerations as a motive for constitutional reform. His main problem with the old constitution was that it had "held our schools back for more than 100 years." He likened the 1901 document to "a wagon that wasn't sturdy enough to carry its load when it was first put together—a wagon which has hindered progress in education." However, Siegelman cautioned that the contemporary revision movement might not have success right away, possibly not until he was out of office, because of the numerous formal and political obstacles that would have to be overcome. He did not outline a program for constitutional reform.[25]

In a speech on April 16, 2001, to the Alabama Commerce Commission, Governor Siegelman endorsed a constitutional convention as the preferred method of bringing about constitutional change for the state. "On this one we need to trust the people," Siegelman said. One specific provision he would like to see in a new constitution would be permission for local communities to increase their property taxes for schools through popular referenda without securing the approval of the legislature. Still, the governor did not summon the legislature to set in motion the steps leading to the meeting of an assembly of delegates to rewrite the constitution. He would instead travel around the state and listen to suggestions from voters as to how they would change the old constitution.[26]

Presumably in response to his conversations with Alabamians, in the State of the State address delivered at the opening of the regular legislative session beginning on January 8, 2002, Governor Siegelman asked the legislature to give the voters the right to call a constitutional convention by putting this question on the November general election ballot. In his speech, the governor pitted himself against "special interests" and argued that a new constitution would enable "the people" to retake control of state government from those who were more concerned with their own interests than with the general good. The primary motivation for constitutional reform, in the governor's mind, was the need to adequately fund public education, which was in an even more perilous condition than usual due to the nationwide recession and the downturn in revenues earmarked for schools.

Immediate prospects for favorable legislative action were dampened, however, when both key Democrats and minority Republicans expressed doubts that Siegelman's convention call would be endorsed before the regular session ended in the spring of 2002. Critics of the governor professed to believe that Siegelman, astute politician that he is, did not really expect legislative action in 2002, but mostly wanted an issue to run on as he sought a second term. Either Lieutenant Governor Steve Windom or U.S. Representative Bob Riley appeared, at the beginning of the year, to have the best chance of winning the Republican gubernatorial primary and thus being pitted against Siegelman on the November general election ballot. Both Riley and

Windom had also committed themselves to achieving a new state constitution. Windom said he preferred one drafted by a constitutional convention.

To win his own party's renomination, Siegelman faced Charles Bishop, the agriculture commissioner, who favored legislative initiatives for constitutional reform as opposed to a convention. Republican Tim James, son of former governor Fob James, was the only aspirant for the governorship from either of the major parties to specifically oppose comprehensive constitutional reform.

Within the legislature, the speaker of the House, Seth Hammett, expressed support for legislative reform of the 1901 constitution through an article-by-article revision, and simultaneous with Governor Siegelman's advocacy of a convention, the House began rapidly to approve "cleaned-up" versions of several relatively noncontroversial sections of the old document. The Senate, however, either refused to act on the House's proposals or made changes that were unacceptable to the sponsors.

Opposition to Reform

Opposition to constitutional reform in Alabama remains very strong. One legislator observed: "If what they're talking about is taking out the antiquated language, that's easy, but if we're talking about tax reform, that's problematic, and if we're talking about giving county commissions home rule, that's problematic." The Alabama Farmers' Federation (ALFA) is especially opposed to changes in Alabama tax laws. Elaine Witt, political columnist for the *Birmingham Post-Herald*, identified ALFA as "the protector of large landowners who are essentially untaxed." One of the organization's lobbyists said he "believe[d] that the folks who promote the idea of constitutional revision are focused on tax [reform] and land use planning."[27]

The new Republican chief justice, Roy Moore, became in the spring of 2001 the most quoted cautionary voice with respect to making major changes in Alabama's old constitution. He was particularly opposed to the legislature's drafting a new constitution, because "If you put changing the constitution in one branch of government, isn't there a conflict in the balance of powers?" Moore also saw what he considered strong points in the existing constitution, which in his view "has kept our taxes reasonable. It has kept things like the lottery out of the state. It has held down special interests."[28]

An anti-reform rally was held simultaneously with the pro-reform rally in Montgomery headlined by Governor Siegelman. Literature publicizing the rally had this advice: "Let's not destroy or revise. Let's preserve our constitution." The sponsoring organization for this much smaller event was identified as the Association for Judeo-Christian Values. Lobbyist Joyce Perrin, one of the speakers at this program called the "Keep Our Constitution" rally, asserted that the 1901 constitution was "written by godly men" and deserved to be retained rather than scrapped. The Alabama Constitution was founded on the Ten Commandments (the public display of which had made Roy Moore's reputation), Perrin claimed, and it was doubtful that a new document, formed in a much more secular time, would have the same basis. Opponents of change have also expressed anxiety that a new constitution could "remove references to God contained in the 1901 constitution," as well as facilitate the increasing of property and income taxes without popular votes, authorize comprehensive zoning, and enlarge the sphere of gambling operations in Alabama.[29]

Conclusion

In this chapter we have examined efforts dating from 1915 to achieve comprehensive constitutional reform in Alabama. While these initiatives must be viewed as failures as judged by the inability to achieve a new constitution to replace the existing document so roundly condemned, there are nonetheless important lessons that can be learned by both present and future generations of reformers.

Race has historically been the most important factor in Alabama politics. Beginning with the first small movement toward constitutional reform in 1915, race was prominently mentioned in connection with proposed changes. At that time, however, white supremacy was so firmly entrenched that Governor Emmet O'Neal was able to say that what black Alabamians might or might not desire was now irrelevant because they had been effectively excluded, presumably indefinitely, from the political process. By the mid-1930s, although blacks were still politically impotent, there were, as we have seen, a few both within and outside of government who were willing to assert some of their claims to fairer treatment from the majority whites.

In the current constitutional reform movement, racial issues have not been dominant thus far, and the divisions pro and con related to the concept of a new constitution seem to be between competing groups of whites. The overwhelming number of black Alabamians who have expressed a position, however, favor a new constitution that would eliminate the present offensive racial language (even though it has no legal effect) and one that features a reformed tax system that stresses ability to pay much more than is the present case.

At present, one of the most commonly heard objections to a constitutional convention to draft a new basic law for Alabama is that it would be dominated by interest groups. Interest groups have indeed been very visible in some previous constitutional reform movements. For example, during the effort led by James E. Folsom, Sr., most opposition came from the Alabama Farm Bureau Federation (the precursor of ALFA). A combination of interests, again including organized agriculture as well as big business and industry, worked against some of the proposals of the Constitutional Commission in the early 1970s, particularly the suggestion for annual legislative sessions the first time it went on the ballot. In the current movement for constitutional reform in Alabama, however, the reactions of most major interest groups, again with the notable exception of organized agriculture (ALFA), have initially been favorable. How long this support would last would seem to depend on the specific proposals for change that emerge from the deliberative arenas for reform and their potential impact on these groups' interests.

As previously noted, a new dynamic in the equation of constitutional reform in Alabama is broader than interest group affiliation. It is the tie of political party. In none of the struggles related to constitutional reform prior to the late 1990s and early 2000s was the tie of political party significant. Since Democrats are likely to continue to dominate the legislature (perhaps heavily), whence all items short of an actual constitution drafted by a convention must come, the burden will be on Republicans in the statehouse to resist playing the role of spoiler by using their greatly strengthened position to kill constitutional reform for the sake of partisan advantage against a Democratic governor and his or her legislative allies.

It is also only in recent years that the media—overwhelmingly newspapers—have become important actors in the constitutional reform drama. The earliest constitutional reform efforts in the twentieth century went virtually unnoticed by the press. Toward midcentury, the newspapers did take notice but were mostly opposed because of their antipathy toward James Folsom, Sr. Beginning with the constitutional reform movement of the 1960s, the press has been mostly supportive, and now it provides the most incessant support for a new constitution.

Public opinion has never played a sustained role in shaping the outcomes of any of the constitutional reform efforts discussed in these pages. In the traditional Alabama political culture, citizens generally have been passive and have not attempted to pressure their leaders to act in favor of any desired comprehensive constitutional changes. The ultimate success of the present constitutional reform movement may hinge on whether large numbers of

Alabamians come to see that their constitution does indeed have a great impact on both the quality of their families' lives today and the lives that their children and grandchildren will lead in the future.

Notes

1. Emmet O'Neal's most recent biographer, R. B. Rosenberg, does not even mention O'Neal's recommendations related to constitutional reform. See *Alabama Governors: A Political History of the State*, ed. Samuel L. Webb and Margaret Armbrester (Tuscaloosa: University of Alabama Press, 2001), 157–62. Michael A. Breedlove, Thomas Kilby's biographer in the same volume, also ignores that governor's advocacy of comprehensive constitutional change; see 166–70. These omissions are regrettable, particularly since national public administration scholars were well aware of these governors' contributions and made reference to them; *Journal of the House of Representatives of Alabama* (1915), 1:310.

2. *Journal of the House of Representatives* (1915), 1:310–24.

3. Ibid. (1923), 135–36.

4. Brookings Institution, Institute for Government Research, *Organization and Administration of the State Government of Alabama*, vol. 1 (Montgomery: By the Institution, 1932), 51.

5. *Birmingham Age-Herald*, July 16, 1938, February 10, 1939; *Bulletin of the Alabama Policy Committee: Democracy and the Constitution*, April 14, 1945, 33.

6. *Birmingham News*, July 28, 1950.

7. Ibid., August 4, 1950.

8. Ibid., April 13, 1955.

9. *Opinion of the Justices*, 81 So.2d 678 (1955) 697.

10. *Birmingham News*, January 3, 1956.

11. *Journal of the House of Representatives of Alabama* (1967), First Special Session, 548; quoted in William H. Stewart, Jr., *The Alabama Constitutional Commission* (Tuscaloosa: University of Alabama Press, 1975), 6, 8. Most of the material relating to the work of the Alabama Constitutional Commission which appears in the following pages is drawn from this work.

12. Alabama Constitutional Commission, *Interim Report* (Montgomery: By the Commission, 1971).

13. Alabama Constitutional Commission, *Proposed Constitution of Alabama: Report of the Constitutional Commission* (Montgomery: By the Commission, 1973), iii.

14. This discussion relies mainly on James D. Thomas and William H. Stewart, *Alabama Government and Politics* (Lincoln: University of Nebraska Press, 1988), 47–48.

15. Ibid., 48–49.

16. *State v. Manley,* 441 So.2d 864 (1983).

17. Also in 1995, Auburn University's Center for Governmental Services presented a symposium on the Alabama Constitution in Montgomery at which prominent speakers from government, academia, and interest groups addressed the subject of reform, most being supportive. See the *Symposium on the Alabama Constitution: Selected Papers and Constitutional Articles Prepared for the Symposium on the Alabama Constitution,* December 13–15, 1995, Montgomery, Alabama (Auburn: Center for Governmental Services, Auburn University, n.d.).

18. *Tuscaloosa News,* February 18, 2001.

19. The group's website is www.constitutionalreform.org.

20. *Tuscaloosa News,* February 16, April 9, 2001.

21. Quoted in *Birmingham News–Birmingham Post-Herald,* April 7, 2001; *Birmingham News,* March 13, 2001; *Tuscaloosa News,* February 16, 2001.

22. *Birmingham News,* October 18, 2000, April 4, 6, 2001.

23. *Tuscaloosa News,* March 18, 25, 2001.

24. Ibid., February 15, 2001; *Birmingham News,* March 25, 2001.

25. *Birmingham News,* April 8, 2001.

26. Ibid., April 17, 2001.

27. *Tuscaloosa News,* February 11, 2001, quoting Senator Jeff Enfinger; *Birmingham News–Birmingham Post-Herald,* April 7, 2001; *Tuscaloosa News,* October 14, 2000.

28. *Tuscaloosa News,* April 8, 2001.

29. Ibid., April 1, 5, 8, 2001.

5
Missing
Local Democracy

Joe A. Sumners

T HE CLEAR INTENT of the framers of the 1901 Alabama Constitution was to stifle democracy in the state. These men, mainly wealthy plantation owners and Birmingham industrialists, sought to protect their property and privilege from populist demands for responsive government. To achieve this goal, they conspired to silence the democratic voices of small farmers and laborers—black and white—through poll taxes, literacy tests, and other tools of disfranchisement. By maintaining a submissive and cheap workforce while denying poor whites and blacks the right to exercise full citizenship, the framers would guarantee and preserve their control of the state.

The framers also were responsible for another, though less obvious, restraint on democracy in Alabama. They centralized political power in such a way that even today citizens have little say in how they are governed. The Alabama Constitution contains none of the provisions that empower citizens—recall, initiative, and referendum. Most important, Alabama's local governments lack the power to govern themselves. Instead, the framers centralized governing power at the state level in Montgomery, depriving Alabama counties, cities, and towns of self-government, or "home rule."

The framers believed that local governments had to be restrained lest they devise programs that men of property would have to pay for. Thus convention delegates imposed strict constitutional limits on local borrowing and taxing authority as a way of keeping cities and counties from spending money. To overcome these restrictions, many constitutional changes would be needed over the next century in the form of hundreds of local amendments.

Actually, the 1901 constitutional convention had a few dissenters on the subject of home rule. Some delegates argued that city and county elected officials would be more accessible to the public than would be the legislature and that voters would elect good people to local office if those officials were given decision-making power. These delegates wanted to grant county commissions the power to act on any matter not covered by general law and to give cities of over twenty thousand the power to adopt home-rule charters.[1]

The majority of delegates, however, wanted all power concentrated in the legislature. Opponents of home rule argued that legislators clearly were more capable of making decisions than were local officials and that unrestrained city and county officials would foolishly get themselves into all manner of mischief. These opponents could point to a few examples of local governments that made unwise investments for railroad construction following the Civil War.

Arguing against home rule, Thomas Bulger of Dadeville voiced the contempt of many in the legislature for local officials when he said, "No gentleman on this floor will contend that his Commissioners' Court at home is more capable of legislating for the people of his county than the General Assembly of Alabama, comprised of 100 select men." That argument prompted a rebuttal from John A. Rogers of Gainesville in Sumter County, who asked, "Why is it that these people can select such fine representatives to the Legislature and yet it be feared that they won't be able to select satisfactory County Boards to handle these matters?"[2]

Opponents of local self-government carried the day. As a result, local governments in Alabama operate under a constitution that prevents them from exercising the powers of self-government. For example, county governments lack the authority to pass ordinances, raise taxes, zone land, or do much of anything else without first going "hat in hand" to beg the legislature for approval. This bottlenecking of lawmaking power in Montgomery provides a focus for special-interest money and politicizes the smallest of county decisions.

State-Local Relations in Alabama

In 1868, Judge John F. Dillon of the Iowa Supreme Court expressed the principle—commonly known as Dillon's Rule—that localities can exercise only those powers conferred upon them by state government. According to Dillon, "Municipal corporations owe their origin to, and derive their powers and rights wholly from the Legislature. It breathes into them the breath of life, without which they cannot exist. As it creates, so it may destroy. If it may destroy, it may abridge and control."[3]

While most states subscribe to Dillon's Rule to some degree, none adhere to it more tenaciously than does Alabama, whose local governments are forbidden to do anything unless the legislature has first authorized them to take action. By contrast, the clear trend in other states has been to grant broad home-rule powers that enable local governments to do anything not specifically prohibited.

Lacking home rule, Alabama operates local government through the slow, cumbersome routes of constitutional amendment and local legislative act. In fact, local bills account for about half the legislature's workload. And more than seven hundred amendments inflate the state's fundamental charter—about 75 percent of them affecting only specific cities and counties.

Local acts are hardly new. In the decades prior to 1901, the legislature adopted far more local and private acts than general laws (local legislation applies to specific counties or municipalities rather than the state as a whole; private acts are concerned with specific individuals or corporations). There was general agreement in the 1901 constitutional convention that the legislature's power to adopt local laws should be constrained. As a result, the new constitution prohibited local acts on a long list of subjects. Moreover, the legislature could not pass a local act on any matter already covered by a general law.

Despite these constitutional constraints, the legislature since 1901 has used local acts as a primary means for governing cities and counties. Shortly after ratification of the new constitution, the legislature began to loosen its restrictions on the use of local acts. For example, Section 96 of the Alabama Constitution specifically prohibits the legislature from altering court costs and charges, or the pay of county officials, except by a general act applying to all counties. To get around this limitation, the legislature in 1912 adopted Amendment 2, allowing it to set salaries of county officers and court fees in Jefferson County. Today the provisions in Section 96 remain completely effective in only one Alabama county. About one hundred local amendments, applying to specific counties, have been adopted that relate to court fees, the pay of county officials, or both.[4]

In other areas where no amendment empowered the legislature to adopt local acts, the legislature developed other strategies to manage local affairs. One legislative tactic to circumvent the constitutional restriction on local legislation was the enactment of "general laws of local application." Without naming a specific county or municipality, a law was written so specifically—usually defined by a very narrow population range—that it could apply only to the targeted jurisdiction. In 1978 the Alabama Supreme Court invalidated such "general laws of local application." In response, the legislature created eight classes of municipalities based on population and began to write general laws for each class. Counties, however, were not included under this new law.

To expedite legislative action on local laws, the legislature follows the well-worn custom of "legislative courtesy." Under this practice, legislators representing the affected jurisdiction determine the fate of local bills. The House and Senate simply agree to the wishes of the locality's legislative "delegation." This practice gives the individual legislator great power back home.

Legislative courtesy made more sense many decades ago than it does today. Prior to reapportionment of the legislature in the 1970s, there was some accountability in this practice, since the 1901 constitution provided for a single senator for each of the larger counties. It also prohibited the splitting of any county between two or more senatorial districts. However, this arrangement disappeared with reapportionment, as legislative districts began to cross county lines to ensure fair representation.

Lee County, for example, is represented by three people in the Senate and five in the House, but only three of the eight actually live in Lee County. The situation may become even more complicated when a sixth representative to the legislature is approved following the decennial reapportionment. It is already difficult to get all Lee County representatives together to discuss and agree on local legislation. Any one of these members can prevent the adoption of a local bill, and none of them may have a particular reason to feel personally responsible for the smooth functioning of county or municipal government. According to Senator Larry Dixon of Montgomery, "If you are one of those legislators that has four or five counties in your district, you have unbelievable local power. Everyone is beholden to you."[5] In the absence of home-rule powers, local governments must continually ask their legislative delegation for help in matters big and small. One example of the absurd reach of local legislation is Alabama Legislative Act 647 (1973), "to permit flea markets to remain open on Sunday in Etowah County." Another is a local act in the 2000 legislative session that repealed a bounty on beaver tails in Fayette County.

Alabama has the longest constitution in the United States—and probably the longest in the world. While the average state constitution has about 26,500 words, Alabama's constitution weighs in at around 315,000 words. It is almost forty times longer than the U.S. Constitution. It is over twelve times longer than the typical state constitution. In fact, the combined constitutions of our neighbors—Mississippi, Georgia, Tennessee, and Florida—are only a third as long as the Alabama Constitution.

The Alabama Constitution was long even prior to the adoption of its first amendment. It included language that outlined, in very specific detail, what state and local governments could *not* do. Because of these constitutional restrictions, the smallest changes required amending the state's fundamental law. This constitutional straitjacket explains why throughout the twentieth century hundreds of changes had to be made for the state to adjust to modern life. The result is a constitution with an unbelievable 706 amendments as of this writing, each representing an attempt to loosen the original restrictions of the 1901 constitution. Over five hundred of these amendments—almost 75 percent of the total—apply only to specific counties and municipalities.

In the area of county finances, for example, there are more than one hundred local constitutional amendments that authorize counties to levy property taxes for specific purposes, including education, public hospitals, parks and recreation, youth services, rural fire protection, trade schools, economic development, roads and bridges, libraries, and debt service. Section 94 of the 1901 constitution prohibits the legislature from authorizing local governments to have any interest in a private enterprise. Voters have approved more than fifty amendments authorizing specific counties and cities to engage in economic development activities. Section 65 prohibits the legislature from authorizing "lotteries or gift enterprises for any purposes." Fifteen amendments have been adopted to allow the operation of bingo games in specific counties.

Amendment 555 provides that any proposed amendment that affects only one county is submitted to that county's voters alone unless one or more legislators object, in which case the proposal must be referred also to voters statewide. This procedure leads to ridiculous situations, as in 2000, when voters statewide considered an amendment that would allow the little town of White Hall in Lowndes County to operate bingo games.

The absurdity of the Alabama system of doing local government by constitutional amendment is well illustrated by the following list of topics for amendments to the 1901 constitution:

• Amendment 502 allows Morgan County to have a sheriff's posse.
• Amendment 351 provides for mosquito and rodent control in Mobile County.
• Amendment 482 allows Lauderdale County to dispose of dead farm animals.
• Amendment 497 prohibits the overgrowth of weeds and storage and accumulation of certain junk, motor vehicles, and litter in Jefferson County.
• Amendment 520 allows Madison County to excavate human graves.
• Amendment 34 permits Limestone County to tax for malaria control.

In 1907, the Alabama Legislature authorized the incorporation of cities and towns in places with as few as three hundred residents. It also gave municipal governments the power to "adopt and enforce ordinances not inconsistent with the laws of the state." Thus on most local matters, a municipality has the ability to act on behalf of its residents without having to seek legislative permission. For example, municipal governments have some flexibility in generating local revenue, and their partial grant of police power allows them to pass ordinances that address most of the health, safety, and welfare issues that concern their residents. They also have the power to zone and plan for development. However, Alabama municipalities do not have complete home-rule authority. For example, they are limited by constitutional taxing restrictions and debt limits, and they cannot change the structure of their city government.

In Alabama, cities are divided into five classes based on population, with all cities of similar size granted comparable powers under state law. Counties, on the other hand, are established as political subdivisions of the state, and whatever authority particular counties may possess has been granted to them piecemeal. In other words, there is no power for county governments except that which is delegated by the Alabama Constitution or authorized by the legislature. This means, for example, that Mobile County, which has more than 125,000 residents in unincorporated areas, cannot adopt zoning regulations, while the town council of Loachapoka, which has 259 residents, can. The Alabama Constitution allows county government little control over its own structure, functions, or many of its processes.

Despite the constitutional constraints, the demands on county governments have increased dramatically in recent years. An analysis by the Public Affairs Research Council of Alabama (PARCA) shows that 44 percent of Alabama's population growth during the 1990s was in unincorporated areas.[6] As migration from the inner city continues outward, counties, especially those in fast-growing metropolitan areas, face increasing demands for municipal-type services. In response, counties are being challenged to address issues of planning and land-use zoning, solid waste services, general economic development, and a range of other services demanded by citizens. County governments in Alabama are ill-prepared to meet the challenge. Even those counties with hundreds of thousands of residents have never been given general ordinance-making power resembling that of the smallest town.

Consequences of the 1901 Constitution

The 1901 constitution damages Alabama's communities and weakens local democracy in a number of ways. As the following sections will demonstrate, it contributes to wasteful and ineffective governments, anemic citizens, haphazard growth and development, and unrealized economic potential.

Wasteful and Ineffective Governments

These days governments at every level face an increasingly difficult question: How do they meet increasing demands for high-quality services in an environment characterized by stable or declining revenues and great public resistance to increased taxes? One solution, or at least a partial answer, is for governments to institute reforms to become more efficient and productive. Achieving such efficiencies in Alabama, however, would require a significant change in the nature of the existing state-county relationship.

The absence of local democracy means that both state and local governments perform poorly. At the state level, legislators' time is wasted on matters that could, and should, be dealt with by city and county governments. The term economists use to describe such a situation is "opportunity cost." The time and energies that legislators spend on local concerns could be spent addressing systemic statewide problems, such as public education. A recent study sponsored by *Governing* magazine ranked Alabama last in managing state government.[7] This ranking indicates that state legislators have plenty of statewide concerns to occupy their time and attention.

At the local level, an enormous amount of time—sometimes months and years—is wasted trying to get state permission for matters that might otherwise be handled in one city council or county commission meeting. Having to rely on the legislature means that only during a few months a year during a legislative session can a county government get a problem fixed, and that usually occurs only if there is unanimous support from the local legislative delegation. All it takes is one lawmaker to stop a local bill in its tracks. The way Alabama does local government is, in effect, a huge "tax" burden on the people of Alabama—the equivalent of an enormous "inefficiency tax." This waste constitutes lost opportunities for dealing with pressing concerns for both the state and the local governments.

The problem was outlined by Jim Williams, executive director of PARCA, in remarks he made to the Birmingham Area Chamber of Commerce: "We can't hold local officials accountable for results until we give them control over the services they manage. Inefficiency is inevitable as long as the people we elect to make policy for the state government also have to worry about local government, and as long as the people we elect to run local government can't make basic decisions without asking permission."[8]

Section 2 of the 1901 constitution states that the people have "an inalienable and indefeasible right to change their form of government in such manner as they deem expedient." The legislature has carried out this principle for municipalities, providing methods by which voters can choose among three forms of government: the commission form, the council-manager form, or the mayor-council form. However, the state legislature has retained for itself the power to change the form of county government; there is only one form of county government allowed under general Alabama law. Other states have expanded options for county organizational structures. In South Carolina, for example, county voters may choose among a range of governmental forms created by state law. Florida, Louisiana, and Tennessee go even farther, allowing voters to adopt local charters that create the form of county government they prefer.[9]

It is hard to imagine a structure less suited to efficient and accountable administration than is county government in Alabama. Its authority is fragmented among county-level offices filled by popular vote, creating a government of elected equals with no one in charge. The sheriff, tax assessor, tax collector, probate judge, and coroner are all elected independently and are not accountable to the county commission. For example, the county commission funds the county jail, but the sheriff runs it and does not answer to the commission. Also, it is difficult to defend the existing practice of electing such highly technical and professional positions as the county tax assessor, sheriff, or coroner.

Compare counties to Alabama's municipal governments, where department heads such as the police chief and finance director are selected based on qualifications and professional experience. Some city councils hire a city manager, who has authority to hire and manage these department heads. With such a structure, the municipal governing body exercises centralized control over the functioning of the city government, and voters can hold elected officials accountable for the city's successes and failures. Of course, no such accountability exists for Alabama county governments.

Around the state one sometimes hears citizens criticize the performance of their county government and county commissioners. But in the absence of adequate resources, efficient organizational structures, and sufficient authority to act, it is surprising that county governments are able to accomplish as much and perform as well as they do.

Anemic Citizens

"Popular sovereignty" is a pillar of democratic society; sovereignty rests neither in the government nor in the rulers, but in the people. Indeed, the highest office in a democracy is that of citizen. All other offices are filled by action of the people, and the people delegate to elected officials certain responsibilities. The 1901 constitution, however, provides very limited power to the people, and citizens remain a relatively unimportant force in Alabama's government and politics. While we may talk a lot about grassroots government and local control, Alabama has none of the constitutional provisions that provide for the people to act as the primary source of political power—referendum, initiative, recall, and home rule. The 1901 constitution is a formidable barrier to citizens who want to control their government.[10]

Government closest to the people is most responsive to the people. Local officials know more than those in Montgomery about local conditions and the needs of local citizens. City councils and county commissions meet twice a month, every month, giving constituents plenty of time to air their concerns.

By making government more responsive to local citizens, home rule would address the growing feeling of powerlessness and distrust that citizens have toward government. Under home rule, citizens could also hold county and city elected officials more accountable for the results of local government actions—or inaction.

To exercise the duties of citizenship, people need to have a basic understanding of their government and laws. This is nearly impossible for anyone trying to understand local government in Alabama. Laws and regulations for counties are made by statewide and local constitutional amendment, by general and local acts of the legislature, and by actions of the county commissions. It is increasingly difficult to know what the law is in a particular county. According to Alabama attorney general Bill Pryor, "It would be very difficult for the experts on my staff to be experts on the constitution, and we're the law firm for the state of Alabama."[11] Although this confusion works to the benefit of special interests that understand and manipulate the system, it works to the disadvantage of citizens who wish to exercise their role in the democratic process.

Haphazard Growth and Development

The most urgent problem facing metropolitan-area counties in Alabama is managing growth and development. The need to address such problems through land-use planning and zoning has become especially apparent in the state's fastest-growing counties: Shelby, Baldwin, Elmore, St. Clair, Autauga, Madison, Marshall, Blount, and Limestone.

The Alabama Legislature granted zoning powers to municipalities in 1907. Alabama counties, however, have never been given comparable planning and zoning authority, and instead they have received piecemeal authority. Three counties have limited zoning authority. The legislature also authorized all counties to regulate subdivision development, and later it expanded that authority to include mobile home parks. And in the mid-1990s, counties were authorized to adopt and enforce residential building codes.[12]

With such limited tools for planning, county governments can do little to stop a hog farm, rock quarry, racetrack, junkyard, or strip club from moving into a residential area. Counties cannot control nuisances, even when they may threaten citizens' health or safety. While localities in other states use development impact fees to help offset the costs of services that development requires, Alabama counties do not have that authority. Well-run localities in other states also require developers to provide normal infrastructure—paved streets, curbs and gutters, water and sewer lines—before they plat subdivisions. Not in Alabama.

The following are examples of how the absence of home rule can lead to absurd situations for Alabama counties:

• In Madison County, a company proposed a rock quarry near a quiet neighborhood. The residents protested, but Madison County has no zoning powers. Residents could seek relief through an act of the legislature, but the next legislative session was months away. The only solution for residents was annexation into the city of Huntsville, which could stop the quarry by exercising the zoning powers that Alabama grants to cities.
• The Gulf Shores Parkway is the gateway to Baldwin County's beaches, one of the state's most valuable tourist attractions. Yet what a tourist sees while driving down the parkway is a wall of ugly double-stacked billboards. Alabama counties do not have the authority to adopt sign-control ordinances.
• About three thousand people are moving into Blount County each year. Development is replacing farmland, packing schools with new students and filling roads with extra traffic. But Alabama does not allow development impact fees to pay for the services required by this growth.
• A family built a nice home in an unincorporated part of St. Clair County, which like most Alabama counties has no zoning restrictions. All was well until a huge hog farm moved next door. According to the homeowner, "Does it stink? Good God, yes! We can't even open the windows in our house."
• The Platinum Club, which features topless dancing, opened in the middle of a residential neighborhood on the outskirts of Anniston. Calhoun County commissioners were powerless to do anything about it.
• In Tuscaloosa County, people want to protect Lake Tuscaloosa from pes-

ticides and other pollutants caused by rapid growth in the area. Because the county lacks zoning power, however, citizens must depend on the legislature for a solution—which could take years.[13]

Many rural county commissioners will probably not want to tackle the hot political issues of zoning and land-use control. Many farmers and other rural residents do not want to be told what they can do on their land and are vocal in their opinions. As St. Clair County Commission chairman Stanley Bateman says, "One thing people are out here for is the freedom. Part of that freedom is being able to do what you want with your property." But in other fast-growing metropolitan counties, many commissioners feel a sense of urgency to prevent public nuisances and control haphazard development. Also, the nature of these former rural counties is changing. According to Lyman Lovejoy of the St. Clair County Economic Development Council, "The makeup of the county has changed so much over the past five years. You've got an urban population moving out here that doesn't think like your old country people."[14]

Unrealized Economic Potential

The issue of economic development in Alabama is tightly interwoven with the issues of taxes, education, and home rule. It is difficult to discuss economic development without exploring these other linkages. The Alabama Constitution outlines, in extraordinarily specific detail, the property tax system that funds local schools in Alabama. And the quality of local schools is the key determinant of the economic prosperity of the state and its communities. Without home rule, citizens are prevented from making basic decisions about funding their local schools. It is this interconnectedness that leads many to oppose piecemeal reform. In order to address issues of tax inadequacy and unfairness, the lack of local self-government, weak educational performance, and stagnant economic development, one must first attack the origin of these problems—the 1901 constitution.

The Alabama Commerce Commission, which Governor Don Siegelman appointed in 1999 to develop the state's economic strategic plan, recognized these connections. For that reason, the commission recommended that "the Governor should initiate activities to develop a plan for addressing constitutional revision and tax reform which will lead to the improvements necessary to allow this State to move forward rapidly in economic development."[15]

The seeds of Alabama's current economic development strategy—low taxes and minimal government regulation and services—were sown in the 1901 constitution. The constitution was designed for a nineteenth-century economy that depended upon the labor of poor, uneducated workers who planted fields and dug coal and iron ore. Throughout the twentieth century, Alabama's approach to economic development continued to rely on unskilled cheap labor and low taxes. With this strategy, the state managed to attract many low-wage manufacturing industries. By the late twentieth century, however, manufacturing companies were leaving the United States—and Alabama—for foreign nations where labor costs a fraction of what U.S. workers earn. In addition, high-quality industries now are less interested in low taxes. Instead, they look for a highly educated labor force, modern infrastructure, and public amenities that contribute to a high quality of life.

Progressive states saw early the limited potential of the old-style economy. They embraced the possibilities of high technology and welcomed the information age. But political leaders in Alabama remain mired in the antiquated model of low taxes and cheap labor. As a result, Alabama is poorly positioned to compete now that the question companies are most likely to ask is not "What does labor cost?" but rather "What does labor know?"

In today's economy, education is central to development and quality of life. Economic developers know that what industries need in the twenty-first century is an abundant, educated, and trainable workforce. Communities that can provide a sufficient number of well-educated workers will get the jobs. And business executives will be willing to locate only in communities with high-quality schools for their companies' employees.

Unfortunately, education has never been highly valued in Alabama. Recent comparisons show that Alabama ranks forty-seventh in the nation in average spending per pupil—just 74 percent of the national average.[16] It is no coincidence that Alabama's property taxes—the primary source of local education funding—are by far the lowest in the nation. Indeed, the state would have to more than triple its rates just to meet the national average! Taxing property at the national average would mean an additional $2.7 billion per year for public education and other vital state services.[17]

Local leaders who pursue economic development must struggle to overcome the obstacles created by the 1901 constitution, particularly the strict limits it imposes on the ability of communities to raise adequate property taxes to support good schools. Amendment 373, known as the Lid Bill, ensures that increasing local property taxes will require not only a local popular vote, but also a favorable vote of the entire legislature.

Counties and cities must be able to move quickly to put together incentive packages when major companies show interest. Yet Alabama's constitution forbids cities and counties from engaging in practices that are basic to economic development efforts in other states. For example, Section 94 prohibits cities and counties from lending or providing public dollars, or transferring publicly held assets, to private industries as part of an incentives package. It also prevents cities and counties from pooling resources to lure industry. Because of Section 94, cities and counties have been forced to ask the legislature—and voters—to approve constitutional amendments when they want to use financial subsidies to attract new industries.

Because the constitution restricts the ability to raise state and local revenues, communities often have been unable to build the infrastructure that companies look for when seeking plant sites. Crumbling roads and bridges, inadequate sewer and water mains, and lack of utility and telecommunications links in many areas are serious disadvantages when recruiting industries.

Most companies look at more than labor costs, taxes, or incentives before deciding where to locate a plant. They examine cultural attractions, recreation, health facilities, and other public amenities that define the quality of life in a community. The 1901 constitution, however, defines Alabama as a low-tax, low-services state. This means there is relatively little money for parks, libraries, the arts, and other amenities that help a company attract and keep talented workers. For many high-tech, high-paying companies, the lack of these extras in a community can be a big liability.

Conclusion

Alabama is the only southern state to deny home rule to county governments. Alabama counties, especially the fast-growing metropolitan counties, need the authority to make any local decisions that do not conflict with general state law. Without home rule, those governments closest to problems are prevented from resolving them. County government works best at the county courthouse, not at the state capitol.

Providing increased self-government for our communities will help to reduce waste and increase government effectiveness at both the state and local level, reconnect citizens to their local government and energize Alabama's democracy, reduce haphazard development and public nuisances in unincorporated areas, and allow communities to realize their economic potential.

Not all counties will want the increased decision-making authority that comes with self-rule. Some rural residents and county commissioners may want things left just as they are now. Home rule, however, should be an option for all Alabama counties that need it and want it. Local citizens should have the right to decide how they will be governed. This means some may prefer to retain the status quo. And some may be cautious and prefer to see how home rule works in other counties before taking the step themselves. That's what democracy is all about.

In *Essentials of County Reform,* Richard Childs, a local government reformer in the early twentieth century, wrote of the need for counties to have the freedom to adapt county reform efforts to their own particular circumstances: "A satisfactory solution of the many problems can be worked out only by a steady process of evolution, under conditions that give scope for experiment, free from needless constitutional restrictions. The counties must be free to advance individually and not in perpetual lockstep. Let the more progressive counties feel their way cautiously forward, to be followed by others when the value of a given step is clearly proved by experience."[18]

The Association of County Commissions of Alabama (ACCA) supports home rule with the creation of a classification system for counties similar to that used by municipalities. According to the ACCA:

Constitutional Reform in Alabama is long overdue and the public's renewed interest in this important endeavor can be the catalyst for change in our state. . . . The Association supports the enactment of a Local Government Article to the Constitution that would prescribe the basic authority and duties of both county and municipal government. In drafting such an article, consideration should be given to the enactment of a classification system for county government, similar to the existing municipal classification, which would allow for the passage of general laws that would apply to only specific counties categorized according to population.[19]

The local government article of a new constitution should give local governments the option to do the following:

• Establish alternative forms of county government—for example, commission, county council/manager, and elected county executive.
• Authorize the adoption of any of the alternative forms of government by local referendum.
• Allow the creation of city and county government structures in addition to the standard forms through a charter commission and referendum.
• Provide for the consolidation of city and county governments into a single entity.

• Grant city and county governments the authority to adopt ordinances to protect the health, safety, and public welfare of their citizens and to impose penalties for violation of those ordinances.

• Include in the grant of local ordinance authority the ability to adopt zoning regulations and development controls and to impose development impact fees.

• Allow functional consolidation or transfer of local government services among cities or between cities and counties.

• Allow county governments to reduce the number of elected department heads.

• Require consolidated budgeting and management of all local government funds.

Constitutional reform and home rule are no panacea. And an obsolete constitution is not the only problem we face in Alabama. But it is a *fundamental* problem. It is at the root of so many of the other problems we face, especially in our local communities. The 1901 constitution was written for a time that has long since passed. It embodied all the things the framers really cared about: low taxes on landowners, minimal government regulation and services, and white supremacy. Alabama has never really let go of those principles. The state will never realize its great potential until it rids itself of this outdated and dysfunctional constitution and restores faith in local democracy that has been missing in Alabama for at least one hundred years.

Notes

1. The PARCA Report, no. 18, Fall 1993, The Public Affairs Research Council of Alabama.

2. John Peck, "Study: Legislature Deep in Local Issues," *Huntsville Times*, June 21, 2000.

3. Elliott C. McLaughlin, "Officials: Home Rule Makes Government More Efficient," *Opelika-Auburn News*, March 19, 2000.

4. The PARCA Report, Fall 1993.

5. Thomas Spencer, "Home Rule Debate Commenced before 1901 Constitution," *Birmingham News*, July 8, 2001.

6. The PARCA Report, no. 32, Spring 1998, The Public Affairs Research Council of Alabama.

7. Katherine Burnett and Richard Greene, "Grading the States 2001: A Management Report Card," *Governing* 14, no. 5 (2001): 38. Available at http://governing.com/gpp/gp1intro.htm.

8. Jim Williams, "Why Business Needs to Be Involved in Constitutional Reform," Remarks to the *Compass on Business* Economic Forum and Luncheon, Birmingham, Alabama, March 23, 2000.

9. The PARCA Report, Spring 1998.

10. Gerald W. Johnson, "The Alabama Constitution: The People's Fundamental Document?" in *Proceedings of the Symposium on the Alabama Constitution* (Center for Governmental Services, Auburn University, 1995), 6–8.

11. Elliott C. McLaughlin, "Officials Say Constitution Is Proof Enough for Rewrite," *Opelika-Auburn News,* February 27, 2000.

12. Bessie Ford, "Big Brother Government—The Alabama Model," *Business Alabama Monthly,* January 1999, 13–17.

13. Examples taken from Bailey Thomson, "Alabamians Start to Rally for a New Constitution," *Birmingham News,* April 2, 2000; Gene Owens, "Capital Has the Power in Alabama, *Mobile Press Register,* December 11, 1994; Verna Gates, "Country Charm with Vigilance," *Business Alabama Monthly,* January 1999, 37–38; Linda Long, "Upwind of Unpleasant Aroma," *Business Alabama Monthly,* January 1999, 25–26; and Matthew Korade, "Alabama's Constitution: Delegates Decide Many Local Issues," *Anniston Star,* April 1, 2001.

14. Long, "Upwind of Unpleasant Aroma," 26.

15. Report of the Alabama Commerce Commission, Executive Summary, March 23, 2000.

16. Kendra A. Hovey and Harold A. Hovey, *CQ's State Fact Finder 2002* (Washington, D.C.: CQ Press, 2002), 208.

17. Ibid., 146.

18. Quoted in National Civic League, *Model County Charter, Revised Edition* (Denver: National Civic League Press, 1990), xiii.

19. "ACCA Takes Constitutional Reform Stand," *County Commissioner* 44 (Fall 2000): 17.

6
Alabama's Dysfunctional State Government

Bradley Moody

In 1978, AUBURN historian Malcolm C. McMillan deplored how the 1901 Alabama Constitution was a "legislative document" rather than a charter of fundamental laws and principles "rigid enough to protect the rights of all people and give them good government but not so restrictive and unpliant that it cannot be interpreted to meet the changing needs of succeeding generations." This antiquated 1901 constitution has remained "a straitjacket from which the state government has tried to extricate itself by piecemeal operations, each time patching the document but not removing its basic statutory nature."[1]

McMillan's criticism, offered in an introduction to the reprint of his acclaimed 1955 study of Alabama's constitutions, rings just as true a generation later. This chapter will document the ways in which the 1901 constitution, now amended more than seven hundred times, continues to make it difficult for the executive and legislative branches of Alabama state government to be responsive to the preferences and needs of citizens and to develop solutions for the short- and long-term problems facing the state.

Six specific issues will be examined: the requirement that many of the heads of departments in the executive branch are chosen by popular election; the power of the governor to make appointments to important policy-making and administrative positions in state government; the governor's veto power; the earmarking of state taxes for specific purposes; the constitutional amendment, adopted in 1984, that makes state budget appropriations the "paramount duty" of each regular session of the legislature; and the contemporary role of the lieutenant governor in the Alabama political process.

Elected Executive Department Heads

Because of their general distrust of government, and particularly because of their fear of concentrated power in the hands of one individual, Americans have tended to restrain the power of state governors—and they began doing so even before the ratification of the U.S. Constitution. The growing reliance on the "long ballot" during the first half of the nineteenth century, in response to the ideas connected to the kind of democracy associated with President Andrew Jackson, reinforced the already-present belief that the power of state chief executives should be limited by the popular election of many heads of state administrative departments. While some states have managed to move away from selection by popular vote, most still choose significant numbers of department heads through popular ballot. In one study completed early in the 1990s, Keon S. Chi examined data for eleven executive branch departments from 1972 to 1992 and concluded that 254 heads of these departments were popularly elected in the 1990s as compared with 256 in 1972, although there is considerable variation from state to state. States such as North Dakota and North Carolina elect more than eight department heads, while Maine, New Jersey, Alaska, Hawaii, New Hampshire, and Tennessee elect fewer than two.[2]

The most current information on popularly elected executive branch department heads is found in the 2000–2001 edition of the *Book of the States,* published by the Council of State Governments.[3] Data for ten of the most significant departments in state government are as follows:

Attorney-General	Elected in 42 states, including Alabama
Treasurer	Elected in 39 states, including Alabama
Secretary of State	Elected in 36 states, including Alabama
Auditor	Elected in 25 states, including Alabama
Comptroller	Elected in 18 states, not including Alabama
Education	The chief administrator, usually the superintendent of education, is elected in 14 states. Alabama does not elect its state school superintendent, but does elect the state board of education, the policy-making body for K–12 education in the state.
Agriculture	Elected in 9 states, including Alabama
Public Utility Regulation	Elected in 7 states, including Alabama, which elects the three-member Public Service Commission
Insurance	Elected in 6 states, not including Alabama
Labor	Elected in 5 states, not including Alabama

The average number of these ten executive department heads who are elected for all fifty states is 3.7. As the preceding list indicates, Alabama chooses six of this group of department heads by popular vote, a position shared with five other states (Florida, Georgia, Idaho, Kentucky, and South Carolina). Thus Alabama ranks among the top fifth of the states in this regard. Alabama's popularly elected state board of education is not included in the above calculations, nor are the boards of the seven additional states (Colorado, Kansas, Louisiana, Michigan, Nebraska, New Mexico, and Texas) who elect such bodies.

Several questions might be asked about the information presented above, but two seem to be particularly appropriate. First, does a state really need all of these officials? In Alabama, for example, could not many of the duties of the treasurer and the auditor, both elected, and those of the appointed comptroller be combined into two positions, or even one, especially given that the Alabama Department of Public Examiners, a legislative branch agency, also has similar responsibilities? A second question is more pertinent to a discussion of the overall effectiveness of the executive branch and particularly of the governor. It is well documented that the governor is the most visible and most recognized public figure among a state's citizens and that this greater visibility results in the governor's being given credit for the state's successes while being held responsible for its failures, even if neither is earned or deserved. Given these circumstances, would not citizens be able to render fairer and more accurate judgments of the performance of their governors if those elected leaders had more influence over the policy areas for which we hold them responsible?

Every year, the state of Alabama spends more than $4 billion on education—significantly more than it spends in any other single policy area. More than two-thirds of that spending is controlled by the state board of education, a body that includes eight members elected by voters in separate districts, along with the governor, who serves as president of the board. The board, created in 1969 by Amendment 284, replaced the elected superintendent of education and became the chief body for making and carrying out policy for all elementary and secondary education in Alabama. It also exercises budgetary and ultimate policy responsibility for the two-year community and vocational college system. While the governor serves as a member and as president of the board, he has only one vote on policy decisions. Likewise, he has only one vote when the board names a state superintendent of education or chooses presidents of the two-year colleges. If citizens, parents, and educators are concerned about the level of funding for education and about how the present funds are allocated among the various educational entities in Alabama, placing decisions about these matters clearly within the responsibilities of the governor by eliminating the elected state board of education and by making the superintendent of education a gubernatorial appointment, subject to confirmation by the Alabama Senate, would make accountability for these decisions much clearer.

Both the effectiveness and the accountability of state government would be improved if Alabama reduced the number of executive department heads that are popularly elected. Effectiveness would be enhanced by reducing the potential for conflict and inconsistency in making and implementing policy when different groups and departments are responsive to different constituencies and individuals. Moreover, accountability would be clearer and fairer if ultimate responsibility for successes and failures in policy were centered on one individual and one office. The present circumstances are an invitation to both ineffectiveness and inefficiency and make it more difficult for citizens to render fair and accurate judgments when giving credit or placing blame for the actions of state government.

The Governor's Appointment Power

In addition to popular election, the three most frequently employed methods for selecting heads of executive branch agencies are gubernatorial appointment without legislative confirmation, nomination by the governor with confirmation by the upper house of the legislature, and appointment by either a multi-member board that governs a department or the head of an agency within which a policy or service area is located. The first of these methods places the fewest restrictions on the power of the governor to select the heads of these departments, while appointment by a board or agency head generally imposes the greatest number of limitations on gubernatorial influence. The appointive power of Alabama's governor was compared with that of the governors of the other forty-nine states in twelve policy areas (not including those mentioned in the discussion of popularly elected department heads) using data provided in the 2000–2001 edition of the *Book of the States*.[4] The following table presents the results of this analysis.

Two points need to be made about the information in this table. First, the states use almost as many methods to select department heads as there are states. While the table includes the most frequently used methods, none of the totals for the most frequently used methods for the twelve policy areas in this table equal fifty because of the diversity of mechanisms employed. For example, the head of the budget office in Maryland is elected by the legislature, as mandated by the state's constitution. Officials in charge of economic

Methods of Selecting Heads of Executive Branch Departments

Policy Area	Number of States Using Each Method of Selection
Budget	Appointment by governor = 22 (Alabama) Nomination by governor, confirmation by upper house = 6 Appointment by board or agency head = 9
Corrections	Appointment by governor = 11 (Alabama) Nomination by governor, confirmation by upper house = 26 Appointment by board or agency head = 7
Economic development	Appointment by governor = 13 (Alabama) Nomination by governor, confirmation by upper house = 17 Appointment by board or agency head = 9
Environmental protection	Appointment by governor = 9 Nomination by governor, confirmation by upper house = 15 Appointment by board or agency head = 16 (Alabama)
Finance	Appointment by governor = 15 (Alabama) Nomination by governor, confirmation by upper house = 11 Appointment by board or agency head = 11
Health	Appointment by governor = 9 Nomination by governor, confirmation by upper house = 19 Appointment by board or agency head = 16 (Alabama)
Mental health	Appointment by governor = 4 (Alabama) Nomination by governor, confirmation by upper house = 7 Appointment by board or agency head = 22
Natural resources	Appointment by governor = 11 (Alabama) Nomination by governor, confirmation by upper house = 23 Appointment by board or agency head = 7
Personnel	Appointment by governor = 12

	Nomination by governor, confirmation by upper house = 9
	Appointment by board or agency head = 25 (Alabama)
Social services	Appointment by governor = 12
	Nomination by governor, confirmation by upper house = 20
	Appointment by board or agency head = 12 (Alabama)
State police	Appointment by governor = 10 (Alabama)
	Nomination by governor, confirmation by upper house = 18
	Appointment by board or agency head = 14
Transportation	Appointment by governor = 9 (Alabama)
	Nomination by governor, confirmation by upper house = 24
	Appointment by board or agency head = 12

development in Montana and Wisconsin are selected through civil service personnel procedures. The same is true for officials in charge of environmental protection in Colorado and North Dakota; for the leaders of mental health in Colorado, Hawaii, Montana, North Dakota, and Wisconsin; for the heads of natural resources in Connecticut and North Dakota; and for the chief administrators of the state police in Colorado and Nevada.

Second, no clear consensus exists among the states concerning the most effective method for selecting leaders for the various departments in the executive branch. A majority of the states have agreed on one method of selecting the head of the department only in the policy areas of corrections (where twenty-six states provide for nomination by the governor and confirmation by the upper house of the legislature) and personnel (whose head is named by either a multi-member board or an agency head in twenty-five states). Most states employ all three of the most frequently used methods; no state relies exclusively on only one of them.

Nomination by the governor with confirmation by the upper house of the legislature is the method adopted by a plurality of the states in seven policy areas: corrections, economic development, health, natural resources, social services, state police, and transportation. Selection by agency head or by governing boards is the method used by the largest number of states to select chief administrators in the areas of environmental protection, mental health, and personnel. The most prevalent method used for selection of the heads of the budget and finance departments is gubernatorial appointment with no requirement for confirmation by any other body.

Describing the power of the Alabama governor to appoint the heads of important executive branch departments is difficult. In none of the twelve policy areas included in the table does the state employ the method of gubernatorial nomination with confirmation by the upper house of the state legislature, the most commonly used method of the three included in the table. By contrast, in eight of the policy areas (budget, corrections, economic development, finance, mental health, natural resources, state police, and transportation) the governor has no restraints, other than public opinion, on his choices for the heads of these departments. But in the areas of environmental protection, health, personnel, and social services, the chief administrator is determined by the choice of multi-member boards, which are responsible for the management of these departments. While the governor often appoints the members of these boards and can influence their choices of departmental administrators, the board members are also free to ignore the governor's preferences.

This pattern of almost unlimited gubernatorial power to make appointments in some policy areas and very limited influence in other areas amounts to the worst of all possible worlds if the goal is an effective and accountable state government. Eliminating legislative confirmation—the method used in almost 40 percent of the cases identified in the table, as well as the method specified for appointment of the members of the president's cabinet in the U.S. Constitution—means that the governor is not required to make a case for his nominee to either state legislators or the general public. This deficiency removes an important check on the chief executive's powers, and it reduces the incentive for making certain that the nominee has both the knowledge and character required to lead the department.

At the same time, it makes little sense to hold the governor responsible, as the state's most visible public figure and as its chief executive, for developments in environmental protection, public health, and social services when he plays only a limited role in the selection of the person who will be responsible for proposing and carrying out policies in these areas. (A strong case can be made for retaining board selection of the head of the personnel department, on the grounds that the governor has no reason to be interested in personnel policies and decisions that affect persons who occupy nonpolitical positions in the state's various agencies.) Certainly, the governor often is able, in effect, to select the chief administrator of these departments by making his choice known to the board members who comply with the governor's preferences. Requiring the governor to go through the board, however, creates the potential for complications and unacknowledged bargains that could be avoided by direct gubernatorial selection.

A process that combines nomination of department heads by the governor with confirmation by the Alabama Senate by majority vote would provide, in most circumstances,[5] the most desirable combination of effectiveness and accountability for citizens. The state's chief executive could choose someone who is knowledgeable in the policy area in which he or she will serve. At the same time, the governor could feel confident of being able to work with this person, and a majority of state senators could be persuaded that this person is qualified and fit to lead the department. This approach to gubernatorial appointment would enhance accountability by making both the governor and a majority of the Senate's members responsible for the performance of each departmental head. It also would reduce the potential for conflicts and confusion in making and carrying out policy that can arise when a top-level administrator is selected by someone other than the governor.

The Governor's Veto Power

The veto power given to Alabama governors is described in Sections 125 and 126 of Article V of the 1901 constitution. These provisions make four important points concerning this power:

1. Gubernatorial vetoes of legislation enacted by the legislature may be overridden by a majority of the members of both the House and the Senate, acting separately. Note that this is not a majority of those present and voting, but a majority of the entire membership of each body.

2. A governor who objects to any provision or provisions of bills passed by the legislature may propose amendments that will eliminate his objections. If those proposals are accepted by a majority of the members of both houses—again, not just those present and voting—the bill is returned to the governor for his consideration. If a majority of the membership of either house refuses to accept the amendment, the bill can be passed by majority vote of both houses over the governor's objections.

3. The governor has six days, excluding Sundays, to act on bills the legislature has approved while it is in session. Otherwise, legislation not acted

on by the governor within six days while the legislature is in session becomes law. Bills passed within five or fewer days before the legislature adjourns do not become law unless the governor approves them within ten days of adjournment.

4. Section 126 appears to give the governor the right to veto specific items in appropriations bills—but only appropriations bills—subject to the majority override provisions described in Section 125.

Anyone familiar with the legislative process who closely examines Section 126 quickly realizes that this provision does not make clear whether the governor has the power to veto certain items within appropriations bills passed in the five days prior to adjournment of the legislature. Given this uncertainty, no Alabama governor attempted to veto individual appropriations in budget bills at the end of a legislative session until Governor Guy Hunt eliminated $25 million from the $2.6 billion education budget passed by the legislature in August 1991. However, a Montgomery Circuit Court subsequently declared Hunt's action unconstitutional, and the Alabama Supreme Court upheld the ruling.[6]

The results of this litigation underline two substantial limitations on the veto power of the Alabama governor:

1. A majority of the legislature's members can override a governor's veto. By contrast, forty-four states require the votes of either two-thirds or three-fifths of either the members elected or of those present to override the veto.[7]

2. Alabama's chief executive does have the power to veto certain items within appropriations bills—a power that governors of only six other states do not have.[8] The Alabama governor cannot use this power, however, when the legislature passes appropriations bills within the last five days of its session, a common practice.

These limitations greatly restrict the governor's ability to influence the legislative process in general and the budget process specifically. Government could be more effective and accountable in terms of both policy and administration if the constitution strengthened the governor's veto power. After all, the governor is the one leader who is charged with and held responsible for the successes and failures of state government in Alabama. A stronger veto power (including a requirement that two-thirds of the membership of the

House and Senate would be needed to override gubernatorial vetoes) and more ability to delete individual provisions of legislation passed by the legislature (including budget bills) would make it much more difficult for governors to deflect blame for policy failures. For example, governors would be more accountable when both the Education Trust Fund Budget and the General Fund Budget face proration because state revenues fail to reach levels needed to fund fully the amounts appropriated by the legislature.

Earmarked Tax Revenues

A fourth cause of dysfunctional state government in Alabama is the practice of "earmarking" the vast majority of state tax revenues for specific programs. Two political observers who have studied earmarking define this practice as "reserving a specific revenue for a specific expenditure." They use the reservation of monies collected from motor fuel taxes for highway construction programs as an obvious example of earmarked revenues.[9] A report by the General Accounting Office indicated that, on average, states earmarked 24 percent of tax revenues in the 1993 fiscal year. Of all the states, Alabama earmarked the largest portion of its tax revenue—87 percent. Montana, with 64 percent, ranked a distant second. The only other states that earmarked more than 50 percent of their tax revenues were Tennessee (60 percent), Nevada (57 percent), and Utah (55 percent). Eight states—Wisconsin, Alaska, New York, Delaware, Georgia, Hawaii, Rhode Island, and Kentucky—earmarked less than 10 percent of their tax revenues.[10]

Almost all of the revenues generated from Alabama's two largest tax sources, the personal income tax and the general sales tax, are earmarked for education. In the first instance, earmarking is done by the constitution, and in the second it is done by statute. Education also receives all of the monies collected from the income tax on corporations. Alabama designates more than 90 percent of revenues from its tax on public utilities for either education or mental health.

The entire proceeds from the gasoline and motor fuel taxes are earmarked, with the largest portions going to the construction and maintenance of state highways and to city and county governments. Three-fourths of the fees collected to register motor vehicles also are earmarked for highways and local governments. Meanwhile, the state earmarks two-thirds of the revenues raised from taxing alcoholic beverages, and these funds benefit various state departments, including human resources and mental health.

The financial straitjacket created by this reliance on earmarked taxes makes it much more difficult for both the governor and the legislature to have the necessary flexibility to respond effectively to changing economic, technological, social, and political circumstances. Programs that were once effective and timely continue to receive designated funding, while new needs cannot be met because of a lack of needed revenues.

Supporters of earmarking emphasize how it provides stability in funding for essential programs such as elementary and secondary education. They also argue that earmarking makes a desirable connection between those who benefit from a service and those who finance it, as is the case when motor fuel taxes are used to build and maintain highways. In addition, advocates of earmarking contend, with some justification, that it is easier to build support for new taxes when the expected revenues can be used only to pay for popular programs such as education or services for senior citizens. Although Alabama's voters defeated Governor Don Siegelman's lottery proposal in 1999, one of the strongest arguments presented by supporters was that lottery revenues would be used only for college scholarships, for a pre-kindergarten program, and for enhancing technology in Alabama schools.

Nevertheless, authorities on state revenue systems generally agree that the problems that result from earmarking are much greater than its alleged benefits. They conclude that earmarking reduces gubernatorial and legislative control over state budgets by removing revenues and expenditures from budgetary review. Reducing flexibility within budgets also impedes the ability of governors and legislators to respond effectively to important issues of policy or administration as they arise.[11] Clearly, if Alabama earmarks 87 percent of its tax revenues, while other states earmark on average only 24 percent, both the constitutional and statutory requirements for earmarking deserve serious attention to determine if this practice enhances the effectiveness and accountability of state government.

Jonathan Walters, in a recent description of Governor Siegelman's efforts to reform state government, suggests that another benefit of a substantial reduction in earmarking of state education revenues might be less temptation for state lawmakers to use state education dollars to fund projects in their districts that have minimal relationship to education. According to Walters, the legislators add money to an already-earmarked expenditure category in the education budget with the understanding that the money will "pass through" the budget of the education department and be returned to specific legislators for projects that often have little to do with education.

Walters believes that the incentive to use this deceptive approach to funding new projects might be mitigated by reduced earmarking, which would leave more funds available to fund new programs.[12]

Results of Making Budgets the "Paramount Duty" of the Legislature

Without question, the most important responsibility of each regular session of the Alabama Legislature is the appropriation of money for the operation of state government during the next fiscal year. This requires passage of both the Education Trust Fund Budget, whose primary purpose is funding elementary, secondary, and higher education programs provided by state government, and the General Fund Budget, which includes revenues for all other departments of state government.

During the 1950s and 1960s, the legislature exhibited a tendency to wait until the very end of the legislative session to pass bills that made appropriations for state departments and programs. In a few instances, this practice resulted in stopping the legislative clock just minutes before midnight on the final night of the session so the legislature could complete its work. On numerous occasions, the legislature was so deadlocked that it failed to pass one or both of the appropriations bills before the end of the regular session. That meant one or more special sessions were necessary to enact the two budget bills. This tendency seemed to become more pronounced with the adoption of annual legislative sessions, which began in 1976.

During the first administration of Governor Fob James, from 1979 to 1983, he and the legislature agreed to attempt to end this practice by proposing a constitutional amendment that would make the passage of "basic appropriations" bills the "paramount duty" of each regular session of the legislature. This amendment was adopted by the legislature in 1981 and submitted to the voters, who ratified it in November 1984 as Amendment 448 to the Alabama Constitution. In effect, the amendment states that no bill may be adopted by the House or Senate or transmitted to the governor until bills making basic appropriations for the "ordinary expenses" of state government are passed.

However, the amendment also included an emergency or "escape" clause which provides that the requirements of the amendment do not apply to the passage of resolutions or to actions necessary for maintenance of normal legislative activities. Moreover, provisions of the amendment do not apply if either legislative body, by a three-fifths vote, adopts a resolution stating that the provisions of the amendment do not apply in that house for a specific bill under consideration. Thus, in effect, any bill can be passed following the adoption of the appropriate resolution.

In practice, the effect of Amendment 448 is that every bill enacted by either house of the legislature must first survive a vote on what has become known as the "Budget Isolation Resolution," or B.I.R., as it is generally called. The reason is that the legislature still waits until near the end, if not the last night, of every legislative session to enact the General Fund and Education Trust Fund Budgets. This step requires support of three-fifths of the members present and must occur prior to final passage, where support of only a majority of the members voting is necessary for adoption.

How does this requirement affect the effectiveness and accountability of state government? First, it means that adoption of any regular session bill, other than appropriations bills, requires support of 60 percent of the members voting. This provision is inconsistent with American democracy, which relies on a majority of votes to enact new programs and policies except in exceptional circumstances. Second, the provision makes accountability more difficult because legislators can "play games" with their constituents by both supporting and opposing specific legislation through voting for the bill's B.I.R. and against the bill on final passage or voting against the bill's B.I.R. and for the bill's final passage. Third, the B.I.R. requirement adds an element of confusion and complexity to a process that is already difficult for average citizens to comprehend. Given the present high levels of mistrust of public officials and cynicism about government—particularly in Alabama—anything that adds to citizens' alienation from the process is of dubious value and deserves serious reconsideration. As is often the case with reforms that superficially appear to have great potential for improving the effectiveness of government, Amendment 448 has not made budgets the first order of business in each regular legislative session. Meanwhile, the amendment has made the work of the legislature more confusing and has made it more difficult for citizens to hold legislators accountable.

Role of the Lieutenant Governor in Contemporary Alabama Politics

For most of the years since the position of lieutenant governor was created by the 1901 Alabama Constitution, its occupants have behaved as if the office were part-time, with its primary responsibility being to preside over the Alabama Senate. The lieutenant governor did not compete with the governor for political power and most frequently was not considered a rival.[13] However, this situation changed with George Wallace's national campaigns for the presidency and after the 1972 assassination attempt against him, which resulted in his absence from the state for several months. Alabama's lieutenant governors, beginning with Jere Beasley, who held the office during Wallace's second term, began to challenge the governor for political power. In every gubernatorial election since 1978, the person serving as lieutenant governor has mounted a significant campaign for the governorship, either in the party primary or in the general election. The competition for political influence between the governor and lieutenant governor has become even more pronounced since 1998. With that year's election of Republican Steve Windom as lieutenant governor, members of different parties for the first time occupied the offices of governor and lieutenant governor. The result has been a more pronounced rivalry between the two officeholders, as both men appear to be likely candidates for the top office in 2002.

Lieutenant Governor Windom's Democratic predecessors all had significant control over the operations of the Senate through their power to select committee members and chairs and their power to refer bills to committees of their choice for hearings and deliberations. The Democrats, who held an advantage of twenty-three to twelve over their Republican rivals in the Senate, determined, with the somewhat covert support of the sitting lieutenant governor and soon to be governor, Don Siegelman, to revise the operating rules of the Senate with the goal of stripping most of the lieutenant governor's powers to influence the actions of the Senate.

Meeting in an organizational session in the middle of January 1999, with Siegelman presiding since his inauguration occurred a week later, a closely divided Senate agreed to a new set of rules that removed the lieutenant governor's powers to refer bills to committees and to name committee members and their chairs. The eighteen-vote majority included only Democrats, while five conservative Democrats joined with twelve Republicans who supported Windom in his effort to retain the powers held by his predecessors. The deciding vote was cast by Democrat Phil Poole of Tuscaloosa County, whose district, two months later, received $12 million from the Alabama Department of Transportation for work on a ten-mile bypass in Tuscaloosa County.[14]

When the regular legislative session convened in early March, by voice vote with Windom presiding and over the loud objections of the Democratic opposition, the powers of the lieutenant governor were restored in a tumultuous session. Democratic Senate president pro tem Lowell Barron asserted that he thought it might be necessary to call up the National Guard, and Mobile Democrat Vivian Figures told Windom that she thought he had "obviously lost his mind."

The eighteen Democrats immediately began to boycott sessions of the Senate, which meant that no business could be transacted because the Senate lacked a quorum. Ten days of the thirty-day session were consumed with litigation, press conferences, and negotiations, all of which failed to break the deadlock between the two bitterly divided groups. On Thursday, March 25, Governor Siegelman called a special session to find a compromise that would resolve the differences. On both Friday and Saturday, the Senate convened but made no progress. An eight-hour Sunday session was described in one headline as a "brawl" and featured the lieutenant governor relying on a plastic jug to perform certain biological necessities because he feared that if he left the floor he would lose control of the Senate. However, negotiations continued and two days later the Senate agreed on a compromise set of rules. Windom took a "victory lap" by airplane around the state, though most observers agreed that he had failed to retain much of the power held by his predecessors.[15]

This rivalry reduces the incentives for the governor and lieutenant governor to build a consensus and find common ground in seeking solutions for the problems facing the state. It also increases the likelihood that each officeholder will use the political rivalry as a means for boosting his own popularity with the state's citizens while attempting to erode the support of his rival. Furthermore, this competition almost guarantees that debates on some important issues will result in legislative deadlocks, as the governor and lieutenant governor concentrate more on how their actions affect their standing with voters and less on finding workable solutions to problems.

The competition between the governor and the lieutenant governor can produce situations that are both difficult for the state to resolve and embarrassing. When Jim Guy Tucker, who replaced Bill Clinton after Clinton's successful campaign for the presidency in 1992, left Arkansas to attend Clinton's inauguration, acting governor and Senate president pro tem Jerry Jewell granted two pardons and executive clemency to two inmates. When Tucker had to travel to Minnesota for medical reasons, Jewell proclaimed Christian Heritage Week, something Tucker had refused to do.[16] While Massachusetts governor Michael Dukakis was with a trade delegation in Germany, his lieutenant governor, Evelyn Murphy, announced her own plans to cope with the state's financial crisis, including executive orders that would have required state agencies to reduce significantly the workforce and salaries of remaining state workers and to cut their budgets by 10 percent. These actions, apparently intended to strengthen her candidacy for governor, backfired, leading her to withdraw from the race within a week.[17]

What is an alternative? First, eight states, including Tennessee, have decided that the office of lieutenant governor has no significant role and either have abolished it or never had such a position. However, less drastic options exist. The lieutenant governor presides over the upper house of the state legislature in only twenty-six states. In twenty-four states, the governor and lieutenant governor are elected jointly, following the method used to elect the president and vice-president. In nineteen of these states, the lieutenant governor also serves as a member of the governor's cabinet or in some other type of advisory position to the governor. (In nine of these states, the lieutenant governor also presides over the upper house of the state legislature.) Since the potential for a persistent and perhaps even more intense rivalry between the governor and lieutenant governor is significant and because the effect of this competition for political power is likely to make state government less effective, a serious examination of the need for the position and of its proper role in state government should be a part of any effort to restructure the operations of the legislative and executive branches.[18]

Conclusion

This chapter has examined how certain practices of the legislative and executive branches in contemporary Alabama contribute dramatically to government's ineffectiveness. The changes considered in this discussion would address this problem by strengthening the governor's appointment and veto powers, a change that would provide the chief executive with more of the power necessary to accomplish the responsibilities already assigned to the office. These changes would also contribute to the accountability and responsiveness of the legislative and executive branches by giving both of them greater flexibility in the use of state revenues, by eliminating the need for a three-fifths vote to enact new legislation in most circumstances, and by modifying the role of the lieutenant governor.

Notes

1. Malcolm Cook McMillan, *Constitutional Development in Alabama, 1798–1901: A Study in Politics, the Negro, and Sectionalism* (1955; reprint, Spartanburg, S.C.: The Reprint Company, 1978), v. Anyone interested in the events leading to the calling of

the 1901 constitutional convention, the motives and goals of the delegates to that convention, and the events of the convention would benefit greatly from examining McMillan's description of the 1901 convention in chapters 14–20.

2. Keon S. Chi, "Trends in Executive Reorganization," *Journal of State Government* 65 (April–June 1992): 33–40.

3. *The Book of the States*, 2000–2001 (Lexington, Ky.: Council of State Governments, 2000), 31–32.

4. Ibid., 33–38.

5. A requirement for Senate confirmation of the appointments of presidents and governors has its own problems, as anyone familiar with recent controversies over confirmation of presidential nominations to federal judicial positions and gubernatorial appointments to university boards of trustees in Alabama can readily attest.

6. *Hunt v. Hubbert*, 586 So.2d 848 (Ala. 1991). See also *Montgomery Advertiser,* September 19, October 3, 1991.

7. *The Book of the States*, 2000–2001, 101–2.

8. Ibid., 20–21.

9. Martha A. Fabricus and Ronald K. Snell, *Earmarking State Taxes*, 2nd ed. (Denver: National Conference of State Legislatures, 1990), 2.

10. U.S. Congress, General Accounting Office, *Earmarking in the Federal Government* (Washington, D.C.: Government Printing Office, 1995), 11.

11. Fabricus and Snell, *Earmarking State Taxes*, 11–21.

12. Jonathan Walters, "Raising Alabama," *Governing* 14 (October 2000): 28–30, 32; see esp. 30 and 32.

13. Only two Alabama lieutenant governors, Thomas Kilby in 1918 and Don Siegelman in 1998, have been elected governor. Russell Cunningham served as acting governor in 1904 and 1905 during the illness of William Jelks, and Jere Beasley served as acting governor in 1972 while George Wallace was hospitalized following an assassination attempt. Albert Brewer became governor in 1968 after the death of Lurleen Wallace, and he was defeated by George Wallace when he ran for governor in 1970. Brewer ran again in 1978 but lost in the Democratic primary. James E. Folsom, Jr., became governor in 1993 when Guy Hunt was impeached and removed from office. Folsom's effort to win a full term failed when he was defeated in the 1994 general election by Fob James. See Samuel L. Webb and Margaret E. Armbrester, eds., *Alabama Governors: A Political History of the State* (Tuscaloosa: University of Alabama Press, 2001), 147–50, 166–70, 235–40, and 254–56.

14. *Montgomery Advertiser,* January 10, 12, 13, March 17, 1999.

15. Ibid., March 3, 4, 26, 28, 29, 30, 31, 1999.

16. Thad L. Beyle, "The Executive Branch: Organization and Issues, 1992–1993,"

in *The Book of the States,* 1994–1995 (Lexington, Ky.: Council of State Governments, 1994), 65–66.

17. Thad L. Beyle, "The Executive Branch: Organization and Issues, 1990–1991," in *The Book of the States,* 1992–1993 (Lexington, Ky.: Council of State Governments, 1992), 57.

18. *The Book of the States,* 2000–2001, 15, 45–46.

7
Alabama's Revenue Crisis

Three Tax Problems

James W. Williams, Jr.

JUSTICE OLIVER WENDELL HOLMES rightly said that taxes are the price we pay for civilization. In every state of the United States, taxes are levied to pay for services that benefit all citizens generally—services such as education, roads, public safety, and public health.

The term "tax" refers to a compulsory payment for services of general benefit, based on a definition of ability to pay. There are three broad definitions of ability to pay, or "tax bases": the value of income earned, the sale price of goods or services purchased, and the value of property or other assets owned.

Nobody likes to pay taxes. Why, then, do we finance public services with taxes? It may not be a perfectly satisfactory answer, but nobody has found a better way to distribute the burden for general societal benefits. Would you pay for prisons unless you had to? Probably not—surely you have no plan to spend the night in one! Yet you undoubtedly agree that we all benefit from locking up criminals. We also benefit from universal public education, which is clearly a good investment for all taxpayers—including those who have no children in school. States with better-educated residents tend to have high personal incomes, and this advantage creates many benefits throughout society. Even so, it is often difficult to win voter support for school taxes.

Seeds of a Revenue Crisis

The problem is that the costs of a public investment (that is, the taxes) often seem much more real to each of us personally than the benefits we might receive. So we find it hard to think of the costs and benefits together, as the two sides of an investment. We are tempted to look at the taxes alone, as if they were a complete loss, while taking the direct benefits for granted and ignoring the indirect benefits altogether. This is particularly true if there is the slightest hint of governmental waste.

None of us want to pay more taxes than we have to. We all would prefer to take a free ride on someone else's tax dollar. Unfortunately, it is entirely possible to shift the tax burden from some taxpayers to others, to waste tax dollars that are collected, or to pass the tax burden on to tomorrow's taxpayers even though they will pay far more as a result of the delay. When these things happen, and everyone finds out (as they will), no rational taxpayer wants to invest again until the rules are changed for the better.

Think about these dynamics for just a minute and you will understand why public confidence in the tax system is so crucial. Taxpayers must have faith in the fairness, adequacy, and efficiency of the tax system to make the necessary connection between the benefits and the costs of a public investment. Where the tax system commands no respect, the willingness to invest in public services simply dries up. Indeed, this situation is why, in a nutshell, the state of Alabama has a revenue crisis.

The following section describes the condition of our state's tax system in terms of those three key factors that relate to public confidence—adequacy, efficiency, and fairness. The discussion highlights the role that the state constitution plays in these problems. A final section looks at the options for improvement.

Alabama's Tax Problems

Creating Tax Adequacy

Taxes are collected to produce results; without results, the public loses confidence and the willingness to invest in tax-supported activities. The catch is that, after a period of low confidence, revenues become so inadequate that government lacks the means to do a good job. This creates a problem that is difficult to solve. As the following discussion indicates, Alabama has an adequacy problem. Options for solving it are limited by constitutional restrictions on certain taxes and by the unbalanced tax structure that has evolved.

How do Alabama's taxes compare with those levied by other states?[1] The U.S. Census Bureau has been publishing data on state and local taxes for a number of years.[2] Since the early 1990s, Alabama's tax collections have been lower than those of any other state when measured on a per-person (or per capita) basis. The gap between our state and the rest of the nation is substantial: Alabama's state and local tax collections per capita are only two-thirds of the national average. In other words, Alabama's governmental units are trying to produce results that compare favorably with the average state while spending one-third less money.

Tennessee ranks just ahead of Alabama, at number forty-nine, but the gap between neighbor and us is also very large. To see just how large this gap is, imagine that Tennessee had the same population as Alabama. If this were the case, Tennessee's state and local governments would have collected $591 million more in tax revenues during 1999, the latest year for which figures are available. Put another way, even if Alabama had raised taxes by $590 million in that year, we still would have ranked behind every other state in tax collections.

Mississippi ranks just ahead of Tennessee in state and local tax collections per capita, at number forty-eight. If Mississippi had the same number of people as Alabama in 1999, its state and local governments would have collected $836 million more than ours. This means that if Alabama had raised taxes by $835 million in that year, we would have risen only to forty-ninth place in the tax rankings.

Mississippi and Tennessee are not high-tax states; everywhere in America, except Alabama, they are considered low-tax states. Their cost of living is about the same as Alabama's, and both spend their state and local tax dollars pretty much as Alabama does—for education, roads, police and fire protection, and other services that are important to the quality of life and to economic development. When a state is in last place for a number of years and as far behind even the closest states as the numbers indicate Alabama is, then revenue adequacy is clearly an issue.

Why is Alabama so far behind? All too often the rationalization has been simply that "we are a poor state." The truth is more complicated. It is possible to compare the taxable resources per person that each state can draw on. Basically, these are the personal income and business profits that make up each state's economy.[3] When these taxable resources are compared, we find that Alabama's tax base is about 78 percent of the national average. This is low, but remember that our state and local governments generate tax revenues at only 67 percent of the national average. Five states, including Arkansas and Mississippi, had smaller tax bases than Alabama in 1999, yet every one of them raised more revenues than Alabama did by levying taxes at rates that were closer to the national average.

When we compare the amount of tax revenue collected to the size of the tax base in every state, we have a broad measure of the overall tax rate. By this measure, Alabama's tax rate is about 85 percent of the national average. Six states, including Tennessee, had lower tax rates than Alabama in 1998, but all of them had greater resources to tax. They were able to raise more revenues than Alabama did, even with the lower rates.

Therefore, the reason for Alabama's last-place ranking on revenues is that our state combines a small tax base with a low tax rate. No other state ranks lower on *both* measures. Mississippi has a smaller tax base, but its resources are taxed at the national average. Tennessee has a lower tax rate, but its larger resource base produces more revenue even with the discount.

The Alabama Constitution contributes to the adequacy problem through its limitations on the rates and bases of certain taxes. The limitations are very stringent for property and income taxes but almost nonexistent for sales taxes. Constitutional limits on inheritance and estate taxes will become important in the future. The following analysis examines each of these taxes:

1. *Property taxes.* Article XI of the Alabama Constitution, titled "Taxation," contains four sections that limit both the rate and the base of the property tax, as well as the procedures for adopting property taxes. Article XIV, titled "Education," contains a section authorizing counties to levy a property tax for public schools. There also are numerous constitutional amendments related to city, county, and school property taxes.

Section 214 limits the state property tax rate to 6.5 mills on the value of taxable property (a mill is one-tenth of a percent). An amendment related to the state income tax requires a homestead exemption of $2,000 in assessed value from the state property tax.

Section 215 limits county property taxes for operating and debt purposes to a rate of 7.5 mills. There are six statewide amendments authorizing county property taxes for health and library purposes and about sixty local amendments authorizing county property taxes for fire protection, health, libraries, roads, and other purposes. These local amendments apply only to specific counties.

Section 216 limits municipal property taxes to rates that range from 5.0 to 15.0 mills, but a number of cities have specific limits set by statewide or local amendments.

Section 217, as amended, divides all taxable property in the state into four classes; specifies assessment of these classes for tax purposes at different percentages of value; creates a three-step process for adopting property taxes that requires approval of the local legislative body, the state legislature, and the voters; and sets overall limits on the amount of property taxes that can be collected from each class. The classes are:

• Utility property (Class I), assessed at 30 percent of market value.
• All other business property (Class II), assessed at 20 percent of market value.

• Agricultural, forest, and single-family residential property (Class III), assessed at 10 percent of market value, except that the owner may elect to have it taxed on the basis of current use rather than market value.
• Private passenger automobiles and pickup trucks (Class IV), assessed at 15 percent of market values.

Section 269 allows counties to levy a 1.0-mill property tax for public schools. Three statewide amendments authorize another 14.0 mills of school property taxes, and eighty-six local amendments provide specific authorizations for school property taxes in various jurisdictions.

2. *Income taxes*. The state income tax on individuals and corporations was authorized initially by Amendment 25. This provision has been amended four times. It now sets the tax rates at a maximum of 5.0 percent for individual income and 6.5 percent for corporate income, sets minimum amounts for personal exemptions, and requires deductibility for federal income taxes paid or accrued.

3. *Sales taxes*. The state sales tax is not limited as to rate or base in the constitution. Local sales taxes also are not limited generally, although there are local amendments that involve sales taxes (usually authorizing them).

4. *Inheritance and estate taxes*. The Alabama Constitution allows such taxes only if the federal government levies them, and only to the extent of absorbing the deduction or credit allowed by a federal tax. Current federal law calls for phasing out such taxes within a few years, which will trigger the repeal of Alabama's taxes.

When tax revenues in every state are compared with the taxable resources from which they are drawn, it turns out that some of Alabama's taxes are much lower than others. The tax structure in most areas of the state is dominated by sales taxes and makes very little use of property taxes, although there are exceptions. The imbalance in the tax structure contributes to the adequacy problem.

Alabama's state and local sales tax burden was 122 percent of the national average in 1998. Sales taxes also are the largest source of municipal revenues and are second only to the income tax as a source of state revenue. Most counties also receive sales tax revenues. However, state and local sales tax rates in Alabama have reached the range of 8 percent or higher in many areas, and there is little room for increases. Tax competition is emerging in the state's metropolitan areas, with cities competing for commercial development and some businesses moving into county areas with lower tax rates.

Alabama's income tax burden was 80 percent of the national average in

1998. The constitutional limits on maximum income tax rates and the requirement for deductibility of federal income taxes are major impediments to the increased utilization of this revenue source.

Alabama's property tax burden was only 37 percent of the national average in 1998. However, the constitutional limitations on this tax base and the procedures required for tax increases are formidable obstacles to the state's increased reliance on property taxes.

Creating Tax Efficiency

The tax limitations and imbalances just described raise another issue related to results—efficiency. Tax limitations often are portrayed as enhancements to accountability, but at the extreme they interfere with the management of tax dollars. Limitations may occur directly, through provisions that govern the spending of tax revenues, known as "earmarking," or they may occur indirectly, through tax reductions that affect one service more than others. Alabama's tax limitations have created extreme conditions of both types. Among all states, Alabama has the lowest state and local tax revenue per capita, the lowest property tax revenue per capita, and the highest level of earmarked state taxes. Together, these extreme conditions amount to an efficiency problem that is difficult to overcome.

About 87 percent of Alabama's state tax dollars are earmarked for specific purposes. This is four times the national average, and Alabama ranks first in this practice by a big margin. A state that ranks last in tax revenues per capita *and* first in tax earmarking clearly suffers from a crisis of public confidence in those who manage tax dollars. Yet it is just as clear that managing well in such a fiscal environment is virtually impossible.

Earmarking is widely considered to be appropriate when those who pay the tax benefit directly from the expenditure, such as when gasoline taxes are earmarked for highways and transit services or when hunting and fishing licenses are earmarked for conservation programs. In Alabama, however, earmarking goes much farther:

- *Property taxes.* Section 260 of the Alabama Constitution earmarks 3.0 mills of the 6.5-mill state property tax for education. These tax dollars are appropriated to the public schools.
- *Income taxes.* Revenue from the state income tax, the largest source of tax revenue to the state government, is earmarked entirely for paying public school teacher salaries and replacing revenue lost through the homestead exemption to the state property tax.

• *Sales taxes.* There is no constitutional earmarking of state sales tax revenue. However, only 7 percent of state sales tax revenue goes into the general fund of the state government. Most of the revenue is earmarked by statute for education, with smaller amounts for conservation and human resource programs.

• *Gasoline and motor vehicle license taxes.* Two constitutional amendments earmark these taxes for use in construction and maintenance of roadways and enforcement of traffic laws. The provisions are restrictive and do not allow these state revenues to be spent on mass transit services.

• *Hunting and fishing licenses.* A constitutional amendment restricts these license revenues to the state game and fish fund.

Earmarking channels most of the state's income and sales tax revenue to education, but it also focuses the economic risk there. Income and sales taxes are economically sensitive; while they normally increase with the economy during growth years, they also follow its path during recessions. For the last half century, a midyear cutback in the state's education budget (known as "proration") has occurred on average once every four years. The state has never created a reserve fund to cushion this risk, and as a result, proration has been very disruptive to school systems' operations.

The interruption of state revenues is a significant problem for school systems in Alabama because of the very low property taxes in most communities. Schools and counties are the governmental units most affected by a tax structure that minimizes property taxes. Alabama's public schools have lower tax support at the local level than do the public schools in every other state except New Mexico and Hawaii, which has only one statewide school system. In Alabama, local communities are required to provide the equivalent of 10.0 mills of property tax effort for their schools. On average statewide, this effort raises about $2.30 per student per day—an amount that is insufficient even though it is paired with a relatively large contribution from the state. The 10.0-mill requirement is ineffective as a counterweight to the risk of proration that comes with the state's support. These tax provisions for financing the public schools create another efficiency problem in Alabama.

Creating Tax Fairness

Adequacy and efficiency are important characteristics to develop in a state tax system, but fairness is absolutely essential. If a state has low tax revenues but accomplishes this condition by treating certain classes of taxpayers unfairly, it has sacrificed any benefit sought by its low-tax status. Alabama's tax revenues are low, but they are not collected through broad-based, low-rate taxes that treat every taxpayer the same. In fact, quite the opposite is true: exclusions are large, tax rates vary from one taxpayer to another, and sometimes those who can least afford it carry the largest tax burden. This unfairness is the biggest tax problem faced by Alabama.

Alabama's property tax is a classic case of tax rates that vary from one kind of taxpayer to another. Because of the classification system that is built into the Alabama Constitution, four types of property have average effective tax rates that vary by ratios of as much as four to one:

- Utility property (Class I), taxed at 1.22 percent of market value.
- Commercial property (Class II), taxed at 0.78 percent of market value.
- Privately owned automobiles (Class IV), taxed at 0.65 percent of market value.
- Single-family homes, farms, and timberland (Class III), taxed at 0.33 percent of market value.

This variation in the tax burden borne by different classifications of property is not just a fairness issue among taxpayers. It also widens the revenue differences among rich and poor school systems. Urban counties have much of the commercial property in the state, and that property is assessed for taxation at 20 percent of its market value. In rural counties, most property value is assessed in Class III, at 10 percent of its value. Utility property, assessed at 30 percent of value, also is not spread evenly among the state's sixty-seven counties. This means that the state's 10.0-mill requirement raises much more money in urban and other areas with large concentrations of property value in Classes I and II than it does in rural areas where most property value is in Class III.

In today's economy, most individuals own savings accounts and other financial investments as well as real estate and automobiles, but Alabama's property tax applies only to tangible assets. Alabama's taxpayers reported $3 billion in earnings from interest and dividends to the Internal Revenue Service in 1997, suggesting a value of at least $60 billion for such intangible assets. None of this intangible wealth is on the property tax rolls.

The best-known fairness problem with Alabama's taxes is regressivity— the fact that the system taxes the least-wealthy families more heavily than others in terms of the percentage of income paid in taxes. A recent study showed that Alabama's personal income tax hits families at a lower income level than does the income tax of any other state. In Alabama, a family of four starts paying income tax at $4,600 of income, while in neighboring Mississippi the threshold is $19,600. Studies also show that when income, sales, and property taxes are combined, Alabama's low-income families pay a higher tax burden than do middle- or upper-income families.

Options for Resolving the Three Tax Problems

The three tax problems discussed above—fairness, efficiency, and adequacy—are related to one another. An adequate amount of tax revenue is necessary to achieve good results in public services, but no taxpayer wants to invest when the tax system treats him or her unfairly. It is difficult to improve tax fairness when the revenue from specific taxes is owned by providers of services who don't want to give up any of "their" money. Taxpayers turn to this kind of earmarking because they do not trust those who will spend their tax dollars, but the restrictions actually create inefficiencies and prevent the good management that taxpayers say they want. Lack of results produces even more mistrust, further eroding the willingness to invest. And so on.

The only way out of this vicious cycle is to attack all three problems together. The common denominator is that the three problems are embedded in the state constitution, which specifies many details of the rate and base for property and income taxes as well as much of the tax earmarking. The many separate constitutional specifications make it all but impossible to create tax improvements if they involve more than one tax source, or even more than one change within a particular tax source. Such specifications simply make change too complicated to manage unless it is too simple to be productive.

The first step to resolving Alabama's interrelated tax problems would be to remove the details of particular taxes and their uses from the constitution. This would allow the legislature to develop solutions that would make the tax system more fair, efficient, and adequate.

What would ensure accountability if the constitutional tax specifications were removed? Alabama has a representative democracy, and true accountability comes from electing good people to office and then holding them accountable for managing government in a way that carries out the public will. Thus we hold the legislature accountable through the electoral process. However, there is another accountability tool available.

Decisions that we do not trust our representatives in Montgomery to make should be brought home to be decided by those we elect to local school boards, city councils, and county commissions. Raising money statewide, sending it to Montgomery for distribution, and then arbitrarily tying the hands of those who make spending decisions is a prescription for inefficiency and waste, not accountability. If we do not trust the state government to manage our tax money, then we should keep more of it at home and elect people we trust to manage it locally, where we can keep a closer eye on it.

Once the constitutional impediments to a fair, efficient, and adequate tax system were removed, there would be a number of options for improvements. In the early 1990s, two tax reform committees were appointed to make recommendations for improving Alabama's tax system. The two studies remain viable as starting points for tax reform discussions today. Their recommendations are discussed below.[4] Recommendations that could not be made without constitutional change are indicated by "(C)."

The Alabama Commission on Tax and Fiscal Policy Reform

The legislature created this group in 1990. The report of this commission, presented in 1991, recommended changes that would produce a broad-based, low-rate tax system "capable of producing adequate revenues, in a fair way, and without compromising economic development in the state." The commission's recommendations included the following:

1. A personal income tax (C) with a flat rate based on federal adjusted gross income. The federal income tax deduction would be eliminated. Such an income tax would be simpler, reducing the costs of compliance and administration. It would reduce the tax burden on low-income families, offsetting the regressive effect of Alabama's high sales taxes and producing a more even distribution of the tax burden across income levels. The rate would be reduced from the current maximum of 5 percent to about 4 percent for revenue neutrality.

2. A sales tax broadened to include services, with fewer exemptions. This would decrease the regressive nature of the sales tax, since higher-income taxpayers purchase more services. The statewide rate would be reduced from the current 4 percent to about 3 percent for revenue neutrality. Local taxes of up to 3 percent, using the state tax base, would be permitted.

3. A property tax (C) in which all property would be assessed at 100 percent of value, with dramatically reduced tax rates. Intangible personal property would be taxed at 1.0 mill by the state only. A reformed version of current-use assessment would be available for homes, farms, and timberland. Cities and counties would be able to authorize votes on property tax increases without legislative approval.

4. A corporate income tax (C) based on federal taxable income, and a

corporate franchise tax based on capital employed in Alabama by both corporations and limited partnerships. Reliance on the franchise tax would be reduced, and the revenue would be replaced by eliminating the federal income tax deduction from the corporate income tax.

5. An end to tax earmarking (C) except for highway user taxes. Education would be defined as an essential function of state government, and all state functions would be subject to equal proration during budget shortfalls.

6. A reduction in the use of tax incentives for economic development, which would be granted only after an independent cost-benefit analysis. School taxes could not be abated.

The Tax Reform Task Force

In October 1991, Governor Guy Hunt appointed this group to formulate a plan for reforming the state's tax system and producing additional revenue for state services. In its deliberations, the task force decided to develop accountability reforms for state government as well, on the premise that any increased funding must be accompanied by better performance and accountability. Among the task force recommendations:

1. A personal income tax (C) based on federal taxable income, with rates set at 4.6 percent on the first $35,000 of income and 5 percent on the remainder. This basis, while more progressive, would incorporate the deductions in the federal tax code. Deduction of federal income taxes would be eliminated.

2. A sales tax expanded to include certain types of services. The rate would be kept at 4 percent, with the automobile rate increased from 2 to 3 percent.

3. A corporate income tax (C) of 6.5 percent with no federal income tax deduction, coupled with a reduced corporate franchise tax levied on the same basis for foreign and domestic corporations and limited partnerships.

4. A change in utility taxes. Utility privilege license taxes would be repealed; utility gross receipts tax rates would be increased, and cable TV service would be included in the base.

5. Higher property tax rates (C). The state tax would rise from 6.5 to 14.0 mills, and a floor of 20.0 mills (rising eventually to 30.0) would be set for local school property taxes. All business property, including utility property, would be taxed at 20 percent of value, with the change phased in so

that no revenue loss would occur. Local taxing authorities would be allowed to call ad valorem referenda. Intangible property would be taxed at the state level, collected through the income tax.

6. Limits on tax incentives, and required reporting of tax-exempt property.

7. Accountability measures for state government, including strategic planning, performance-based budgeting, a quality improvement program, financial and operating reviews of agencies, and a cap on expenditure growth. Separate accountability measures were proposed for elementary and secondary education and higher education.

Combining the Two Approaches

The two tax reform committees took different strategic approaches to the tax problems facing Alabama. In order to create what was considered an acceptable package at the time, neither of the reports attacked all of the state's tax problems fully.

The Alabama Commission on Tax and Fiscal Policy Reform focused on resolving the fairness and efficiency problems, leaving the adequacy question to the legislature. The report recommended that, as tax bases were broadened, taxes could be reduced to produce the same amount of money as before. The argument was that if the tax system were made fair to all taxpayers and the fiscal policy of the state were made efficient, the legislature would be able to decide later how much money to raise for public services.

The Tax Reform Task Force focused on resolving the adequacy problem by raising additional revenue, particularly for education, leaving a number of fairness and efficiency issues to be resolved later. For example, property tax increases were achieved mainly through rate increases rather than by equalizing the tax base. To achieve more efficiency, the report recommended that the legislature approve a number of accountability measures for state government rather than addressing the earmarking issue.

In the end, neither of these partial approaches succeeded. Today it seems clear that a tax reform proposal will have to attack all three problems—adequacy, efficiency, and fairness—to earn the public confidence that will lead to its adoption.

Notes

1. The data discussed on the following pages are included in analyses of Alabama's tax system published biennially by the Public Affairs Research Council of Alabama.

These reports and other information on Alabama's taxes can be found on the Internet at http://parca.samford.edu.

2. The U.S. Census Bureau data can be found on the Internet at http://www.census.gov.

3. This analysis, done by PARCA staff, compares the Census Bureau's tax-revenue data with data on gross state product and personal income produced by the Bureau of Economic Analysis.

4. The full text of these reports can be found on the PARCA website, at http://parca.samford.edu, under taxes.

8
Economic-Cultural and Political Gaps in Alabama

Anne Permaloff

In RECENT YEARS, public officials in Alabama at both the local and state levels have increased their efforts to promote economic development. The decision by DaimlerChrysler AG in 1993 to locate an automobile assembly plant at Vance near Tuscaloosa was the first major breakthrough in attracting a new industry to the state. Its successful operations resulted in an ongoing expansion of the plant. Meanwhile, Honda and Toyota have since joined DaimlerChrysler in choosing Alabama for locating assembly plants.

Each major company that comes to Alabama brings jobs associated with plant construction and operation, including added power sources, roads, and communications equipment. Many businesses, large and small, benefit. New industries form or move into the state in support; established companies expand, often developing more modern operating processes. They too hire workers, buy goods and services, and add to the state's business infrastructure. The economy benefits from a multiplier effect that ripples beyond the original plant.

Attracting the Mercedes plant to Alabama cost the state about $250 million in construction support payments, tax incentives (delayed or canceled tax collections), development, and support of training programs for the plant workforce. Large financial incentives were needed by Alabama not only to counter offers from other states but also to combat a badly blemished image. Newspaper stories in business sections of the newspapers rarely cast Alabama's workforce, schools, government leaders, courts, and race relations in a positive light. Alabama is almost never characterized in national media as a destination for those seeking an improved quality of life.

Quality of life concerns everyone. Increasingly, businesses and industries look to measure quality of life in a prospective state along with assessing economic and political conditions such as taxes, unemployment levels, political climate, and available markets. Corporate leaders are concerned about how the families of their employees will live, if only for reasons of morale and personnel retention. In particular, they are concerned about educational quality, access to good health care, environmental conditions, recreational and culture opportunities, and housing.

Alabama falls behind most of the nation on virtually every key indicator in measuring quality of life—a predicament the state has suffered throughout the modern period of its history. This gap between Alabama's performance and the national average is a deficit that the state has had to combat in seeking to attract new businesses and industries, particularly those relying on new technologies serving a global marketplace.

Those seeking the causes of Alabama's long-standing malaise are quick to settle on the state constitution as a major contributor. The Alabama Constitution, enacted in 1901, created a governmental wet blanket that weighs down the state's economy.

The Impact of the 1901 Constitution

The 1901 Alabama constitutional convention and the state government it created were dominated by some of the state's largest industrial and agricultural interests—a group I refer to as the Big Mule Alliance. In effect, the 1901 constitution served as a sort of treaty between the alliance's partners, who sought to block the political development of the state and to achieve other common interests. The welfare of the state as a whole was not the alliance's concern.[1]

The alliance's goals included low taxes, a limited educational system designed to supply largely unskilled farm and factory labor, a small electorate, and racial segregation. The alliance did not promote widespread economic development. After all, educational and economic progress would require increased taxes, expand the number of players seeking entry into the political process, and threaten the power held by the alliance members. The Big Mule Alliance's members used disenfranchisement of blacks and poor whites, segregation of the races, racial fears, and control over the legislature as major tools for accomplishing their ends. They enhanced their political control by preventing reapportionment of legislative districts, even though the 1901 constitution required the legislature to reapportion itself after each federal census. Legislative control was reinforced by locally based machine politics that controlled elections and voter registration in counties where the alliance dominated. By maintaining a ruling majority of eighteen seats in the Senate, the alliance could block any law or constitutional amendment that threatened its power. In those very rare instances where a majority in the Senate might be able to pass unfavorable legislation, the lieutenant governor could prevent votes from occurring; failing that, a friendly governor's veto could be used.

The entire system was built upon and reinforced by a traditional political culture. A traditional political culture reflects an agrarian, pre-commercial attitude. It considers a hierarchical society as part of the natural order of life and limits the role of government to preserving the existing social order and its control over the economic and political systems. The traditional political perspective includes the notion that only those with the correct quasi-aristo-cratic social and economic background should serve in government or par-ticipate in the political life of the community. A system built and maintained on such beliefs is not responsive to the needs and concerns of the average citizen.[2]

This political environment and the limitations placed on state and local government by the 1901 constitution created a set of political lags and eco-nomic-cultural gaps. A lag is a failure in the responsiveness of the state's po-litical system. The political lags in twentieth-century Alabama centered on civil rights, urban-rural disparities and regional inequities within the state, the lack of party competition, and a regressive tax system. These lags helped to create and maintain economic-cultural gaps that separated Alabama from the nation as a whole.[3] The gaps are most evident in terms of the quality of life of the average citizen.

Economic-Cultural Gaps

Throughout the first half of the twentieth-century, Alabama trailed the rest of the nation in terms of every major measure of public well-being, includ-ing health, educational attainment, public assistance to the poor and elderly, and political participation. Over time, however, the gaps began to narrow, and Alabama (along with other southern states) moved toward the national averages.

Several factors assisted in narrowing the gaps. Chief among them were federal legislation and financial assistance during the Great Depression; eco-nomic growth and cultural and social changes produced by World War II; federal assistance programs that expanded after the war; migration patterns; and economic change in both the South and the nation.

Despite these improvements, the quality of life for most Alabamians re-mained inferior to that found in many other parts of the nation. In 1950, for example, almost 40 percent of Alabama farms were located on dirt or unimproved roads, and only eight states ranked below Alabama on this indicator. While this condition might be viewed as simply an inconvenience for people who lived along such roads, one should keep in mind that utility companies bring service to areas along paved roads. Mud roads often meant no electricity, telephone, or natural gas.

Education

Another indicator of a gap is found in a 1955 study by the Alabama Business Research Council. It noted that 70.3 percent of top management personnel and nearly 45 percent of all middle managers working in the state had received their education outside Alabama. Income and education are perhaps the most important indicators of quality of life. Income pays for goods (for example, food, shelter, clothing) and private and public services such as health care, education, and roads. Education is directly linked to income. Better-educated people tend to earn more. They buy the goods and services that drive the economic system and supply government with the tax revenues needed to provide and then improve services.

The *Statistical Abstract of the United States* summarizes various social, economic, health, and other characteristics of the nation as a whole. Often it presents state-by-state comparisons as well as relative rankings of the fifty states and the District of Columbia. Its 2000 edition indicates that in 1999 Alabama ranked forty-eighth in the average amount of money it spent on students in grades K–12. Alabama spent on average $4,818 that year toward the education of each student attending public school. This amount represents funds from all sources—local, state, and federal funds. Alabama spent approximately $1,916 less than the national average of $6,734 per pupil. Only North Dakota (ranked forty-ninth), Mississippi (fiftieth), and Utah (fifty-first) spent less per pupil. States with the four highest or best rankings were Alaska ($10,611), New Jersey ($10,420), New York ($9,786), and Delaware ($9,589). These states do not only spend more on education; a larger share of the funds they spend on schools comes from the local community through the property tax.

Another way to look at educational gaps is to focus on how many Alabamians hold high school diplomas and how many have graduated from college. Here, too, Alabama continues to lag behind the national averages, although the size of the gap expressed as a percentage of the national figure has been closing over time. The percentage of Alabamians twenty-five years of age or older who hold a high school diploma or a high school equivalency certificate (GED) is depicted in figure 1. The numbers presented are based on U.S. Census data since 1940, a time when few Americans and even fewer Alabamians graduated from high school. Notice that in 1940 only 24.1 percent of Americans and 15.7 percent of Alabamians graduated from high school. This figure represents an 8.4 percentage point difference between the national and the Alabama levels, but a 34.9 percentage difference (percentage differences allow us to compare the magnitude of difference between two figures). Over time, the numbers for each group grew steadily. Since at least 1980, the gap between the national average and the Alabama percentage has been closing as well. By the year 2000 just over 84 percent of Americans and 77.5 percent of Alabamians were high school graduates or GED holders—a 6.6 percentage point difference but a 7.8 percent difference. The movement from a 34.9 percent difference to a 7.8 percent difference is a very positive change, but a high school diploma alone does not prepare a student for the new technological age.

Another area of positive change is the percentage of citizens twenty-five years of age or older who hold the bachelor's degree. Figure 2 presents that information for the period 1940–1990. It also shows estimated percentages yearly for the period 1996–2000. Notice again the overall rise in both sets of percentages as the decades pass. In 1940, only 4.6 percent of Americans held a bachelor's degree; Alabama's figure was 2.9 percent. The percentage point difference was only 1.7, but again the percentage difference is larger—nearly 37 percent. By 2000, 25.6 percent of the national population and 20.4 percent of Alabamians held a bachelor's degree—a 5.2 percentage point difference and a 20.3 percent difference. The second number shows the gap still existing but narrower.

Now look at the height of the bars for each year. The gap between them increases, decreases, and increases again with no pattern of steady narrowing. While the bars representing Alabama climb at each point from 1940 to 1999, the bars representing the nation often rise at a faster rate. Thus the gaps vary in size from year to year even though Alabama is making progress. Note too that while the U.S. figure inches up a little in 2000, the Alabama figure actually drops. In fact, a slowdown in the rate of increase in Alabama really started in 1996.

Another important factor in education is the quality of teachers. Most informed observers argue that teacher quality is to a great degree dependent upon salary. Alabama's teachers in both K–12 and in higher education traditionally have been paid much less than the national averages. In 1930, Alabama public school teachers earned on average 55.8 percent of the national

Fig. 1. Percentage of those twenty-five and older with at least a high school diploma or GED

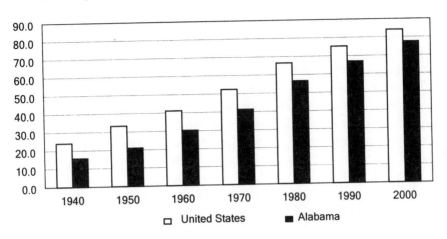

Source: U.S. Census Bureau, Current Population Surveys.

Fig. 2. Percentage of those twenty-five and older with a bachelor's degree

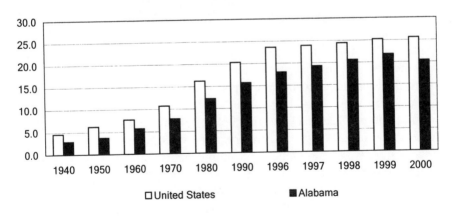

Source: U.S. Census Bureau, Current Population Surveys.

average. This figure dropped to 51.6 percent by 1940. Steady improvement then occurred each decade from 1950 (73.8 percent) to 1970 (79.8 percent). By 1981 and 1986, Alabama's salaries were up to 87.9 and 90.5 percent of the national average, respectively. Then, in 1990 they dropped 8.8 percentage points to 81.7 percent of the national average, only to rise again in 1999 to 88.2 percent, or $35,800. This increase brought the state back to the percentage level attained in the early 1980s.

Salaries for those teaching in the state's institutions of higher education show a different pattern. Figure 3 begins with 1970 and shows Alabama's average salary compared as a percentage of the average salary nationally. The salaries represent 1996 constant dollars—that is, they have been adjusted to account for inflation. In 1970, Alabama salaries ($43,114) were at 84.5 percent of the national average. From then on, however, the pattern is erratic. The percentages rise and fall throughout the period 1970–1996. And, by 1999, the U.S. Census Bureau reported, the figure is 82.6 percent of the national average. The average salary reported for 1999 ($42,006) and the salary reported for every year between 1970 and that date is lower than that reported in 1970.

Scores on the Scholastic Aptitude Test are often used to compare schools because the SAT is given throughout the nation and is widely used by colleges and universities to evaluate the potential performance of applicants. It is difficult, if not impossible, to compare Alabama's scores with those of other states because traditionally, few Alabama high school graduates have taken the examination.

States such as Alabama, which traditionally have had 20 percent or fewer of their high school graduates take the SAT, tend to have much higher average scores than do states such as Connecticut, where higher percentages of graduates take the SAT. The reason is simple: in the low-percentage states, only the best academic performers take the test, while in the high percentage states, those participating are more representative of a cross section of high school graduating classes.

The Southern Regional Education Board (SREB) reports other disturbing information in its *2000/2001 Fact Book on Higher Education*. State appropriations per student in higher education dropped greatly in Alabama between 1995 and 2000. The drop (adjusted for inflation) was $906. Tuition increases have been used to fill the gap, placing greater financial burdens on families who are sending children to college. In Alabama the impact of these tuition increases is greatest on families with lower incomes, because only 27 percent of scholarships and grants are given to undergraduates based on

Fig. 3. Alabama higher-education salaries as percentage of the national average (in 1996 constant dollars)

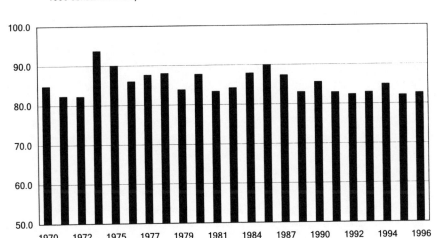

Source: U.S. Department of Education, National Center for Education Statistics, Higher Education Information Survey (HEGIS).

financial need. The national average is 80 percent (a 53 percentage point difference but a 66 percentage difference), and the figure for SREB's member states is 40 percent (a 13 percentage point difference or 33 percentage difference). Here elements of the traditional culture belief system and the Big Mule Alliance myth system are still at work. Particularly evident is the belief in a natural hierarchy and the importance of bloodlines. Lower family income and poverty are said to indicate inferior abilities which do not deserve to be rewarded by special treatment—in this case, need-based scholarships.

Expenditures indicate a state's commitment to the education of its residents. Alabama's expenditures for education have been consistently low in comparison with that of other states and the national average. This pattern exists for spending on both primary and secondary schools and on higher education. In October 2000, *Governing* magazine ranked Alabama fortieth in total per capita educational spending (K–12, junior colleges and technical schools, four-year colleges and universities, and other education spending) and forty-seventh in per capita spending on education for just K–12.

Income

The economic well-being of Alabama's residents is similar to their educational condition. From 1930 to 1990, Alabama's per capita personal income as a percentage of the national average rose steadily. In 1930, for example, the per capita income in Alabama, $267, was only 43.1 percent of the national average. By 1940 the figure was up to 47.3 percent, or $280. The impact of the war and postwar assistance—including the GI Bill, which made higher education possible for many veterans—caused the figure in 1950 to jump to 60.3 percent of the national average. Thereafter, the state's per capita income continued to climb. By 1980 the figure had reached 79.4 percent of the national average, and throughout the 1990s the percentages stayed in the low eighties. But by 1999, per capita income had dropped to 80.5 percent of the national average, or $22,978. In 1990, Alabama ranked forty-second on this indicator; by 1999 the state had dropped one place, to forty-third.

Figure 4 shows these changes from a different perspective. The negative numbers indicate the results of calculations that show how far below the national average per capita income in Alabama is. The fact that the bars grow downward in length over time shows that the per capita income gap between Alabama and the nation is growing. These income figures are reported in real rather than constant dollars. If reported in constant dollars (adjusted for inflation), the decline would be even greater.

The income figures presented above and others like them show that from about 1930 until 1980, Alabama steadily improved its situation compared with that of the nation as a whole. Then in the 1980s and 1990s (the decade depends on the data being examined), this progress slowed or ended. In some cases, Alabama's condition worsened relative to that of the nation; in other cases, the pattern fluctuated. At best the state climbed toward the national average. It did not meet or exceed it.

Poverty Rates

Alabama has shown improvement in reducing the rate of poverty among its citizens. Figure 5 shows the poverty rates for the state and nation since 1980. Initially, the state's poverty rate was around 23 percent. That rate dropped slightly thereafter and then moved up again. But by the late 1980s, the rate had fallen below 20 percent and stayed below that level. By the end of the 1990s, the rate had dropped below 15 percent. Just as important is the fact that the gap between the state and the nation narrowed significantly.

Less encouraging is the fact that during the 1990s, when the overall pov-

Fig. 4. Gap between U.S. and Alabama per capita personal income (real dollars)

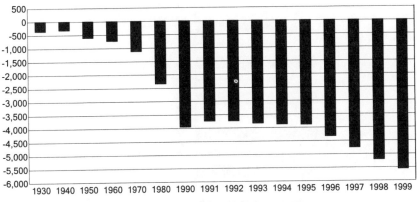

Source: U.S Department of Commerce, Bureau of Economic Analysis.

erty rate declined, the percent of children (those under age eighteen) living in poverty did not decline. Instead, the rate for children in poverty fluctuated between 23 and 25 percent. The greatest improvements in poverty rates were among adults, including the elderly, and not among the young. Poverty among the young is associated with lower levels of educational attainment, movement into lower-paying jobs, and other factors that serve as a drain on economic development.

Additional Rankings

The October 2000 issue of *Governing* magazine cited above also ranked Alabama in comparison with the other states (and Washington, D.C.) on several other important measures. All measures represented per capita figures. On all but two measures, Alabama ranked near the bottom: forty-seventh in personal income; fiftieth in tax revenues collected; forty-fifth in corrections spending; fortieth in highway spending; forty-third in welfare spending; fortieth in total educational spending; forty-seventh in spending on education for K–12; and forty-seventh in environmental spending. The two "high" rankings in fact are not good: twenty-first in the number of state employees per capita and seventh in the rate of incarceration. In other words, we have a relatively large state government, and we put large numbers of people in jails and prisons. However, we do not spend enough to build and maintain correctional facilities, pay for an adequate staff, or supply necessary support services.

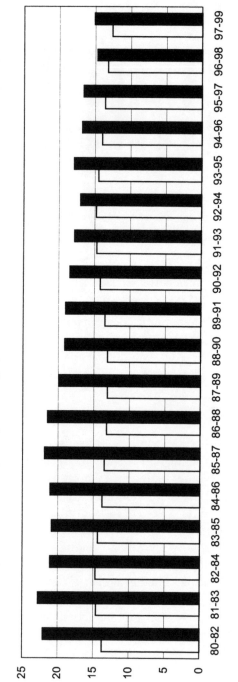

Fig. 5. Poverty rates, 1980-1998 (three-year averages)

□ United States ■ Alabama

Source: U.S. Census Bureau, Current Population Surveys.

Other Issues

All of the examples and figures discussed above represent information on the state as a whole. Each set of figures presented could have been broken down into comparisons based on the racial composition of state residents (black-white) or by region of the state (north-south or Black Belt–non-Black Belt). Such comparison would show that in almost every case each group being compared falls below the national average on the indicators, but that large differences exist between the groups.

Political Institutions and Functional Gaps

The weaknesses in state governmental structure created by the 1901 constitution are documented elsewhere in this book. Another consideration, however, is the degree to which daily operations of government fail to meet modern standards for management performance. Perhaps the most systematic examination of state performance available is the Government Performance Project conducted by the University of Syracuse's prestigious Maxwell School of Citizenship and Public Affairs and *Governing* magazine.[4] Their work was based on a thorough examination of three different sources of information. First, the Maxwell School worked with public officials, management experts, and scholars to develop a survey that was sent to state governments. Second, the Maxwell School systematically sought and then analyzed a specific set of public documents from each of the fifty states. These documents included general and transportation capital improvement plans, performance audits, budget documents, strategic plans, and more. They represent the types of documents one would expect a well-run organization with a large budget to have in place and use for everyday management and long-term planning. Finally, reporters from *Governing* interviewed four governmental officials as well as one knowledgeable source outside of government in each of the fifty states.

Five sets of quantitative measures were developed from these data, and the states received a report card for each as well as an average grade. The study was conducted in both 1996–97 and 2000–2001, with the results for each reported in 1997 and 2001. This method allows not only comparisons across states but also examination of whether a state improved its performance over time.

Alabama received the lowest average grade given in each year. In 1997, Alabama's average grade was a D; none of the other states received an average grade lower than a C-. In 2001 Alabama's average grade rose to a C-; no other state received a grade lower than a C. All of our neighboring states did better, sometimes much better. Mississippi received a C+ in both years, while Tennessee received two B- grades. Georgia and Florida both moved from a C+ to a B-.

The average Alabama grade improved because the state improved its grades for four of the five areas examined. In financial management, the grade moved from a D+ to a C+. Here the study examined whether the government viewed budgeting from a multi-year perspective; used mechanisms aimed at preserving financial stability and health (for example, balanced revenues and spending and used mechanisms to handle the impact of economic downturns on revenue); had sufficient financial information and made it available to policy-makers, managers, and the public; and had appropriate measures in place to control financial operations. Alabama has been credited with finally introducing long-term fiscal planning into the budget process; however, the process is just being developed and the legislature and the executive branch are operating separately from each other.

Alabama's capital management grade moved from D- to D+. This grade reflected how well state government linked its capital budgeting (big ticket items such as buildings and major equipment purchases that last a number of years) to a coordinated plan, analysis of future needs, and its operating budget (which pays for everyday operations). The grade also indicated how well the state handles capital projects (for example, whether it maintains them adequately once purchased). As *Governing* pointed out, Alabama had no capital plan in 1999; it did not even have a list of what buildings the state owns and where they are located. In 2001, the administration of Governor Don Siegelman gave the Finance Department responsibility for establishing a planning document.

The human resources grade moved downward from a C- to a D+. Here the emphasis is on whether the state does a strategic analysis of its present and future governmental workforce needs; is able to obtain, train, and keep a skilled governmental workforce; motivates that workforce to perform effectively; and can develop human resources to achieve the state's workforce goals.

Governing noted that hiring state employees takes twice as long in Alabama as it does in any other state and that there is little long-term planning or analysis of workforce needs. A good example of this problem, although it was not reported in *Governing*, occurred a few years ago when the governor and legislature, hoping to reduce the size of the state payroll during an economic downturn, offered additional retirement incentives for state workers who were eligible to retire. The incentive was so popular that some agencies lost most of their senior workers. This situation left the agencies with largely inexperienced workers and no senior workers to train them. Moreover, the agencies were unable to hire replacements due to a hiring freeze. When the freeze was finally lifted, the agencies were unable to find enough qualified people because the personnel system had too few applicants available for hiring. New testing and certification of candidates takes time.

Information technology grades improved from a D to a C-. This component focused on the state's computer hardware and software systems as well as on their quality and quantity. For example, researchers looked at whether such systems were standardized across agencies and divisions, designed for effective management usage, and tied to strategic planning at the state and agency levels.

Managing for results was the final area graded. Its focus was decision making and leadership. Here the concerns included whether government used results-oriented strategic planning, whether leaders communicated strategic planning objectives to all employees, whether the planning process was responsive to citizens and stakeholders, whether government developed indicators to measure progress and evaluated the quality and validity of the data, and whether the data are used for policy making, management, and evaluation. Also considered was whether government communicates the results of its activities and evaluations to people with a stake in its operations. From 1999 to 2001, Alabama's grade moved from being "an abject failure" to a D+. *Governing* sarcastically observed, "Against, any other background, the current state of affairs wouldn't look so great."

Conclusion

Due to space limitations, this discussion focused on a small portion of the evidence available to document the economic-cultural and political gaps between Alabama and the nation. I have emphasized education and income statistics because they are important for economic development. I have included management gaps because poor management techniques further waste the limited resources available for the delivery of needed public services.

When the 1901 Alabama Constitution placed restrictions on state economic development activities and supported the interests of the Big Mule Alliance, the document either reinforced existing gaps or created new ones. In its amended form, the constitution has helped to maintain the gaps by limiting the revenue base available for taxation, restricting funding of vital services such as education to tax sources heavily dependent on economic conditions (state and national), earmarking funds for specific purposes, and limiting government operations in so many other ways documented throughout this book.

Alabama's greatest periods of gap narrowing occurred because the rising tides of good economic conditions nationwide moved the state upward. Those tides, however, swept the state along without direction and purpose. Meanwhile, we are left with the certain knowledge that rising tides always recede.

Notes

1. Big Mule Alliance development, goals, and political strategies are documented in Anne Permaloff and Carl Grafton, *Political Power in Alabama: The More Things Change*... (Athens: University of Georgia Press, 1995), and Carl Grafton and Anne Permaloff, *Big Mules and Branchheads: James E. Folsom and Political Power in Alabama* (Athens: University of Georgia Press, 1985).

2. See Grafton and Permaloff, *Big Mules and Branchheads,* 52–55.

3. See Permaloff and Grafton, *Political Power in Alabama,* chapters 1–2.

4. Information on Government Performance Project goals and evaluation criteria is available on-line at http://www.maxwell.syr.edu/gpp/about.htm.

9
Lessons of Reform

Alabama in National Perspective

G. Alan Tarr

ALABAMA'S ADOPTION, in 1901, of its sixth constitution was not particularly noteworthy. After all, the American states have periodically replaced their constitutions. Altogether they have operated under 146 constitutions, with most states adopting three or more. The southern states have been particularly active constitution-makers. Among Alabama's neighbors, Georgia has adopted ten constitutions, Florida six, Mississippi four, and Tennessee three. Constitutional reform has occurred through piecemeal amendment as well as through more comprehensive revision. Almost half of the current state constitutions include more than one hundred amendments each, and in recent years most states have added amendments at a rate of better than one per year. However, no state constitution rivals Alabama's with its encrustation of more than seven hundred amendments.[1]

The states' extensive experience with writing and amending constitutions offers valuable lessons, both positive and negative, about how to introduce constitutional reform. Indeed, one important advantage of our federal system is that it encourages learning from the experience of other states, permitting states to assess the success of reforms pioneered in other states and then to adapt them to local needs, circumstances, and preferences. In this chapter I seek to foster such learning by surveying states' experience with constitutional reform and analyzing how this bears on Alabama. More specifically, I describe the various mechanisms devised by the states for instituting constitutional change, evaluate the states' experience with these mechanisms, and identify those factors that have been crucial to the success of campaigns for state constitutional reform.

Constitutional change can occur either by constitutional revision (replacement of one constitution by another) or by constitutional amendment. During the nineteenth century, the American states adopted ninety-four constitutions, but during the twentieth century the number of new constitutions fell to twenty-three, as constitutional amendment replaced revision as the primary mechanism of constitutional reform. This shift from revision to amendment has meant that by 2002, thirty-four states were operating with constitutions at least a century old. It also has meant that many of those constitutions, extensively amended for more than a century, had lost whatever coherence they initially possessed.

Constitutional Revision

The National Picture

On occasion, state legislatures have written new constitutions and proposed them for ratification. In Alabama, however, this option is unavailable. In *State v. Manley* (1983), the Alabama Supreme Court ruled that the constitution of 1901 does not authorize the legislature to propose a complete revision of the constitution.[2] Even if this option were available, experience suggests that such legislative initiatives have rarely fared well. When the Louisiana Legislature declared itself a constitutional convention in 1992 and proposed major constitutional changes, all its proposals were resoundingly defeated. The constitution proposed by the New Jersey Legislature in 1944 suffered a similar fate. Voters tend to view such legislative involvement in constitutional revision as a usurpation of a power belonging to the people. In addition, they tend to assume (often correctly) that legislative constitution-making represents an attempt by those with political power to safeguard their positions, an inappropriate intrusion of ordinary politics into what should be an act of extraordinary political solemnity.

These problems with legislative constitution-making led to the emergence of the constitutional convention as the preferred instrument of constitutional reform. Altogether, the states have held more than 240 constitutional conventions. What is perhaps most attractive about the constitutional convention is that it maximizes the opportunities for popular participation in the process of constitution-making. First, the people determine whether or not a convention should be called. In most states, the procedure is for the state legislature to put the question of whether to call a convention on the ballot, with the issue decided by the voters. Second, if a convention is called, the people select the delegates who will represent them at the convention. Third, the people decide whether to ratify or reject the proposals put forth by the convention. Each of these votes represents an important opportunity for the exercise of popular sovereignty. Voters can refuse to authorize conventions and in fact have often done so: from 1970 to 2000 they defeated twenty of twenty-four proposals for conventions. In addition, voters can reject the constitutions proposed by conventions, and they have likewise done so, rejecting seven of fourteen proposed constitutions during the 1960s and 1970s alone.[3] It is thus no exaggeration to say that the constitutional convention represents the closest institutional approximation of a gathering of the entire populace to deliberate on its constitutional future.

One sticking point, however, is that legislators may refuse to put the question of calling a convention on the ballot, particularly if they fear that constitutional changes might jeopardize their political power. One solution to this problem, currently employed by fourteen states, is a constitutional requirement that the question of whether to call a convention be placed on the ballot periodically. Eight states require submission of the convention question every twenty years, five require it every ten years, and one (Hawaii) requires it every nine years. Although these automatic votes on whether to call a convention can circumvent legislative efforts to block constitutional change, they do not necessarily ensure needed constitutional reforms. For one thing, the timing of the convention vote may be inconvenient, given political realities within the state. For example, although Missouri has an automatic vote in 2002, this provision has not produced any significant discussion of constitutional reform, because political forces in the state are focused on the reapportionment of the state legislature. In addition, voters may be reluctant to call a convention, even when constitutional reform is needed, for fear that a convention would be dominated by existing political elites. The failure of the campaign for a constitutional convention in New York in 1997 can largely be attributed to this fear.[4]

Alabama

The national success of the constitutional convention as an instrument of popular sovereignty stands in striking contrast to the situation in Alabama. Alabama has not held a constitutional convention since 1901, when it adopted its current constitution. Moreover, the Alabama Constitution's provisions regarding conventions raise serious questions about its framers' commitment to popular rule. One concern involves the procedure for calling a constitutional convention. A majority vote in each house of the Alabama Legislature suffices to submit the convention question to the voters. However, even if a majority of voters favor a convention, it is not clear that one would be called. Section 286 of the Alabama Constitution requires that a convention call "must be approved by a majority of those voting at such election." Two different interpretations of this language are possible. One could read the provision as authorizing a convention whenever a majority of those voting on the issue favor a convention, thus aligning Alabama with the practice in the vast majority of states. However, one could also read it as imposing a more stringent standard, requiring the affirmative votes not of those voting on the convention question but of those voting in the election at which a convention is proposed. Under this latter interpretation, if 1,000 voters participated in an election, then 501 votes would be required to authorize a convention. This would remain true even if only 600 people voted on the convention call, hence the convention call would fail even if 450 of those 600 voters supported it. Put differently, under this latter interpretation, a failure to vote on whether to call a convention has the same effect as a vote against a convention. This is more than a theoretical concern. When New Yorkers voted in 1997, almost 40 percent of voters ignored the ballot question on calling a convention.[5] Thus, adopting the more restrictive interpretation of Alabama's constitutional language could thwart the will of the majority of those voting on whether to call a convention.

A second concern under the Alabama Constitution involves the ratification of convention proposals. Unlike most state constitutions, Alabama's makes no provision for popular ratification, thus leaving it unclear whether a convention would be obliged to submit its proposals to the people. The absence of such a provision could be inadvertent, an oversight in constitutional drafting, or it could be intentional, an attempt to deter citizens from calling a constitutional convention by raising the prospect that the convention's proposals would take effect even without popular approval. Whatever the cause, this lack of clarity—like that regarding the popular majority necessary to call a convention—could easily be remedied by a constitutional amendment, drawing on the provisions of sister states for appropriate language. (Indeed, the legislature in 2001 approved such an amendment, and voters will consider it during a general election in 2002.)

Constitutional Amendment

The American states have developed four procedures for proposing constitutional amendments: proposal by the state legislature, proposal by a constitutional commission, proposal by constitutional initiative, and proposal by constitutional convention. The vast majority of amendments are proposed by state legislatures. In some instances, legislatures rely on constitutional commissions to develop the proposals they will submit to voters. Florida goes further, permitting its constitutional commission to submit proposed amendments directly to the people for ratification. Eighteen states also permit voters to propose constitutional amendments via the constitutional initiative. Finally, states may convene constitutional conventions to propose amendments, although the difficulty of calling conventions and the time and expense associated with them make this an unattractive alternative.

It is worthwhile to examine each mechanism for constitutional amendment, both to show what is distinctive about this procedure in Alabama and to survey alternatives that Alabama might consider should it revise its current constitution.

Proposal by State Legislature

More than 90 percent of the amendments proposed each year originate in state legislatures. State constitutions are amended more frequently than the U.S. Constitution, in part because the process of amendment is easier. Whereas the federal Constitution requires a two-thirds majority in each house of Congress to propose an amendment, seventeen states require only a simple majority in each house, and nine require a three-fifths vote. To amend the U.S. Constitution, amendments must be ratified by three-quarters of the states, usually by vote of the state legislature. All states but Delaware require ratification of legislatively proposed amendments by popular referendum, but forty-three require only a simple majority of those voting on the amendment. Yet ease of amendment is not the sole factor affecting the frequency of amendment in a state. Alabama amends its constitution far more frequently than any other state, yet the procedure prescribed by the Alabama Constitution—proposal by three-fifths majorities in both houses of the legislature and ratification by a majority vote on the amendment—is more onerous than that in sixteen states and the same as that in five others.

During the twentieth century, state legislatures increasingly relied on constitutional commissions to provide expert analysis and advice on constitutional problems and to develop proposals designed to address those problems.[6] Utah has by statute created a permanent Constitution Revision Study Commission, and the Florida Constitution provides for the periodic appointment of a constitutional commission. Most often, however, constitutional commissions are temporary bodies whose members are appointed by the state legislature and report to it. For example, the Alabama Legislature in 1969 created the Alabama Constitutional Commission to recommend needed changes in the constitution, and its recommendations ultimately led to a 1973 amendment overhauling the judicial article of the constitution and a 1975 amendment establishing annual legislative sessions.[7]

The membership of a constitutional commission usually includes political leaders (even perhaps some state legislators themselves), constitutional experts, and other notable citizens from throughout the state. Whatever the composition of the commission, the legislature retains the power to accept, modify, or reject the proposals.

From the point of view of the legislature, the use of a commission offers several advantages. First, the commission enables busy legislators to promote in-depth study of constitutional issues and to draw upon the advice of experts. Second, commissions can provide political cover for legislators. Legislators can point to the commission and claim to be addressing constitutional concerns, and they can survey public reaction to the commission's recommendations in deciding whether to support or attack the commission's work. Third, in contrast with the constitutional convention, the commission approach allows the legislature to address constitutional problems while retaining control over the process.

From the point of view of commissioners, the knowledge that their recommendations must gain legislative approval before they can be submitted to the voters discourages proposals likely to antagonize legislators or major interest groups with influence in the legislature. The experience of the California Constitutional Commission in 1996 provides an object lesson in what happens when a commission ignores these political realities, as the legislators refused to endorse any of the commission's recommendations.

Proposal by Constitutional Commission

The Florida Constitution, adopted in 1968, provides for an automatic, periodic review of the state constitution ten years after its adoption and every twenty years thereafter. Although the resemblance to the periodic convention call is apparent, Florida opted for this review to be conducted by a thirty-seven-member Constitutional Revision Commission (CRC), composed of the attorney general, fifteen members appointed by the governor, nine by the speaker of the House, nine by the president of the Senate, and three by the chief justice. What is distinctive about the Florida CRC is that it submits its proposed amendments not to the legislature but directly to the voters for ratification. Thus far, no other state has adopted the Florida model.[8]

This direct submission of amendments to the electorate can be viewed as an attempt to circumvent legislative obstruction. In that respect, too, there is a similarity between the Florida model and the constitutional convention. However, the dissimilarities are even more striking. Whereas voters decide whether to hold a convention and contemplate constitutional reform, the creation of the CRC is automatic, a requirement built into the Florida Constitution. And whereas voters elect the delegates to a constitutional convention, the members of the CRC are appointed. Moreover, because the commissioners are appointed by leading political officials, it is likely that the perspectives of those officials will influence the CRC's deliberations. Thus, despite the fact that the CRC does not submit its proposals to the governor or the legislature, it might not be as independent of the reigning political forces in the state as a constitutional convention would be. Of course, the desirability of such independence is questionable, particularly since proposed constitutional changes must attract political backing to secure ratification. What is clear is that because there is less formal popular participation in the proposal phase, a commission like the CRC needs to tap popular sentiment in the course of its deliberations, lest its proposals be viewed as illegitimate and all go down to defeat.

The CRC has attempted to address this need for public input by conducting public hearings throughout the state prior to devising its proposals. The commission's success in generating popular support for its proposals has varied. In 1978 the CRC proposed eight amendments, all of which were defeated, although when the Florida Legislature endorsed its proposal for a right to privacy in 1980, voters ratified the amendment.[9] In 1998 the CRC proposed thirty-three amendments, contained in nine separate proposals, and eight of the nine, including major constitutional initiatives dealing with the cabinet, education, the environment, and the judiciary, were approved. The effectiveness, as well as the desirability, of this mechanism for constitutional change remains unclear.

Proposal by Constitutional Initiative

Currently, eighteen states permit voters to propose constitutional amendments (but not entirely new constitutions) through the constitutional initiative. In the sixteen states using direct initiative, once proponents of a measure collect the legally required number of voter signatures on petitions supporting it, the measure is placed on the ballot without being submitted to the legislature. In the two states using indirect initiative (Mississippi and Massachusetts), proposals that obtain the required number of signatures are submitted to the legislature before being placed on the ballot. The legislature may adopt the proposals and send them to the people for a vote, or it can revise them and put its own versions before the people for approval.

The use of the constitutional initiative has increased dramatically in recent decades. Yet despite this increase, most state constitutional amendments continue to be proposed by state legislatures, even in states that have the constitutional initiative. Moreover, a relatively small number of states—California, Colorado, and Oregon among them—account for most of the constitutional initiatives.

Proponents and opponents of the constitutional initiative present diametrically opposed assessments of its effects. Proponents assert that the initiative promotes popular control over an otherwise unresponsive government, but opponents contend that the initiative undermines the advantages of representative democracy and substitutes majoritarian for consensual decision making. Proponents assert that the initiative empowers the populace, but opponents respond that it fosters manipulation of the populace by wealthy policy entrepreneurs. Proponents claim that the initiative opens up the political process, but opponents counter that it merely provides another avenue for special interests to advance their agendas. Proponents insist that the initiative fosters thoughtful public consideration of constitutional alternatives, but opponents complain that the process degenerates into "bumper-sticker democracy." Constitutional reformers must carefully evaluate these competing claims before introducing the constitutional initiative in their states.[10]

Proposal by Constitutional Convention

Instead of proposing a new constitution, a constitutional convention may propose one or more constitutional amendments. The scope of a convention's authority to propose constitutional changes is determined by the convention call submitted by the state legislature and approved by the people in authorizing the convention. In most states, the legislature can call either a limited or an unlimited convention. An unlimited convention, as the name implies, has complete discretion in determining the issues it addresses and the proposals it submits for ratification. Conventions that revise state constitutions typically fall into this category. A limited convention, in contrast, is restricted to the agenda specified in the convention call. Whether the convention is limited or unlimited, the procedures for calling the convention, electing delegates, and ratifying convention proposals remain the same.

Alabama's situation differs from that of most other states. The Alabama Supreme Court in 1955 held that the state's constitution does not permit the legislature to call a limited convention.[11] Calling a convention to amend only portions of the constitution thus would require either a constitutional amendment authorizing such a convention or a decision of the Alabama Supreme Court reversing its earlier ruling. Of course, even if an unlimited convention is called, the delegates to the convention have the option of submitting amendments rather than an entirely new constitution.

The Politics of Constitutional Reform

The experience of other states affords important lessons not only about the mechanics of constitutional change but also about the steps reformers can take to maximize their chances for success. What are the lessons for those seeking constitutional revision through a constitutional convention?

One important lesson is that no constitutional convention is likely to be called or is likely to succeed without strong political leadership promoting constitutional reform. When states have revised their constitutions, reform typically has occurred because governors have taken an active leadership role, as occurred with Governor Forrest Anderson in Montana in 1972. Thus, it is not surprising that Alabama Citizens for Constitutional Reform, the state's leading reform organization, made it a top priority to enlist gubernatorial support for its cause. Of course, gubernatorial leadership in and of itself may not always be sufficient, as demonstrated by the campaign to call a convention in New York in 1997, which failed despite the vigorous leadership of former governor Mario Cuomo and the support of Governor George Pataki. For gubernatorial leadership to succeed, the governor must be able to convey a sense that constitutional reform is an urgent priority or that it is necessary to address a glaring problem. Unless citizens become convinced that constitutional reform will improve their lot, they are unlikely to support it. The success of this persuasive effort may depend on circumstances outside the control of reform advocates. For example, during the late 1960s, the U.S. Supreme Court's rulings requiring reapportionment of state legislatures provided the impetus for more far-reaching reform of state governments. However, there has been no comparable impetus for reform in recent decades, and since 1975 there have been only three efforts to devise new state constitutions, of which only Georgia's succeeded.

As noted, in most states constitutional conventions can be either limited or unlimited in the range of changes they are authorized to recommend. One advantage of convening a limited convention is that highly controversial items can be taken off the table at the outset, thereby enhancing the likelihood that the convention's proposals will be ratified. Another advantage of a limited convention is that postponing some issues can encourage potential opponents to support calling a convention. In 1947, for example, Governor Alfred Driscoll of New Jersey pledged that the convention would not address the equal representation of counties in the state Senate, thereby removing an insuperable obstacle to a successful convention. The same effect can be achieved in Alabama, despite the constitutional barrier to calling a limited convention, if delegates agree to limit the convention agenda to a discrete set of issues.

The success of a convention may also depend on how its proposals are presented to the electorate. Typically, a convention's proposals are considered at the next general election after the convention adjourns. If some convention proposals are highly controversial, constitutional reformers have found it useful to submit those proposals separately, rather than as a part of a "take it or leave it" package, lest a few unpopular features doom the entire reform effort. Thus, when Virginia submitted its new constitution to the voters in 1970, it submitted the main body of the document as one question, with separate questions dealing with deleting the ban on lotteries, with broadening authority to issue general-obligation bonds, and with broadening authority to issue revenue bonds.

State constitutional reformers have also discovered that it is not sufficient merely to put reforms before the public. Rather, successful reform requires a concerted campaign to inform the voters and address their concerns. The successful campaign for revision of the Virginia Constitution in 1970 can serve as a model.[12] Proponents of constitutional reform in Virginia formed a statewide steering committee whose broad membership was meant to demonstrate that support for the constitution extended across partisan, racial, and factional lines. This committee—known as Virginians for the Constitution—took the lead in creating themes for the campaign, printing brochures, producing paraphernalia such as buttons and bumper stickers, securing billboard space, buying television advertising time, and otherwise managing the campaign. County and local organizations were also established to handle grassroots operations, including working with local civic groups, canvassing voters, arranging local press coverage of events, handling local newspaper and radio advertising, and manning the polls on election day. Every successful campaign for major constitutional reform, even those facing no organized opposition, has required a similar commitment to informing voters and mobilizing support.

A Cautionary Note

There is little doubt that constitutional reformers in Alabama can benefit from studying the experience of other states that have undertaken constitutional change. Nevertheless, constitutional designs are not like recipes—one cannot borrow them from someone else and, by following the instructions, expect to produce a tantalizing feast. The experience of other states may be informative, even instructive, but it cannot be transferred directly to the very different context of constitutional reform in Alabama. Successful constitutional reformers must take account of circumstances and history, of culture and traditions, of public opinion and community aspirations. In short, they must possess the skills of statesmen.

Notes

1. Data on the number of constitutions and constitutional amendments are drawn from *The Book of the States,* 2001–2002 (Lexington, Ky.: Council of State Governments, 2001), 3, table 1.1. For analysis of the patterns in state constitutional change, see G. Alan Tarr, *Understanding State Constitutions* (Princeton: Princeton University Press, 1998).

2. *State v. Manley,* 441 So.2d 864 (Ala. 1983).

3. For data on voter response to convention proposals, see Gerald Benjamin, "The Mandatory Constitutional Convention Question Referendum 'No' in New York in 1997" (paper delivered at the Annual Meeting of the American Political Science Association, San Francisco, August 29, 2001). For data on voter rejection of proposed constitutions, see Gerald Benjamin and Thomas Gais, "Constitutional Convention Phobia," *Hofstra Law and Policy Symposium* 1 (1996): 69. Benjamin and Gais note that "the constitutions produced by seven unlimited conventions held during the 1960's and 1970's—in New York, Rhode Island, Maryland, New Mexico, North Dakota, and Arkansas (twice)—were rejected at the polls. The 1974 unlimited convention in Texas failed to agree on a proposal at all."

4. Benjamin, "Mandatory Constitutional Convention Question," 9–11.

5. See the website of the New York State Board of Elections: www.elections.state.ny. us/elections/1997.

6. Constitutional commissions may also be established to assist constitutional conventions, providing background study and analysis that can inform the delegates and lay the groundwork for convention deliberations. The most authoritative recent analysis of constitutional commissions is found in Robert F. Williams, "Are State Constitutional Conventions Things of the Past? The Increasing Role of the Constitutional Commission in State Constitutional Change," *Hofstra Law and Policy Symposium* 1 (1996): 1–26.

7. For discussion of the work of this commission, see William H. Stewart, Jr., *The Alabama Constitutional Commission* (Tuscaloosa: University of Alabama Press, 1975).

8. For a particularly thoughtful analysis of the Florida experiment, see Robert F. Williams, "Is Constitutional Revision Success Worth Its Popular Sovereignty Price?" *Florida Law Review* 52 (April 2000): 249–73. This article serves as the foreword to "1999 Florida Constitution Revision Symposium," *Florida Law Review* 52 (April 2000): 249–495.

9. See Rebecca Mae Salokar, "Creating a State Constitutional Right to Privacy: Unlikely Alliances, Uncertain Results," in *Constitutional Politics in the States: Contemporary Controversies and Historical Patterns,* ed. G. Alan Tarr (Westport, Conn.: Greenwood Press, 1996), 73–97; and Rebecca Mae Salokar, "Constitutional Politics

in Florida: Pregnant Sows or Deliberative Revision?" (paper delivered at the Annual Meeting of the American Political Science Association, San Francisco, August 29, 2001).

10. For thoughtful analyses of these competing claims, see Larry J. Sabato, Howard R. Ernst, and Bruce A. Lawson, eds., *Dangerous Democracy? The Battle over Ballot Initiatives in America* (Lanham, Md.: Rowman and Littlefield, 2001); Elisabeth R. Gerber, *The Populist Paradox: Interest Group Influence and the Promise of Direct Legislation* (Princeton: Princeton University Press, 1999); and Shaun Bowler, Todd Donovan, and Caroline Tolbert, eds., *Citizens as Legislators: Direct Democracy in the United States* (Columbus: Ohio State University Press, 1998).

11. *Opinion of the Justices No. 140*, 81 So.2d 678 (Ala. 1955).

12. My account relies on A. E. Dick Howard, "Constitutional Revision: Virginia and the Nation," *University of Richmond Law Review* 9 (Fall 1974): 1–48.

10
A Taste of Reform

The Judicial Article

Robert Martin Schaefer

THE HISTORY OF ALABAMA's judicial branch is noteworthy. Prior to 1973, it had one of the worst reputations in the United States. Academics and journalists throughout the country derisively spoke of Alabama's judiciary. There were frequently heard complaints of backed-up dockets. Sometimes it took years for cases to be heard. Justices of the peace—many of whom were not lawyers—arbitrarily ruled their own "fiefdoms." One commentator proclaimed: "Among state supreme courts, Alabama's was considered to have a particularly notable record for cynical disregard of the law." It was difficult for a lawyer to try a case in a nearby county because judicial procedures were not uniform. Many lawyers spoke of "home-cooking," a euphemism for the arbitrary justice dished out to nonlocals. Alabama also had the reputation of being a state where a "quickie divorce" could be easily obtained: because judges and lawyers were sometimes lax in their interpretation of residency, non-Alabamians could check into a motel room, declare residency, and nullify their marriage.

Exacerbating matters was the Alabama Supreme Court's tendency to imitate the indifference of the legislature and the executive branch to civil liberties. During the 1950s and 1960s judges frequently bowed to political pressure and purposely thwarted individuals' civil rights. As a result, the federal courts overturned many decisions issued by Alabama judges. In 1915, Governor Emmet O'Neal had recognized the disharmony of the Alabama court system, asserting that "in Alabama our whole judicial system has grown up without harmony, unity of scientific arrangement, each legislature creating different courts, until the whole system has become a patchwork which now demands revision and reform."[1] O'Neal's desire for reform, however, would not be satisfied until the late 1960s. In the meantime, Alabama became the popular example of how not to run a judicial system.

By 1975 Alabama's court system had dramatically changed and had become the envy of the rest of the country. Its organizational structure and rules of procedure prompted analysts to speak of Alabama as the model for other states to emulate. How did such a radical change occur?

To properly comprehend the issues surrounding the Alabama Constitution today, and the judicial branch in particular, one needs to appreciate that the framers of the 1901 document were concerned with the rule of law. For them it was a precious thing, but only for themselves. Law is necessary because human beings are imperfect. Consequently, the rule of law replaces despotism. Politicians do not simply rule in the United States; rather, laws are supreme. The writers of the 1901 constitution openly spoke of their disdain at having to fraudulently alter ballot boxes to ensure white supremacy. During the convention it was pointed out that the children of the current leaders might imitate their fathers' tendency to break the law. The children were learning to disregard the law. The rule of law, it was argued, was necessary for the preservation of order and protection of property. Ironically, the 1901 delegates insisted that one more election needed to be stolen to guarantee white supremacy. *Then* the law could be paramount.

Citizens' Conference

Unfortunately, systematic disregard of the law did not cease in Alabama after 1901. Change gradually occurred because many Alabamians worked together, throughout every county and in Montgomery. In 1973 a judicial amendment was proposed on a statewide ballet and passed. Amendment 328 transformed the judiciary. Although many individuals worked hard to secure its passage, Howell Heflin helped to coalesce the grassroots effort. Because of his statesmanship and his unwillingness to succumb to current political pressure, the judicial branch was transformed into a highly respected entity.

Before he was elected chief justice of the Alabama Supreme Court in 1971 (and later to the U.S. Senate), Heflin organized the Citizens' Conference on the Alabama Courts in 1966. The conference, a grassroots coalition of businessmen, lawyers, minorities, and many others, representing a wide range of interests, worked to effect change. They were animated by the judicial branch's lack of professionalism. For decades the conservative planters and the Big Mule industrialists ruled the legislature, which, in turn, effectively controlled the judicial rules of procedure. It was not uncommon for a legislator to adversely affect court procedure in his county—the end result being that for sixty-five years reform was resisted by the state's leaders. The Citizens' Conference slowly but inexorably struggled to alter the judicial landscape. It proposed a number of recommendations, including the following:

- A uniform statewide system of limited jurisdiction trial courts.
- Abolition of the office of the justice of the peace.
- An independent judicial commission for discipline and removal of judges.
- Creation of the Administrative Office of Courts.
- Merit selection of judges.[2]

Prior to 1973, Alabama did not have a uniform judicial code. There were eighty-five limited-jurisdiction trial courts, according to legal scholar Charles Cole, "apart from municipal and probate courts, under 23 different names, each with varying jurisdiction and procedure. Hence, even a lawyer could not know, from county to county, the proper or most convenient forum in which to present a claim for relief."[3]

Another troubling aspect was the fact that many justices of the peace were appointed by mayors for political or nepotistic reasons. Heflin's biographer, John Hayman, notes that "a lot of Justice of the Peace courts were rackets. Justices would be in trailers, and the highway patrol or the sheriff's people would be out on the highways. They would stop somebody, take them to a moveable trailer housing the Justice of the Peace, and collect fees and the fine right there and maybe split the take among themselves."[4]

When local justices or other judges acted capriciously, it was almost impossible to seek impeachment. However, after 1973 a two-tier disciplining structure was implemented. A Judicial Inquiry Commission allows citizens to formally lodge complaints about judges or justices. If the Inquiry Commission deems probable cause, the complaint is forwarded to the Court of the Judiciary, which determines if misconduct occurred and also whether disciplinary action is warranted.

The Administrative Office of Courts (formally called the Department of Court Management) gives the chief justice authority to regulate financial functions, court workloads, juror selection procedures, and various other administrative matters.[5] The courts are no longer overwhelmed with a backlog of cases.

Alabama's judicial system now consists of the Supreme Court of Alabama, the Court of Criminal Appeals, the Court of Civil Appeals, and circuit, probate, district, and municipal courts. Compared to the pre-1973 system, the current one is well organized and coherent. In response to the efforts of the Citizens' Conference, and at the behest of Chief Justice Heflin, the Alabama Legislature created the Permanent Study Commission on Alabama's Judicial System in 1971. The commission examines all areas of Alabama's judicial system, including physical facilities, defense of indigents, criminal rehabilitation, and bail bond practices.

The recommendation of the Citizens' Conference was that the selection of judges be based on merit—a method that is still promoted by many and criticized by others.

Selecting Judges

There are five possible methods of picking judges at the state level. Judges may be selected by the legislature, by the governor, through partisan or nonpartisan elections, or based on merit. The least utilized method is the legislative election. The legislatures of South Carolina, Virginia, and Rhode Island appoint supreme court justices. In most instances, those selected are former legislators who view the position as "a highly valued reward for public service." The obvious problem, recognized by the other states, is that offering judgeships as perks is not conducive to filling the posts with truly qualified individuals.[6]

Various forms of partisan and nonpartisan elections are utilized in twenty-three states. Judicial elections became popular during the Jacksonian period of the 1830s. A wave of democratic sentiment swept the country, causing an endeavor to root out real and imagined corrupt political practices. In an effort to democratize the political system, the checks and balances built into it were altered. Although judicial elections seem democratic in spirit, and therefore appealing, what actually occurs in many states is that sitting judges who are about to retire do so before their term expires. This allows the governor to appoint an interim judge, who usually wins reelection. So in most cases, a genuine election does not occur.

The primary drawback of picking judges through popular vote is that inappropriate partisanship naturally occurs. Many times, candidates accept campaign contributions from parties in a lawsuit. Under normal circumstances, everyday citizens are indifferent to judicial campaigns and rarely give substantial dollar amounts, but special interests, particularly trial lawyers, are more than willing to donate large sums of money. An infamous incident reflects the problems of this situation: during a Texas Supreme Court race, two competing judges accepted "huge campaign contributions" from Texaco and Pennzoil, both of whom were parties in a $10.5 billion lawsuit.[7] One can easily understand the unseemliness when defendants or plaintiffs in a lawsuit expend monies on a campaign that directly affects their own interests.

In six states (and the California Court of Appeals) the governor is allowed to choose judges. Naturally, such appointments are political: the governor normally rewards a loyal party member or former member of the legislature.

If the nominee is approved by the state senate, similar to how federal judges are chosen, the system might work. Overall, though, most scholars dislike this process because of its blatant partisanship and lack of checks and balances.

In 1913 the American Judicature Society proposed that judicial nominating commissions be formed. These commissions would recommend qualified candidates to governors. A similar plan, called the Missouri Plan, became very popular in the 1940s. For many decades scholars and jurists have recommended the Missouri Plan or merit system, currently utilized in one form or another in twenty-two states. A nominating commission composed of representatives selected by the governor, the chief justice, state bar members, and lay citizens reviews credentials of qualified lawyers. Alabama justice Pelham Merrill told the 1966 Citizens' Conference, "I tried to get the legislature to consider such a procedure when I was a member in 1947, but the idea then was too new."[8]

Although the merit plan does not ensure total elimination of politics, candidates are less beholden to the interest groups that support their nomination. Normally the commission recommends three or more candidates to the governor, who then picks a judge. After a predetermined period of time, a retention election occurs. Heflin believed that the "popularity or the unpopularity of a national political party should not be the controlling factor in the election of the justices of the Supreme Court of a state. There was a great feeling among the lawyers that the legal profession ought to go through a cleansing process and straighten up and also should try to move forward with judicial reform."[9] The Citizens' Conference concluded that Alabama "should provide that judges so elected should not be required to run for reelection against opposing candidates but that their names should be submitted to the voters after a reasonable period of time and at the end of each term on a ballot which provides in substance: 'Should Judge _____ be retained in office for another term? Yes _____ No _____.'"[10]

Critics of the merit system claim that "it really does not take judges out of politics . . . but simply gives more political power to the organized bar."[11] The authors of the U.S. Constitution addressed this same issue in 1787 when they defended the selection of federal judges by the president and their confirmation by the Senate. Did this system completely take the politics out of the process? No, but it was argued that two fundamental things do occur: it becomes more likely that a better-qualified candidate is nominated, and also that the president, a person already elected to office, is *responsible* for the choice. The issue of appointing officers is discussed in *The Federalist Papers*

70–72. The author, Publius, firmly believes that many administrative positions ought not be filled by popular vote. The people, though qualified to elect many local officials, do not have the knowledge needed to properly select judges. Publius's comments ought not be construed as undemocratic. On the contrary, he believes that a democratic government requires prudent selection of its officers. Hence, the general populace does not select federal judges because the average person does not fully understand the qualifications for such a position. Alabama, in fact, did not elect judges from 1819 until 1850. Due in part to the spread of Jacksonian democracy, Alabama and a number of other states began to elect judges after that period. By the end of the nineteenth century, however, cries for reform were already being heard. Many judgeships had become "politically" corrupt. This fact should be reflected upon when one considers that millions of dollars are now spent during judicial campaigns in Alabama.

During the last few decades, many state and federal benches have become increasingly politicized. Robert Bork's nomination to the U.S. Supreme Court by President Reagan in 1986 clearly shows how the process has been altered. Thousands of Americans protested for or against Bork because of his political opinions. Due to the judicial activism of the 1950s and 1960s, many Americans have come to believe that policy decisions, and not merely legal decisions, should be articulated by "their" judicial candidate. In recent years, fervor over judicial candidates has calmed down a bit, but the lesson remains the same: any means to limit the politicization of the judiciary is good. Judicial elections do not foster a concern for appropriate application of law.

The Showdown

The Citizens' Conference's energetic and focused campaign to alter the judicial branch came to a head in 1973. Reaching agreement on what ought to be done took at least seven years, but actually persuading the legislature and the people to adopt the new judicial amendment required a well-organized political campaign. In the light of Alabama's political tradition, shaped to a great degree by the 1901 constitution, and exacerbated by the negative atmosphere fomented by Governor George Wallace, it was obvious that reformers would need to expend a great deal of effort. Wallace was not at all interested in changing the political structure in Alabama. To adopt a new constitution, or at least a revised judicial article, would limit Montgomery's power. For Wallace, progress meant preserving the "good-ole-boy" network and keeping blacks in their place. To create change required an immense amount of effort, and it was Heflin who "masterfully managed all the parties and interests essential to obtain court reform."[12] He needed to confront Wallace, who "did not want to 'federalize' the judiciary . . . [and] beat up on us a little bit."[13] Heflin later told John Hayman, "A lot of cooperation between the federal courts and the states courts developed in the years I was chief justice. At the same time, Wallace was ranting and raving about federal judges. He said they ought to give some of the judges barbed-wire enemas and all that sort of thing."[14]

Cooperation was the key element of Heflin's approach. He made it a point to include citizens from all over Alabama, particularly the "opinion leaders." Heflin had been interested in the judicial system since the early 1960s, and his participation in the Alabama State Bar Association allowed him to actively pursue reform. In 1965 he became president of the bar association and vigorously sought ways to improve legal education, judicial ethics, civil procedure, and numerous other important matters. A bar association member recalls that "President Heflin let all of the chairmen of the various committees know that he would not tolerate a dormant committee."[15] Heflin was not afraid of change or the arduous task of effecting it.

He organized the "Muscle Shoals Mafia," composed of editors, mayors, and judges, to lobby the legislature to accept the proposed amendment. In May 1973, shortly before the legislative session was to conclude, Heflin believed that the House would not pass the judicial amendment. Opponents of the bill, hoping it would die in the Judiciary Committee, "delayed and delayed and delayed." Heflin realized that only one more vote was needed to get the bill out of committee. The one legislator who possessed the "key vote" happened to be a Catholic from Mobile. Heflin asked Monsignor Oscar Lipscomb in Mobile for help. A late-night phone call to the resisting legislator from the soon-to-be archbishop saved the day.[16]

The citizens, lawyers, and other Citizens' Conference members benefited from the carefully orchestrated plan to get the amendment passed. Heflin remembers: "The opposition thought they could use all the tricks of their legislative skills to defeat it in committee. There's no question Wallace and all the Wallace people were telling their legislative leaders to defeat it. But they didn't want to get caught doing it."[17] Members of the Citizens' Conference barraged legislators with phone calls seeking support. With only minutes left in the session, the House passed the amendment. House member Ronnie Flippo, holding the bill, rushed to the Senate while surrounded by fellow House members so that nobody could steal it. "If you lost the bill, you lost the issue."[18] The Senate approved the amendment moments before midnight. The only significant recommendation of the Citizens' Conference that the legislature rejected was the merit selection of judges.

This story's dramatic conclusion is instructive. Change in Alabama is difficult to achieve, and organization is absolutely necessary. Reform requires a grassroots movement and a collaborative effort on the part of like-minded individuals. Over fifteen thousand supporters campaigned throughout the state persuading voters to accept the amendment. Amendment 328 was ratified in December 1973, the result of years of relentless struggle.

A Second Citizens' Conference occurred in 1973 with the purpose of offering recommendations on the implementation of the new judicial amendment. Knowing that judicial elections would continue, the conference recommended to the legislature that a nonpartisan system be adopted. Heeding pressure from state judges, the legislature refused to change the system. Justice Hugh Maddox suggests that many judges were "intimately involved in partisan politics" and enjoyed the benefits of their activities. Maddox also suggests that members of the Democratic Party did not want to give up the qualifying fees that judicial candidates were required to pay.[19]

Problems Again

Justice Maddox argued in 1999 that the Alabama judicial system had become the model for the country. The *New York Times, Houston Post,* and *Christian Science Monitor* are a few of the many newspapers that praised the newly reformed judicial system after 1973.[20] Unfortunately, the state's reputation has changed since the mid-1990s. Recent national newspaper stories and journal articles describe Alabama as "tort hell" and as a land of unseemly judicial election wars. Alabama is in the news once again, but this time for all the wrong reasons. The overarching theme is the same: the current system degrades and corrupts the judicial system. The 1995 Third Citizens' Conference again recommended, at the very least, nonpartisan elections, but to no avail.

Critics of both partisan and nonpartisan elections agree that judicial candidates must raise funds—a lot of funds—to compete in the electoral process. Lawyers, who have a stake in the outcome, are the primary contributors. Once again, one wonders how the winners of judicial contests are supposed to respond to their donors.

Alabamians hold dear the democratic notion of electing judges. They are correct, for on the surface it appears to be quite democratic to elect judges.

But a problem arises: judges are not supposed to be partisan politicians; rather, they interpret and apply the law. No doubt such application is sometimes politically prejudiced, but the law is a separate bulwark against the momentary and capricious desires of the people. The very nature of law presupposes our imperfection. To elect judges popularly necessitates partisanship (liberal, conservative, or otherwise) and not the objective application of law. Furthermore, it is supposed that the majority of voters understand correctly when they choose political leaders—that is, that the people know what is best and that their knowledge is reflected in the legislature. But do we know who the most qualified judges are? Judges need to possess an extensive understanding of civil and criminal law. As Publius comments, "Hence it is that there can be but few men in the society who will have sufficient skill in the laws to qualify them for the stations of judges."[21] Another glance at the federal constitution puts this into perspective: the American founders were very much concerned with democracy, but they simultaneously sought to ensure that democracy, and not demagoguery, would prevail. In other words, judges might be required to uphold the law in spite of the momentary passions of the people. Law, not popularity, should prevail. The standard of judicial excellence is found in *Federalist* 78, wherein Publius insists that judges need to be removed from the political arena and kept separate from both the legislative and executive branches. The rule of law must take precedence over the will of legislators. Individual rights must be preserved from the "ill humors" of calculating men. Alabama's history in the first part of the twentieth century proves Publius to be correct. The civil rights of blacks and poor whites were trampled upon with impunity.

Overall, no single plan of selecting judges is perfect, but dissatisfaction with the other plans makes the merit system at least tolerable. Although politics cannot be removed from the process, it is important to realize that "judges who attain their jobs through electoral politics tend to behave like elected officials . . . by emphasizing political—rather than legal—factors in their decision-making."[22]

One theme is common in the popular writings on judicial selection: judicial integrity. The appearance of impropriety is prevalent in partisan elections. Judges are not supposed to make policy—that is the job of the legislature. Allowing candidates to run based on party affiliation causes people to vote for them—whether consciously or unconsciously—for political and not judicial reasons. The contentious 1994 chief justice race between Sonny Hornsby and Perry Hooper, Sr., is a good example of this. Regardless of the merits of each candidate, one must recognize the awkward task confronted by the Alabama Supreme Court. The court, consisting entirely of Democrats, was forced to decide the political contest, and it issued judgments that some considered adverse to the Republican candidate. Braxton Kittrell, former president of the Alabama Association of Circuit Judges, asserts, "This does nothing to maintain public confidence in an independent judiciary and could be avoided if judges were not required to be elected under party labels."[23]

The attempt to reform the judicial system in Alabama has, on the whole, been remarkably successful. Charles Cole sums up this situation best when he asserts, "Judicial reform requires perseverance." He further adds that personal interest must be sacrificed in order to improve Alabama's legal services.[24]

The promulgation of law is fundamentally important in a democracy, yet so is its implementation. Even the founders of the 1901 constitution recognized the importance of law. Unfortunately, they chose to benefit only themselves, leaving the remaining populace—the majority of Alabamians—subject to the capricious will of the state's leaders. In many respects we still are governed by the decisions made during the summer of 1901. Fortunately, our contemporary judicial system offers hope for additional change. Continued improvement of Alabama's judiciary needs to be pursued, but Alabamians can be proud of the goals thus far accomplished. The successful efforts of lawyers, politician, and citizens prove that positive transformation can indeed take place. In the light of Alabama's successes, is it clear that perseverance is the key for future change.

Notes

1. John Hayman with Clara Ruth Hayman, *A Judge in the Senate: Howell Heflin's Career of Politics and Principle* (Montgomery: NewSouth Books, 2001), 154–55.

2. Charles D. Cole, "Judicial Reform in Alabama: A Reflection," *Alabama Lawyer* 60 (May 1999): 188.

3. Ibid., 187.

4. Hayman with Hayman, *Judge in the Senate*, 153.

5. James D. Thomas and William H. Stewart, *Alabama Government and Politics* (Lincoln: University of Nebraska Press, 1988), 113.

6. Ann O'M. Bowman and Richard C. Kearney, *State and Local Government: The Essentials* (Boston: Houghton Mifflin, 2000), 208.

7. Ibid., 209.

8. Quoted in Justice Hugh Maddox, "Taking Politics Out of the Judicial Elections," *American Journal of Trial Advocacy* 23 (1999): 377.

9. Hayman with Hayman, *Judge in the Senate*, 141–42.

10. Quoted in Maddox, "Taking Politics Out," 337.

11. Thomas and Stewart, *Alabama Government and Politics*, 113.

12. Cole, "Judicial Reform," 186.

13. Author's interview with Senator Heflin.

14. Hayman with Hayman, *Judge in the Senate*, 190–91.

15. Ibid., 145.

16. Ibid., 179–80.

17. Ibid., 181.

18. Quoted by Mike House in Hayman with Hayman, *Judge in the Senate*, 182.

19. Maddox, "Taking Politics Out," 338.

20. Ibid., 329.

21. Alexander Hamilton et al., *The Federalist Papers*, ed. Clinton Rossiter (New York: Mentor Books, 1961), 471.

22. Bowman and Kearney, *State and Local Government*, 213.

23. Braxton Kittrell, "Partisan Politics and Judicial Selection," *Mobile Press Register*, September 1, 1996.

24. Cole, "Judicial Reform," 194–95.

11

Options for State Constitutional Reform in Alabama

Howard P. Walthall, Sr.

For any Alabama family that owns an automobile, the day comes when it's time for a replacement. Then the question arises: What are our options? For most of us faced with that predicament, there are three ways to go: We can buy a new car. If that seems too big a step, we can trade for a used car that is a later model. Or we may decide that before we do anything, we need to fix up the old car—give it a tune-up, maybe replace the carburetor—so that we can get a better deal when we trade it in.

Alabamians who have decided that our state's Model T constitution no longer works well in the age of interstate highways face a similar array of options. Calling a constitutional convention to rewrite the constitution completely would be the equivalent of buying a new car. At the end of the process, we could have a totally new constitution ready to carry us through the twenty-first century. A second option is to use the amendment process to revise our present constitution, article by article. Just as with buying a late-model used car, that option at least would give us a more modern document that works better than what we have now. The third option would be to amend the constitutional revision procedure itself to give the legislature power to propose an entirely new constitution. Under a ruling by the Alabama Supreme Court, legislative revision of the entire constitution is not currently allowed.[1] But just as we might install a rebuilt carburetor in our old car before trading it in, we could add the legislative rewrite option before we begin substantive revision of the constitution.

This chapter looks at what is involved in exercising each of these options. We will look specifically at the legal requirements that spell out how each option is to be exercised. These requirements are found in the wording of the present 1901 constitution and in the rulings of the Alabama Supreme Court. We will also look at how one option—a convention—might actually work.

But along the way, we will look back at some of the history that explains the 1901 Alabama Constitution's occasionally peculiar provisions on revision. Justice Oliver Wendell Holmes, Jr., observed that "a page of history is worth a volume of logic."[2] Certainly, that is true in understanding the Alabama Constitution, including its provisions on conventions and amendments.

Most of all, we will be looking at who among us must help to get the job done. One theme runs through each of the options for reform in Alabama, and that is the key role played by the state legislature, where each option for reform must originate. But there are plenty of jobs for each of us as citizens.

Option A: Constitutional Convention

Nineteenth-century Alabamians showed a pronounced preference for the convention as a method of constitutional revision. In the years from 1819 (statehood) to 1901 (our present constitution), Alabamians held a total of six conventions, each of which resulted in a new constitution. During the same period, they adopted a total of only five amendments.[3] Twentieth-century Alabamians, by contrast, have not held a convention since 1901, but they have adopted more than seven hundred constitutional amendments.

The constitutional convention is a unique American invention. During the American Revolution, the concept developed of a body separate from the regular legislature that would be convened specifically for the purpose of drafting a written constitution. Just such a body drafted the U.S. Constitution in the summer of 1787.[4]

As our nineteenth-century forebears appreciated, a convention offers a number of advantages. While amendments simply add to the length and complexity of the constitution, a convention can draft a completely new document. It provides the opportunity to begin anew. That can be an empowering experience, as we learned as a country when we replaced the old Articles of Confederation with the U.S. Constitution.

Another advantage of the convention option is that it is highly democratic. The convention process affords ample opportunity for ordinary citizens to have their say. The people vote twice in calling a convention—first on the question of whether to call a convention and then on the selection of delegates—and almost certainly they would vote a third time on whether to ratify the convention's draft constitution.

Moreover, the convention is devoted specifically to constitutional revision. Convention delegates can focus their energies on that task exclusively. And they do so in a deliberative setting in which, through the exchange of ideas, they may come up with a better product than any one of them could have produced alone.

The basic requirements for calling a constitutional convention in Alabama are set forth in Sections 286 and 287 of the present constitution. Because voters must approve the call of a convention, this method depends upon the support of citizens. But members of the legislature are key, since under Section 286 they must first approve the call for a convention.

The Role of the Legislature

Section 286 spells out exactly how the legislature initiates the call. The act or resolution calling a convention must be approved "by a vote of a majority of all the members elected to each house." So with a total of 35 members of the Senate, 18 senators must vote for the call; with 105 House members, 53 members must vote for the call. Ordinary legislation only requires a majority of a quorum of each house, with a quorum defined as a majority of the total number of members. In the Alabama Senate, 18 senators would constitute a quorum, and a majority of those could pass ordinary legislation. The higher standard for voting for a call of a convention reflects the fact that such a decision is more important than voting on ordinary legislation.[5]

Once an act or resolution calling for a convention has been passed by the legislature, it can only be repealed at that same session. Not surprisingly, there is a story behind this peculiar little provision. In 1898, the legislature, at its regular session, approved the call of a convention. Then in 1899, Governor Joseph F. Johnston, whose political support was among northern Alabama populists who were concerned (quite realistically, as it turned out) that "suffrage reform" was aimed at them as well as at black voters, called the legislature back into special session. The special session repealed the convention call.

Ultimately, the legislature at its 1900 regular session reissued the convention call. When the convention finally met in 1901, it included in the constitution it drafted a proviso that once the legislature has called a convention, that call can only be repealed by the same legislative session that issued it. Thus that particular little provision, preventing the recurrence of the on-again, off-again scenario of 1899, became a part of our constitution.[6]

The Role of the Governor

Just from reading the text of the 1901 constitution, one might think that the governor has no role to play in calling a convention. The last sentence of Section 287 declares that "no act or resolution of the legislature . . . calling a convention . . . shall be submitted to the governor, but shall be valid without his approval." From that, one might think that while the legislature is discussing the call of a convention, the governor might as well take a vacation.

Nothing could be further from the truth. Experts generally agree that the governor plays a pivotal role in constitutional revision.[7] One way a governor might help is by calling a special session of the legislature specifically to address the question of a constitutional convention. Beyond that, the governor's overall political leadership would almost certainly have a great deal to do with the decision made by the legislature on whether to call a convention. The governor's support would doubtless also influence the outcome of the vote of the people on whether to approve the call. Though the governor is not assigned any formal role in the process, his or her participation is nevertheless critical.

Vote by the People

Under Section 286, the legislature's act or resolution calling for a convention must be submitted to the people for a vote. There is some history behind this requirement as well. Alabama's original 1819 constitution did not contain this requirement. Accordingly, the convention of 1861, which voted to take Alabama out of the Union, was called without a vote of the people. The 1865 convention, held after the South's defeat in the Civil War, included a number of northern Alabama delegates who before the war had opposed secession. They believed that if the people had voted, the 1861 convention might not have been called. As a concession to these delegates, the 1865 constitution added a provision that a call of a convention had to be submitted to the voters for approval, and that provision continued in each subsequent constitution.[8]

More Work for the Legislature

Actually, the legislature's role extends far beyond simply calling the convention. The act or resolution it adopts would also include the necessary "enabling legislation." This provides the basic framework for the convention. The enabling legislation may provide for the following:

- How delegates are selected.
- When the convention will begin.
- Where the convention will meet (perhaps the state capitol).
- Designation of a temporary chair of the convention and other arrangements for the organizing of the convention.
- Provision for a research staff or task force to assist the convention with research papers identifying possible alternative approaches to salient issues.

• Provision for other staff and facilities to be available to the convention (for example, secretarial staff, offices and committee meeting rooms, the assistance of the Legislative Reference Service, a press secretary and staff, library and stationery, perhaps a direction to all state departments to provide information and assistance to the convention as needed, and—something no other constitutional convention would have envisioned—computer services, including the capability of hosting a website).

• A requirement that any constitution framed by the convention be submitted to the people for ratification.[9]

Delegate Selection

By far the most delicate issue to be addressed by the enabling legislation is that of delegate selection. Much of the anxiety associated with calling a convention revolves around the uncertainty as to who the delegates would be.

Would the delegates be attuned to the good of the people as a whole rather than to the desires of particular interest groups? Would they be representative of the Alabama's diverse population—black and white, urban and rural, rich and poor? Would the delegates be longtime officeholders—legislators, judges, county or city officials? From one point of view, such delegates would bring experience in working with government to the task of drafting a new constitution. From another point of view, however, delegates with political experience might simply perpetuate "politics as usual."

The delegates chosen might be people from outside politics: civic and business leaders and academics who would constitute a blue-ribbon convention. If so, they might bring a fresh, objective approach to the state's problems. On the other hand, they might lack the political sensitivity to draft a constitution capable of gaining ratification.[10]

The preceding are some general questions and concerns that the legislature would have to keep in mind as it drafted a procedure for selecting delegates. The following, more specific questions would also need to be addressed.

First, would delegates be elected on a partisan (Democrats versus Republicans) basis, or on a nonpartisan basis with no party affiliation indicated? This would be one of the most important questions for the legislature to address. If the election were nonpartisan, it would be more likely to attract nonpolitical blue-ribbon candidates who think of themselves as independents. And if the delegate election were not along party lines, then the convention would be less likely to organize itself along party lines. The enabling legislation for the 1901 convention allowed parties to nominate delegate candidates. When the convention met, its delegates immediately recessed so that the Democrats, who were in a clear majority, could caucus and determine who would be the president.[11] An advantage of a partisan delegate selection process is that it would use the party machinery to nominate candidates. If the election of delegates were nonpartisan, a provision would be necessary for nomination of candidates—for example, by some specified number of signatures on a nominating petition.

Second, how many delegates should be sent to the convention? In answering this question, the enabling legislation must strike a balance. A larger number of delegates would be more likely to include representatives of all or most segments of the state's population. The convention would be more democratic. On the other hand, too many delegates could make the convention unwieldy and deliberation difficult. In striking that balance, one possible reference point is the size of the Alabama House of Representatives (105) or of the entire legislature (140).

And third, how would district lines be drawn? While the enabling legislation might well designate some delegates by virtue of an office currently or formerly held, a substantial number of the delegates would be elected.[12] How would the district lines be drawn? To avoid challenges under the federal Voting Rights Act of 1965, the delegates should probably be from single-member districts rather than elected at large. Single-member districts would provide a greater likelihood that minorities would be selected as delegates, and so such districts have been favored by the federal courts in enforcing the Voting Rights Act. Preference should also be given to districts that are already established and that have already been pre-cleared by the U.S. Department of Justice under the Voting Rights Act.

Obviously, the 105 districts for the Alabama House of Representatives furnish a possible basis for delegate districts. Those districts currently result in the election of representatives who reflect the racial makeup of the state in an approximate fashion. At the same time, using the House districts would result in a number of delegates sufficient to staff the various committees through which a convention would function, while not resulting in so many delegates as to make deliberation and debate difficult.

An "Unlimited" Convention?

The 1901 convention was a limited convention—that is, it was limited to those issues that had not already been declared off-limits by the enabling legislation. For example, the 1901 convention could not have proposed a change in the location of the state capital, because Section 21 of its enabling act forbade that. The 1901 enabling legislation even went so far as to prescribe the exact language of provisions that were to be included in the constitution drafted by the convention.

The convention did as it was told: Section 215 of the 1901 constitution, for example, is copied verbatim from Section 16 of the enabling act. But doubtless this unseemly subordination of a convention to the will of the legislature got under the delegates' skins. And so in Section 286 of the constitution they drafted, they inserted the following provision that had not appeared in any previous Alabama constitution: "Nothing herein contained shall be construed as restricting the jurisdiction and power of the convention, when duly assembled in pursuance of this section, to establish such ordinances and to do and perform such things as to the convention may seem necessary or proper for the purpose of altering, revising, or amending the existing Constitution."

The exact meaning of that language is not self-evident, but arguably it means that any convention called under Section 286 must be a general rather than a limited convention. The Alabama Supreme Court has accepted that argument. In 1955, the Alabama Legislature, at the behest of Governor James E. "Big Jim" Folsom, proposed to adopt a bill calling for a convention limited strictly to the subject of legislative apportionment. But first the Alabama Senate sought an advisory opinion from the Alabama Supreme Court as to whether such a limitation would be valid. By a vote of four to three, the court held that such a limitation would contravene the provision quoted just above, and that the convention, if called, would be free to disregard the limitation.[13] Probably the legislature would not attempt to call a limited convention without seeking a fresh advisory opinion from the Alabama Supreme Court.

Should the People Be Allowed to Vote on the Convention's Draft?

This one is easy. The answer is "Yes." Somewhat surprisingly, however, Section 286 does not require popular ratification of the convention's draft. But according to the same advisory opinion of the Alabama Supreme Court referred to above, enabling legislation can impose such a requirement and the convention must follow it.[14] As a matter of democratic theory, such a requirement is consistent with the principle of popular consent that should underlie the Alabama Constitution. That is why it, like the U.S. Constitution, begins with the statement, "We, the people." And as a practical matter, it is doubtful that the people would vote to call a convention without reserving the right to approve that convention's work.

The issue of whether the people should be allowed to vote on the convention's draft will become moot if an amendment introduced in the 2001 Special Session of the Alabama Legislature is approved. That amendment provides that no proposed constitution, whether adopted by a constitutional convention or by any other method, may become effective without ratification by the people.[15]

At the time and place designated in the enabling legislation, the delegates would assemble and organize themselves. Typically, the enabling legislation would have designated a temporary president, such as the governor or the chief justice. The first order of business would be for the delegates to elect a permanent president from among their number. Committees would be appointed, each focused on a particular topic, such as the declaration of rights, or taxation, or the executive department, to which proposals would be referred for initial review. The convention and its committees might be aided by staff or by a task force or commission already empowered to study the salient issues and have options to propose. Each committee would propose constitutional provisions dealing with the matters within its purview. Sometimes there might be amendments from the floor. Ultimately, the entire convention would vote on the proposed constitution as a whole.[16]

Option B: Revising the Constitution Article by Article

When the old jalopy is on its last legs, our thoughts usually run first to buying a new car right off the showroom floor. But after a Sunday afternoon strolling through new car lots looking at price stickers, we may decide that that's more than we can do. If so, in all likelihood we turn to the option of a good, late-model used car.

An entirely new constitution drafted by convention may be more than we can do. A great deal of political energy would have to be expended, with no assurance of success until the final votes are tallied ratifying the constitution framed by the convention. Opposition to only one or two provisions could, in a ratification election, result in the people's rejection of the entire document. Rather than pursue that option, reformers may instead consider using the amendment process of Alabama's 1901 constitution to amend one article at a time.

There are eighteen articles in the Alabama Constitution. One possibility would be to revise two articles each year, so that over the course of a decade the entire constitution would be modernized. Two revised articles—one to revise Article I's Declaration of Rights and the other to delete Article II, which sets forth the state's boundaries but does so incorrectly—were introduced in the 2000 Regular Session of the Alabama Legislature.[17] In the 2001 Regular Session they were reintroduced along with two additional revised articles,

one revising Article XII, which deals with corporations, and the other deleting Article XIII, which deals with banks.[18] These revised articles passed the
House of Representatives but failed to win approval in the Senate.

There are several advantages in proceeding article by article. Since the
people would be voting on each article separately, opposition focused on a
particular controversial article would not prevent adoption of others. And
Alabamians clearly are comfortable with the amendment process, as evidenced
by the fact that voters have added more than seven hundred changes to the
1901 constitution. Moreover, revision of a single article has already been
shown to work in Alabama. That's how we got our new judicial article in
1973.[19]

But as with buying a used car rather than a new one, there are disadvantages as well. For one thing, one complaint about our present constitution is
that it is the longest constitution in the world. An article-by-article approach
to revision would just make it longer still, as each revised article is added at
the end. Another disadvantage is that it would take a lot longer than a convention would—nearly a decade even if we could do two articles each year.
Also, each article would be drafted by the legislature, rather than by a body
elected by the people for that specific task.

The article-by-article approach would use the Alabama Constitution's
amendment procedure. The basic requirements for amending are set forth
in Section 284 and supplemented by Sections 285 and 287. As with the calling of a convention, the legislature is key. It is the legislature that initiates the
process by proposing an amendment. But overall the amendment procedure
is simpler than calling a convention.

The Role of the Legislature

The legislative vote necessary to propose a constitutional amendment is actually higher than that for calling a convention. "Three-fifths of all the members elected to [each] house" must vote in favor of a proposed amendment.
Thus in the Alabama Senate, which has 35 members, 21 senators must vote
in favor, and in the House of Representatives, with 105 members, 63 members must vote in favor. By contrast, a convention can be called by a majority
of all the members elected to each house (18 of the 35 senators and 53 of the
105 House members).

The difference in the legislative majority required for amendments and
convention calls is somewhat puzzling. Intuitively, one would expect the level
of legislative approval for the calling of a convention to be higher than that
for amending the constitution. One explanation may lie in the fact that each

of Alabama's earlier constitutions had actually required a two-thirds majority of each house to propose an amendment. That was one reason why amendments were so infrequently proposed in the nineteenth century. Focusing on
this problem, the delegates to the 1901 convention quite deliberately liberal-
ized the requirement in order to make the amendment process easier.[20] Little
attention was paid to the approval requirement for calling a convention, however, and the difference in the requirements for the two procedures apparently just went unnoticed.

The Role of the Governor

As is the case with the call of a convention, the Alabama Constitution assigns
no role to the governor in the amendment process. In fact, Section 287 ex-
pressly states that "No act or resolution of the Legislature passed in accor-
dance with the provisions of this article, proposing amendments to this constitution . . . shall be submitted for the approval of the governor, but shall be
valid without his approval." Nevertheless, for article-by-article revision of
the more significant articles of Alabama's constitution—such as Article IV
(Legislature), Article V (Executive), and Article XI (Taxation)—the governor's
leadership might be as important as it would be in connection with calling a
convention and ratifying the constitution it frames.

Vote by the People

All the legislature can do is propose an amendment. It must then be submitted to a popular vote. Section 285 actually spells out the form of the ballot to
be used in voting on an amendment, requiring that the ballot present a choice
of "Yes" or "No."

There is a reason for this specific and somewhat excessive detail. Under
the 1875 constitution and each prior Alabama constitution, amendments had
to be voted on at a general election and had to receive, for approval, the
affirmative vote of a "majority of all qualified electors of the state, who voted
at said election." According to Malcolm Cook McMillan, author of the classic
history of Alabama's constitutions, that provision accounted for the fact that
only one amendment to the constitution of 1875 was ever adopted. As
McMillan states, "The insuperable barrier to amending the constitution was
the requirement that a proposed amendment receive a majority of the whole
number of votes cast at a general election. In a general election all attention
was focused on politics and personalities; large numbers voted for candidates for office and failed to mark their ballots in regard to amendments. . . .
[F]our proposed amendments had failed under the Constitution of 1875

because they did not receive a majority of the whole vote cast in a general election."[21]

That solitary amendment was one to allow the city of Birmingham to levy a special tax for the support of schools. The 1875 constitution had included authorization for such a tax for Mobile, the state's largest city at the time the 1875 constitution was adopted. Birmingham, founded in 1871, grew rapidly and by the 1890s demanded schools on a par with Mobile's. But how could Birmingham get a school tax amendment approved by the people of the state? The device employed to accomplish this goal was to print on the ballot a statement in favor of the amendment. A voter could vote against the amendment only by marking through the statement. If a voter did nothing, that ballot was counted in favor of the amendment. In effect, anyone who did not vote on the amendment was treated as voting "Yes." On that basis, the amendment received a majority of the total votes cast at the election. Naturally, this process prompted a challenge. The Alabama Supreme Court upheld the approval of the amendment, ruling that each voter, in depositing his ballot without striking the statement in favor of the amendment, had made an affirmative act expressive of his approval of the amendment.[22]

Birmingham got its school tax, but the tactics used were a little too much for the delegates to the 1901 convention. So they added Section 285, which mandated that the ballot used in voting on constitutional amendments give the voter a choice of voting "No."

At the same time, Section 284 of the 1901 constitution removed the "insuperable obstacle" that an amendment receive a majority of the votes cast at a general election. Section 284 allows the vote on an amendment to be taken at a general election "or upon another day appointed by the legislature, not less than three months after the final adjournment of the session of the Legislature at which the amendments were proposed." Section 284 also removed the requirement of earlier constitutions that a proposed amendment receive a majority of the whole number of votes cast at the election. All that is required under Section 284 is that a proposed amendment be approved by "a majority of the qualified electors who voted at such election *upon the proposed amendments*" (emphasis added).

An example will illustrate how the rules of Sections 284 and 285 work. Assume that the legislature proposes an amendment revising Article XII (Corporations). The legislature could call for a vote on the proposed amendment at a special election, as long as this election was held at least three months after the legislative session ended. Or the legislature could call for the vote to be taken at the next general election. Suppose the next general election features a hotly contested presidential race at the top of the ballot. Further suppose that one million Alabama voters cast ballots in the presidential race but only 800,000 vote on the proposed revision of Article XII. If 400,001 of those voters choose "Yes" and only 399,999 choose "No" (the ballot choices prescribed by Section 285), then we have a new Article XII. Repeat the same process for each of the other articles, and we have a new constitution.

Option C: Authorizing the Legislature to Rewrite the Entire Constitution

But why proceed article by article? The amendment procedure is clearly much simpler than that for calling a convention. Why not use the amendment procedure to rewrite the entire constitution? The legislature, instead of proposing an amendment that revises a single article, could propose an amendment that rewrites the entire constitution. The people then could vote on it, and if a majority of those voting on the amendment marked their ballots "Yes," we would have a brand-new constitution. In Alabama, unfortunately, that approach is not permitted.

In 1983, the Alabama Legislature drafted a revised constitution to be substituted for the existing constitution, after approval by the people under the amendment procedure. But the Alabama Supreme Court, in *State v. Manley*, refused to let the people vote on the legislature's proposal. The court held that under Alabama's present constitution, only a convention could completely rewrite the constitution.[23]

The absence of any power in the legislature to propose a revised constitution is like having a car that's not firing on all cylinders. It may go forward, but only by jerks and stops. Each of our seven-hundred-plus amendments represents a jerk or a stop. The existence of a legislative power of revision, on the other hand, is like equipping an older car with a new, more efficient carburetor. It opens up all kinds of possibilities for moving forward.

Giving the legislature the power to propose a revision does not necessarily mean that the legislature would draft the new document itself. Consider the course of events in Georgia, where the courts of that state held that the legislature indeed had the power to rewrite the constitution. First, the legislature used its Legislative Reference Service to clean up the old constitution, eliminating redundant and outdated provisions, but without making substantive changes. In 1976, the voters overwhelmingly approved the "cleaned up" constitution. The legislature then created a select committee, chaired by the governor, that drafted a modern constitution. In 1983, the new document won approval by the state's voters.[24]

Florida was once governed by a straitjacket constitution that actually was modeled on Alabama's 1875 constitution. The Florida document had a similarly limited range of options for reform. In 1964, the Florida Legislature and the voters approved an amendment that allowed the legislature to rewrite the constitution. The legislature exercised that power by appointing a blue-ribbon commission that submitted to the legislature a proposed draft. The legislature made some changes in the commission's draft and then submitted the document to the people, who in 1965 approved it.

One of the innovations of Florida's revised document was the establishment of a constitutional revision commission that automatically convenes every twenty years—once a generation. After study and hearings, the commission recommends any needed revisions to the people of Florida for their approval. The revised constitution also reserved to the people of Florida the right to bypass the legislature and initiate constitutional amendments on their own. All this flowed from the simple step of granting the legislature the power to revise the constitution.[25]

In *State v. Manley,* the Alabama Supreme Court, while holding that a convention is the only current way to revise the constitution in its entirety, also recognized that an amendment, approved by the people, could "delegate the power of a complete revision to the Legislature."[26] Once again, the process begins with the legislature. It would be necessary for the legislature to propose an amendment authorizing a legislative rewrite. That amendment must then be approved by popular vote. Such amendments were proposed in the legislature in 2000 and in 2001, but they failed to win sufficient support. Legislators did not seem particularly interested in having authority to draft and present an entirely new constitution—or even a substantially revised one.[27]

If such a proposed amendment were reintroduced and ultimately approved, the legislature would have to decide how to implement its authority. It might proceed, as in Georgia, by first "cleaning up" the constitution as the Georgia Legislature did, eliminating provisions that have been superseded or declared invalid. Then, as in Georgia, it might create a select committee to draft a substantively modernized constitution. Or, like the Florida Legislature, it could create a commission to draft a revised constitution to be reviewed by the legislature. Or the legislature, perhaps in a special session called by the governor, might draft a revised constitution through the ordinary legislative process. In any event, the people would ultimately have to vote in favor of any constitution the legislature might frame.

Conclusion

Alabamians are experienced in deciding what to do when the family car no longer serves its purpose. As citizens, we face a similar array of options when our outdated constitution needs to be replaced. We can call a convention to rewrite the constitution in its entirety. We can revise the present constitution article by article. Or we can increase our options for revision by amending the constitution to allow for legislative revision. Those are the options. The choice is ours.

Notes

1. *State v. Manley,* 441 So.2d 864 (Ala. 1983).

2. *New York Trust Co. v. Eisner,* 258 U.S. 345, 349 (1921).

3. Malcolm Cook McMillan, *Constitutional Development in Alabama, 1798–1901: A Study in Politics, the Negro, and Sectionalism* (1955; reprint, Spartanburg, S.C.: The Reprint Company, 1978).

4. Roger Sherman Hoar, *Constitutional Conventions: Their Nature, Powers, and Limitations* (1917; reprint, Littleton, Colo.: F. B. Rothman, 1987), 1–11.

5. Alabama Constitution, Article IV, Section 52; Robert L. McCurley and Keith B. Norman, *Alabama Legislation,* 4th ed. (Tuscaloosa: Alabama Law Institute, 1997), 152.

6. McMillan, *Constitutional Development in Alabama,* 250–61.

7. Ibid., iii (dedication to the "Alabama governor, as yet unknown, who makes revision of Alabama's constitution a major issue of his administration"); William H. Stewart, Jr., *The Alabama Constitutional Commission: A Pragmatic Approach to Constitutional Revision* (University: University of Alabama Press, 1975), 115.

8. McMillan, *Constitutional Development in Alabama,* 108.

9. John P. Wheeler, Jr., *The Constitutional Convention: A Manual on Its Planning, Organization, and Operation* (New York: National Municipal League, 1961), 6–8.

10. Ibid., 29–36.

11. *Official Proceedings of the Constitutional Convention of the State of Alabama, May 21st, 1901, to September 3rd, 1901* (Wetumpka, Ala.: Wetumpka Printing Co., 1940), 1:5.

12. For example, the legislation might make all living former governors delegates.

13. *Opinion of the Justices,* 263 Ala. 141, 81 So.2nd 678 (1955).

14. *Opinion of the Justices,* 263 Ala. 141, at 146, 81 So.2nd 678, at 683.

15. H.B. 5, 3rd Spec. Sess. (Ala. 2001).

16. Wheeler, *The Constitutional Convention,* 37–51, 63–70.

17. H.B. 191, Reg. Sess. (Ala. 2000) (Article I), and H.B. 192, Reg. Sess. (Ala. 2000) (Article II).

18. H.B. 63, Reg. Sess. (Ala. 2001) (Article I), Ala. H.B. 64, Reg. Sess. (Ala. 2001) (Article II), Ala. H.B. 452, Reg. Sess. (Ala. 2001) (Article XII), and H.B. 451 (Ala. 2001) (Article XIII).

19. Charles D. Cole, "Judicial Reform in Alabama: A Reflection," *Alabama Lawyer* 60 (May 1999): 185.

20. *Official Proceedings,* 3:3924–27.

21. McMillan, *Constitutional Development in Alabama,* 247–48.

22. *May & Thomas Hardware Co. v. Mayor and Aldermen of Birmingham,* 123 Ala. 306 (1898).

23. 441 So.2d 864 (Ala. 1983).

24. Melvin B. Hill, Jr., *The Georgia Constitution: A Reference Guide* (Westport, Conn.: Greenwood Press, 1994), 14–20.

25. Talbot D'Alemberte, *The Florida State Constitution: A Reference Guide* (Westport, Conn.: Greenwood Press, 1991), 11–14.

26. 441 So.2d 865, 876 (1983).

27. For example, see 2000 Al. S.B. 589.

12

Whose Government Anyway? A Call for Citizen-Based Reform

Bailey Thomson

AMERICANS HAVE BEEN retreating from civic participation for at least two generations. That conclusion is the heart of Robert D. Putnam's recent book *Bowling Alone: The Collapse and Revival of American Community*, in which the author charts this depressing trend through various means. For example, he shows the decline of membership in groups as disparate as the League of Women Voters and the Jaycees. For whatever reasons—and there are many—Americans increasingly favor private pursuits over public engagement. The challenge for this generation, writes Putnam, a political scientist at Harvard University, is to get people talking and interacting with one another in ways that are good for democracy. In particular, we need to "transcend our social and political and professional identities to connect with people unlike ourselves."[1]

Putnam's thesis has drawn rebuttals from some other scholars and activists, who question in particular whether lower levels of participation in social and political organizations signal a corresponding decline of democracy. Sociologist Michael Schudson, for example, went back to America's Revolutionary generation to study how Americans exercise their citizenship. He concluded that standards change from one era to the next and that each successive model of citizenship builds upon lessons learned from the predecessor. In Schudson's view, the postwar generation that Putnam extols for its high rate of participation in everything from bowling leagues to civic clubs may have been an anomaly rather than a benchmark. The present generation has found new ways to participate in political life that reflect some profound changes in our society, such as people's intense interest in exercising their legal rights.[2]

I am inclined to agree with Putnam, however, that something is not quite right with our public life in terms of citizens' involvement, which is essential for the survival of our republican form of government. We Americans have lost much of what he and other writers have described as "social capital," which roughly means the dense network of associations necessary to make society work properly. As Putnam argues, "A society of many virtuous but isolated individuals is not necessarily rich in social capital."[3]

With this essay, I hope to show why the present movement in Alabama for a new state constitution provides an opportunity not only to improve government and correct old injustices but also to rejuvenate interest in civic life itself. Putnam's findings notwithstanding, I believe many of our citizens do desire an experience that transcends being mere consumers of goods and services on the one hand and voting and paying taxes on the other. I base much of my optimism upon what I see and hear as I travel across Alabama speaking to diverse groups and listening to citizens talk about the kind of communities they want for themselves and their children.

Simply creating opportunities for civic dialogue to occur is important. As political theorist Benjamin Barber argues, citizens need to develop their civic skills in that crucial third sector that exists between government and the marketplace. In this sector, they can become engaged in public business. They can be responsible members of free associations, such as neighborhood groups, and they can seek common ground where, with members of other groups, they can pursue answers to democratic problems. Indeed, democracy precedes both government and the marketplace in the order of importance for our liberty and happiness. And each generation has a duty to nourish democracy's roots.[4]

Voluntary involvement in public life is what Thomas Jefferson had in mind when he contemplated citizens being full participants every day, not just at elections. Such civic activism, he argued, was the remedy for an unresponsive government whose officials tend to confuse their interests with the public interest. Many developments since World War II, however, have combined to alienate us as individuals from the civil society that sustains our democracy. We see in suburban sprawl, for example, an increasing isolation of people from the kind of healthy republic that Jefferson envisioned. For one thing, there often is not enough public space for citizens to conduct the vital work of democracy. Shopping malls and strip developments have dispersed consumers in contrast to how the old downtowns and main streets attracted people to central locations, where coffee shops, lunch counters, movie theaters, churches, and high school auditoriums beckoned them to talk to one another. The town square or meeting hall symbolized this older communal relationship. We have yet to find sufficient substitutes in the automobile-dependent landscapes that now sprawl away from our cities.

In this atomized society, politics becomes less an art of achieving common goals and more a science of swaying public opinion. Thus the messages of our political campaigns seem to grow shorter and nastier. Money becomes not just the mother's milk of politics but also the poison. The more money special interests pour into the campaigns on behalf of their candidates, the more jaded and distrustful voters become.

How do we reverse such alienation to achieve a more satisfying civic life? In short, how can we make civic renewal a dominant feature of our new century? I suggest we begin at the grass roots and nurture that vital sense of community that is at the heart of our civic being. We must make the center strong so that it can withstand even the kinds of catastrophic events that terrorists have brought to our nation's door. Those attacks taught us Americans something important about our civic life: we no longer can take it for granted. Indeed, the strength of our democracy becomes our greatest defense against those who wage terrorism against us. Our ability to reason together to solve our common problems will mean more for our survival as a free people than the weapons we muster against our enemies.

In response to the recent savagery, Americans have drawn upon a civic foundation bequeathed by generations of unselfish citizens who left this nation better than they found it. Now comes this generation's turn to strengthen that foundation so it can withstand a hundred such tragedies, if need be, to preserve our liberty and our values.

Our first job as civic builders is to ensure that all people have an opportunity to speak about decisions that may affect their lives. One of the common complaints I hear from citizens is that their voices and their votes simply don't count. They believe that decisions are made behind closed doors by powerful economic interests that control government. I do not dismiss this complaint, because there is truth in it. We have to acknowledge the flaws of our system and fix them as we invite more citizens to participate. In particular, we have to reduce the baneful influence of huge campaign contributions on our politics.

The *Birmingham News*, for example, reported that special interests accounted for more than 80 percent of the $13.2 million contributed to the 1998 legislative campaigns in Alabama. Individuals gave only 15 percent. About 70 percent of all campaign money flows through contributions of political action committees. Lobbyists often hide the source of such money by moving it legally from one PAC to another in a shell game. Legislators are obviously so dependent on this money that they refuse year after year to restrict this devious practice.[5]

Rejuvenating our civic life requires that we address such harmful practices and find ways for voters to participate as citizens rather than solely as members of self-interested economic groups. We also have to reduce politicians' dependence on special interest money to fund their increasingly expensive campaigns. Not only do fat cats have more access to our elected leaders than do ordinary citizens under this system, but they are also first in line to reap government's benefits. I am often amazed at how much money the state can waste, particularly on big items such as highways, simply because a governor or some other leader wishes to reward his large contributors with lucrative contracts.

Reforming political methods alone, however, would still leave Alabama laboring under a state constitution that is antidemocratic in nature and antiquated in practice. As essays elsewhere in this book have demonstrated, the 1901 Alabama Constitution is a shameful legacy of political reaction. Its proponents used a crooked election to disfranchise blacks and poor whites and to concentrate power in the hands of a small economic elite. The framers succeeded in achieving their agenda—perhaps beyond even their own expectations—but in the process of protecting their power and privilege they managed to cripple Alabama's democracy and retard its development.

To correct this historic injustice and prepare Alabama for this new century's challenges, we citizens need to set our sights on calling a state constitutional convention to write a modern charter of fundamental laws. We need a constitution that will express the hopes and aspirations of the future—not the prejudices and injustices of the past. To do this great thing, we must find the energy and commitment necessary to demonstrate that democracy is a self-renewing process.

Almost four decades ago, Martin Luther King, Jr., wrote a moving book titled *Why We Can't Wait*. It was his answer to critics who said that civil rights advocates should go slow and be patient for change. But Dr. King didn't wait, and today Birmingham and other southern cities are better places because of his insistence—and that of many other crusaders—on making the practices of democracy consistent with its ideals.

Today, we in Alabama cannot wait for our government to reform itself. We citizens, empowered with inner strength and confident in our ability to govern ourselves, must seize the high ground—the common, civic ground. We must make a new compact with ourselves, one that will bequeath to our children the best democracy we can fashion.

We all benefit from the commitment of people who perform their civic duty. Often, such citizens give back to society more than they receive; they perform their duty to others beyond expectation and seek no recognition. Among the committed citizens of our time, for example, are those who devote themselves to relieving the effects of poverty, whether their service be tutoring a child or organizing a neighborhood cooperative. All of us would gain from the elimination of poverty, yet the ranks of those who actually work toward this goal are relatively thin.

In time, perhaps larger numbers of our citizens—particularly young people—will discover this virtue of civic service. Certainly, those of us who work in the public sphere, such as teachers, ministers, journalists, and officials, can seek new ways to help citizens engage in civic life. If older forms of social engagement have lost their appeal, then let us promote new ideas for connecting people to one another. We have to keep restocking our social capital if we are to pass the freedom and prosperity we enjoy to the next generation.

I understand why, in this individualistic era, the ideal of committed citizenship can be terrifying. People frequently remark how their free time is "golden." The consumerist ethos, meanwhile, equates consumption with personal gratification. But once one embraces a nobler calling, he or she will rise each morning with a fresh expectation of life's blessings. The private matters that often beset us day and night may fade in significance. And most important, one will come to understand that freedom begins with concern for others.

Good citizenship makes us actors in our nation's continuing experiment in self-government. It gives our lives meaning beyond what we simply earn or consume. And most important, it allows us to repair our nation's frayed civic fabric with that most precious thread: a deep and abiding commitment to make our democracy work. It's no wonder that in places where citizenship is highly valued, public life seems to work more effectively for everybody.

Political scientist Daniel J. Elazar noticed this phenomenon many years ago as he pondered why politics functioned differently in various sections of the country, often to the benefit or detriment of citizens. He concluded that a state's "political culture" largely determines its government and politics. Elazar identified three such cultures: traditionalistic, individualistic, and moralistic.[6]

In 1901, Alabama had a "traditionalistic" culture—one based upon its static agrarian economy and reflective of its premodern experience. Authority rested mainly in the hands of the state's planters and its emerging industrialists, who disdained political and social equality. They wanted a cheap, pliable labor force, untainted by education or "foreign" notions such as unions. As many observers have noted, even Alabama's industries—dominated by textiles, mining, and steel—helped perpetuate a colonial economy, subservient to outside interests and unattractive to innovative, technically oriented companies. The captains of Alabama industry, like their political partners in the plantation regions, distrusted democracy and saw no reason to invest in the state's human potential. The constitution that these elites wrote and then promulgated through a fraudulent election helped to sustain their way of life, while leaving blacks and poor whites at the mercy of low-wage jobs and poor social services. This legacy continues in the state's warped and unjust tax system and in its failure to expand democracy in its local communities.

Since the 1960s, however, economic development and the civil rights movement have helped knock the props out from under Alabama's traditionalistic culture, although many of its vestiges remain embedded in the state's constitution. Today, only the most reactionary groups would argue that the past presents any moral or economic roadmap to the future.

As Alabama's traditionalistic political culture fades, the state shows evidence of the two other cultures that Elazar used to explain political life in the United States. The "individualistic" culture is essentially self-centered. Politics provides opportunities for ambitious people to achieve private ends through skillful manipulation and bargaining. In this view, corruption and greed are merely by-products of a rough and often dirty political process. The "moralistic" culture is public-centered. It views civic involvement as an obligation to pursue the highest standards of good behavior. Government is expected to act in the interest of all citizens, present and future, rather than to pit one group against the other for the spoils.

If we were to judge Alabama by the actions of certain special interests and the politicians they influence, we probably would conclude that the self-centered culture, grafted onto the traditional agrarian base, best explains the state's present politics. Yet hopes for Alabama's achieving a vibrant civic life, with all its attendant responsibilities and rewards, rests with developing a public-centered political culture. The state simply cannot achieve its great potential until more of its citizens can engage in the productive and cooperative work of building a strong and responsive democracy.[7]

I can understand why the notion that Alabama might reverse one hundred years of bad government and rule by selfish interests would strike some people as impractical, even absurd. They are like those cynics who greeted the Declaration of Independence with laughter and scorn. They simply cannot conceive of Alabama ever embracing a noble idea, such as replacing its racist, defective state constitution with a document that speaks to modern needs and aspirations. Meanwhile, big landowners and others who have profited from the present system continue to jerk the strings of pet politicians to ensure that reform goes nowhere.

In truth, citizens are not entirely blameless for this shameful mess. Voters around the state regularly reject fair school taxes, and appeals to prejudice continue to resonate with a large part of the electorate. Indeed, there often seems to be a connection between inadequate school revenues and whites' unwillingness to invest in the education of African Americans. Alabama's much-lamented failure to elect a "New South governor" results in no small measure from a political culture that encourages the worst kind of behavior among voters.

So what hope might one hold out in response to the cynics' laughter? Is the Alabama of today really any different from the state that repeatedly gave the opportunist George C. Wallace a convenient soapbox to rail against civil rights and block needed reforms? Have not the majority of Alabamians repeatedly voted against their own children's future by rejecting adequate school taxes, while allowing politicians such as Chief Justice Roy Moore to capitalize on symbolic but ultimately unimportant issues such as whether to display the Ten Commandments in public places?

The first response I give to these "realists" is that a higher percentage of citizens are beginning to connect their state's many failures to the 1901 constitution. This document represents virtually everything that is bad about Alabama's present system, while obstructing the progress that most of our people say they desire. Alabama needs good schools, effective local government, and an adequate tax base, but such practical goals remain largely out of reach so long as the dead hand of the constitution strangles our democracy. I am encouraged as I watch constitutional reform steadily move upward among those issues that citizens say are important to them.[8]

True, Alabamians are far better off today as citizens than were most members of their grandparents' generation. The hated poll tax and other restrictions on voting are gone. African Americans, women, and other groups formerly discriminated against hold prominent public positions. And citizens are now assured through regular reapportionment of the legislature and other representative bodies that their votes count roughly the same as others throughout the state. As a consequence of such reforms, the most egregious injustices from the past have disappeared. And along with those wrongs has gone the overt racism that fueled demagoguery.

But any honest assessment of Alabama's public life would have to concede that many, if not most, of these reforms came through outside intervention.

The federal courts and the U.S. Congress, for example, forced Alabama to extend equal rights to all its citizens, culminating with the 1965 Voting Rights Act. Outside intervention also brought fair labor laws, protection of the mentally ill, and humane treatment of prisoners. Indeed, Alabama's politics has produced remarkably few achievements, beyond stubbornly and skillfully protecting special interests.

Equally distinctive in this cycle of reform is the extraordinary attention that Alabama's newspapers—daily and weekly—are devoting to the 1901 constitution's legacy. They have demonstrated what scholars have long suggested: the press can set the public agenda and persuade politicians to deal with important issues. More important, these newspapers are showing unusual leadership, unlike in earlier times when many publishers and editors were little more than mouthpieces for their local interests. In calling for a new constitution, the papers are embracing a process for change rather than promoting any selfish agenda. On their editorial pages and in their news columns, they are writing about principles of good government, while being guided by practical experience. In this regard, these newspapers are heirs of the philosophical spirit that produced our Declaration of Independence and has infused our nation's most successful ventures in self-government.

Finally, the state now has a citizens organization wholly devoted to achieving a new constitution, and I am proud to have had a modest role in this group's formation. Already we have seen substantial benefits. Alabama Citizens for Constitutional Reform (ACCR) grew out of a rally in Tuscaloosa sponsored by that city's chamber of commerce. As of this writing, ACCR has more than thirteen hundred members, and it operates with the help of a small professional staff. It counts among its leaders some of the state's most distinguished and selfless citizens. Its leader, Thomas E. Corts, president of Samford University, has emerged as a persuasive champion for reform, combining the concern that many of the state's religious people show for social justice with the equally persistent commitment of progressives for better government.

ACCR is unusual in that it actively pursues a grassroots strategy for constitutional change. Indeed, its approach seemed so novel and perhaps even threatening to certain special interests that their spokesmen immediately sought to tar the organization with the brush of tax reform, as if that aspiration were something evil in itself. Corts has insisted, however, that his organization would prefer to take the state's notorious tax system out of the constitution, where it does not belong, and make it a matter of statutory concern. Matters that are constitutional in nature, meanwhile, such as a proper organization of state government, would receive the full attention they deserve from reformers.

ACCR has staked its credibility on its strong faith in citizens' participation in the constitutional process. Toward that end, the group has adopted as a bedrock principle the necessity of drafting a new document through a constitutional convention, with delegates selected through popular election. Furthermore, ACCR has insisted that voters should have the final say in ratifying a new constitution. The group won its first legislative battle in September 2001, when it persuaded the legislature to present to voters a constitutional amendment that would guarantee the people's right of ratification.

Of course, a more enlightened citizenry and an energized press face formidable obstacles in Montgomery, where influence requires lots of money—the kind that the big interests can raise. Citizens who have expressed high civic aspirations for Alabama typically have not been organized to compete in the Darwinian environment of statehouse politics. And the press's attention span can be noticeably short, while that of television sometimes seems to be measured in milliseconds.

On the other hand, if reformers can help enough citizens realize how poorly the current system works and why that failure diminishes future opportunities, I believe we can begin to see a remarkable cultural shift. In other words, citizens can be persuaded through education and good leadership to cross over to what reformers might consider "the right side of history."

I base this prediction on a couple of things. First, information can be a powerful weapon against an entrenched status quo. As Gerald Johnson, now retired from teaching political science at Auburn University, likes to say, "Voters are not stupid." Educate them, and they usually do the right thing. Second, the trend with democracies worldwide is toward broader citizen involvement. Democracy occurs in many kinds of places and involves different classes and races of people, but the common element is a desire of citizens to exercise some control over their destinies.

Certainly, we who live in democratic countries applauded when citizens of Eastern Europe helped topple the Berlin Wall and bring down the Iron Curtain. We thrilled to the inspiring words of leaders such as Václav Havel in the Czech Republic, who articulated this new spirit of freedom. Here in our country, meanwhile, our citizens are also experiencing a civic renewal that shows promising results. We see this development in the current resistance to ugly, dispiriting sprawl; we see it in the fight for campaign finance reform;

and we see it in the concern about violence and gratuitous sex in our enter-
tainment media. Civic renewal also stretches to the neighborhood level, where
residents have taken back their streets from drugs and violence.[9]

Civic renewal has even begun to influence the newspaper industry, in which
I have worked and studied for more than a quarter century. In the last decade, "civic journalism" has emerged to reconnect people to their public institutions and help them deliberate as citizens, rather than merely respond to
campaign propaganda. Journalists have grasped the important connection
between an energized and interested citizenry and the circulation of their
newspapers. The same principle applies for broadcast journalism.

How, then, do civic reformers speed up the democratic process in Alabama? How do we redouble our efforts to educate our citizens while trans-
forming their current role into grassroots activism?

First, as I indicated earlier, the best strategy lies in intensifying the crusade
for a new state constitution. Difficult as this prospect may be, the potential
payoff in terms not only of better government but also of an energized citizenry makes constitutional reform the ultimate expression of a new Alabama.
It holds out hope for the future while encouraging Alabamians to acquire the
political and civic skills they will need to change their state's political culture
so that it values and sustains democracy.

Something in the reformers' favor is the power of truth. After all, it is
relatively easy to persuade a fair-minded citizen why Alabama desperately
needs a new charter. The impenetrable language of the present 315,000-word
document makes a great argument in itself. The problem is not so much the
document's length as what it says or, equally important, fails to say about
democracy in the twenty-first century. It is inconceivable that a representative body of citizens today would draft a document that resembles the 1901
constitution, now amended 706 times as of this writing. Also, our urban voters are beginning to understand the lunacy of denying their local officials the
authority they need to manage growth wisely and provide good schools and
other public services.

Second, advocates for a new constitution can employ the force of moral
leadership. The 1901 constitution deliberately discriminated against African
Americans and working-class whites, while promoting and protecting the
interests of a wealthy elite. It continues to favor the rich and punish the poor
through the nation's most regressive tax system.

Finally, a constitutional crusade can stretch across party, class, and racial
lines to unite Alabamians in favor of positive change. It can draw citizens
into active civic life and perhaps encourage many of them to seek public

office. We could hope to see women comprise at least a third of the delegates to a constitutional convention. Imagine what a difference such representation could make in helping delegates face the issues that most concern our working families.

No doubt many skeptics will argue that until a strong governor steps forward to lead, none of this dream will materialize. I hear this wisdom from my colleagues in political science, and I read similar observations in the press. Yet it is also apparent that we in Alabama cannot wait for a political messiah. We citizens have too much work to do. Our job is to build democracy from the bottom up, rather than be content with crumbs from the top down. When citizens organize to demand better government, the politicians will run quickly to catch up. In other words, we can create a climate in which strong and capable leadership can emerge.

Evidence of this strategy's efficacy can be seen in how Governor Don Siegelman, a Democrat, embraced constitutional reform in the spring of 2001, after having dismissed its chances earlier in his term. In short order, his Republican rival, Lieutenant Governor Steve Windom, publicly endorsed a new constitution as well and, like Siegelman, called for a convention to write a new document. Also in the summer of 2001, Congressman Bob Riley made a strong case for reform when he announced his candidacy for the Republican nomination for governor. (Secretary of State Jim Bennett, also a Republican, had long been a strong advocate for reform.) Siegelman followed through with his commitment by making constitutional reform the centerpiece of his State of the State address to the legislature at the beginning of the 2002 session. Thus as of this writing, reform has firm champions among the two major parties' contenders for the gubernatorial chair in the November election.

What encouraged these leading politicians to become reformers? First, they responded as any good politician would to a growing citizens movement. Second, they realized that there was little to be gained from continuing to ignore the state's fundamental weaknesses, as an educational funding crisis threatened to devastate the state's schools and universities.

I believe constitutional reform will succeed this time in Alabama, but not because this good idea is inevitable. After all, as the essays in this volume make clear, our state is notorious for breaking reformers' hearts. The idea will flourish because for the first time it has behind it the kind of genuine and growing grassroots constituency that ACCR promotes and many politicians now recognize. No reform-minded governor in the last century has enjoyed this kind of support for constitutional change. By concentrating on building support from the ground up, rather than from the top down, reformers can create the all-important popular base that is necessary to overcome the predictable resistance of those who have benefited the most under the present constitution

How long will this process take? There are too many variables for anyone to provide a succinct answer. As we saw with America's declaration of war against terrorism, events and forces outside of Alabama can suddenly change the national discourse. The state of the economy is an important factor, for citizens typically are less inclined to question the status quo when times are good—at least for them. And the continued interest of the press and the politicians who read it will have a large part in keeping reform on the public's agenda. But I think a sufficient foundation has been laid upon which to erect a more efficient and responsive government than the one we have known for at least the last century. Moreover, and I repeat, the very act of laying this foundation through a sustained citizens movement helps invigorate Alabama's civic life and draws more people into the political process.

We citizens cannot make amends to all the many thousands of people who were victims a century ago of the present constitution's antidemocratic provisions. As Thomas Corts likes to point out, no one alive today had anything to do with writing that wretched document. But acting together through a renewed and hopeful civic spirit, we citizens can ensure that no one is left behind in the Alabama of the future. We can write a new constitution and show ourselves—and the world—what kind of people we aspire to be.

Notes

1. Robert D. Putnam, *Bowling Alone: The Collapse and Revival of American Community* (New York: Simon and Schuster, 2000), 411. Putnam continues the conversation about civic participation that began with Alexis de Tocqueville in *Democracy in America*, vol. 2, part 2, chapters 2–8, and continued with such notable works as Robert Neely Bellah, ed., *Habits of the Heart: Individualism and Commitment in American Life*, rev. ed. (Berkeley: University of California Press, 1996).

2. Michael Schudson, *The Good Citizen: A History of American Civic Life* (Cambridge: Harvard University Press, 1999), 296–300.

3. Putnam, *Bowling Alone*, 19.

4. Benjamin R. Barber, *A Passion for Democracy: American Essays* (Princeton: Princeton University Press, 1998), 147.

5. *Birmingham News*, March 14, 1999.

6. Daniel J. Elazar, *American Federalism: A View From the States* (New York: Thomas Y. Crowell, 1966), 79–93, as cited in Putnam, *Bowling Alone*, 346–47.

7. See Anne Permaloff and Carl Grafton for their thoughtful application of Elazar's political cultures to *Political Power in Alabama: The More Things Change...* (Athens: University of Georgia Press, 1995), 63–65.

8. A poll conducted for the *Mobile Register,* for example, and published by the newspaper on May 14, 2000, found that 57 percent of respondents favored a new constitution, and the majority wanted a convention to write the document. More recent polls have shown such support continuing to grow.

9. For a good overview of this development, see Carmen Sirianni and Lewis Friedland, *Civic Innovation in America: Community Empowerment, Public Policy, and the Movement for Civic Renewal* (Berkeley: University of California Press, 2001).

Suggestions for Further Reading

Abernethy, Thomas P. *The Formative Period in Alabama, 1815–1828*. Tuscaloosa: University of Alabama Press, 1965.

Alabama. Constitutional Convention. *Journal of the Proceedings of the Constitutional Convention of the State of Alabama*. Montgomery, Ala.: Brown Printing, 1901.

———. *Official Proceedings of the Constitutional Convention of the State of Alabama, May 21st, 1901, to September 3rd, 1901*. Wetumpka, Ala.: Wetumpka Printing, 1940.

Bailey, Hugh C. *Edgar Gardner Murphy: Gentle Progressive*. Coral Gables: University of Miami Press, 1966.

Barnard, William D. *Dixiecrats and Democrats: Alabama Politics, 1942–1950*. University: University of Alabama Press, 1974.

Bond, Horace M. *Negro Education in Alabama: A Study in Cotton and Steel*. Washington, D.C.: Associated Publishers, 1939.

Brewer, Albert P., and Charles D. Cole. *Brewer and Cole, Alabama Constitutional Law*. Birmingham: Samford University Press, 1992.

Carter, Dan T. *The Politics of Rage: George Wallace, the Origins of the New Conservatism, and the Transformation of American Politics*. New York: Simon and Schuster, 1995.

Doster, James. *Railroads and Alabama Politics, 1875–1914*. Tuscaloosa: University of Alabama Press, 1957.

Ehrenhalt, Alan. *The United States of Ambition*. Times Books, 1992.

Flynt, Wayne. *Poor but Proud: Alabama's Poor Whites*. Tuscaloosa: University of Alabama Press, 1989.

Going, Allen J. *Bourbon Democracy in Alabama, 1874–1890*. Tuscaloosa: University of Alabama Press, 1951. Reprinted 1992.

Grafton, Carl, and Anne Permaloff. *Big Mules and Branchheads: James E. Folsom and Political Power in Alabama*. Athens: University of Georgia Press, 1985.

Hackney, Sheldon. *Populism to Progressivism in Alabama.* Princeton: Princeton University Press, 1969.

Harlan, Louis R. *Booker T. Washington: The Wizard of Tuskegee, 1901–1915.* New York: Oxford University Press, 1983.

Jackson, Harvey H. *Rivers of History: Life on the Coosa, Tallapoosa, Cahaba, and Alabama.* Tuscaloosa: University of Alabama Press, 1995.

McMillan, Malcolm Cook. *Constitutional Development in Alabama, 1798–1901: A Study in Politics, the Negro, and Sectionalism.* Chapel Hill: University of North Carolina Press, 1955. Reprinted 1978.

McCurley, Robert C., ed. *Alabama Government Manual.* 8th ed. Tuscaloosa: Alabama Law Institute, 1991.

Permaloff, Anne, and Carl Grafton. *Political Power in Alabama: The More Things Change . . .* Athens: University of Georgia Press, 1995.

Reynolds, Gerald. *The Alabama Constitution of 1901: Antithesis of States Rights after Seventy-One Years.* Birmingham: Cumberland Samford Law Review, 1972.

Rogers, William Warren. *The One-Gallused Rebellion: Agrarianism in Alabama, 1865–1896.* Baton Rouge: Louisiana State University Press, 1970.

Rogers, William Warren, Robert David Ward, Leah Rawls Atkins, and Wayne Flynt. *Alabama: The History of a Deep South State.* Tuscaloosa: University of Alabama Press, 1994.

Sirianni, Carmen, and Lewis Friedland. *Civic Innovation in America: Community Empowerment, Public Policy, and the Movement for Civic Renewal.* Berkeley: University of California Press, 2001.

Stewart, William Histaspas. *The Alabama Constitutional Commission.* Tuscaloosa: Published for the Bureau of Public Administration by the University of Alabama Press, 1975.

Stewart, William Histaspas. *The Alabama State Constitution: A Reference Guide.* Westport, Conn.: Greenwood Press, 1994.

Stovall, James Glen, Patrick R. Cotter, and Samuel H. Fisher III. *Alabama Political Almanac.* 2nd ed. Tuscaloosa: University of Alabama Press, 1997.

Tarr, G. Alan. *Understanding State Constitutions.* Princeton: Princeton University Press, 1998.

Tarr, G. Alan, and Mary Cornelia Aldis Porter. *State Supreme Courts in State and Nation.* New Haven: Yale University Press, 1988.

Thomas, James D., and William H. Stewart. *Government and Politics of Alabama.* Lincoln: University of Nebraska Press, 1988.

Thomas, Mary Martha. *The New Woman in Alabama: Social Reforms and Suffrage, 1890–1920.* Tuscaloosa: University of Alabama Press, 1992.

Ward, Robert David, and William Warren Rogers. *Convicts, Coal, and the Banner Mine Tragedy.* University: University of Alabama Press, 1987.

Webb, Samuel L. *Two-Party Politics in the One-Party South: Alabama's Hill Country, 1874–1920.* Tuscaloosa: University of Alabama Press, 1998.

Articles

Brewer, Albert P. "Constitutional Revision in Alabama: History and Methodology." *Alabama Law Review* 48, no. 2 (1997): 583–612.
———. "Why Alabama Needs a New Constitution." *Alabama Heritage,* Fall 2002, 6–15.
Flynt, Wayne, and Keith Ward. "Taxes, Taxes, Taxes: Alabama's Unresolved Dilemma." *Alabama Heritage,* Spring 1992, 7–21.
Pruitt, Paul M., Jr. "Defender of the Voteless: Joseph C. Manning Views the Disfranchisement Era in Alabama." *Alabama Historical Quarterly* 43, no. 3 (1981): 171–85.

Symposium Papers (Available at www.constitutionalreform.org)
Brown, Jess. "Legislative Provisions in the Alabama Constitution: Evolution, Commentary and Prescription." In *Proceedings and Selected Papers from the Symposium on the Alabama Constitution, December 13–15, 1995,* 31–35. Center for Governmental Services, Auburn University.
Johnson, Gerald W. "The Alabama Constitution: The People's Fundamental Document." *Proceedings and Selected Papers from the Symposium on the Alabama Constitution, December 13–15, 1995,* 6–8. Center for Governmental Services, Auburn University.
Ward, Keith J. "Taxes and Finance in the Alabama Constitution." In *Proceedings and Selected Papers from the Symposium on the Alabama Constitution, December 13–15, 1995,* 24–26. Center for Governmental Services, Auburn University.

Newspaper Series (Available at www.constitutionalreform.org)
"A New Century—A New Constitution," *Birmingham News,* January 28–February 4, 2001.
"Century of Shame," *Mobile Register,* October 15–21, 2000.
"Dixie's Broken Heart," *Mobile Register,* October 11–17, 1998.
"Future in the Balance," *New York Times* Regional Newspapers (Florence, Gadsden, Tuscaloosa), November 18–25, 2001.
"Sin of the Fathers," *Mobile Register,* December 11, 1994.
"A State Buried in Paper," *Huntsville Times,* May 12–17, 2000.

Contributors

WAYNE FLYNT is Distinguished University Professor at Auburn University. His many books include *Alabama Baptists: Southern Baptists in the Heart of Dixie* (1998), *Dixie's Forgotten People: The South's Poor Whites* (1978), and *Poor but Proud: Alabama's Poor Whites* (1989). He is a prolific speaker and contributor to the state's newspapers on reform in Alabama. In recognition of his work in nonfiction, the University of Alabama presented him its Clarence Cason Writing Award for 2002.

HARVEY H. JACKSON III is Professor of History and Head of the Department of History and Foreign Languages at Jacksonville State University. His specialty is southern history and particularly the history of Alabama. Recent books include *Rivers of History: Life on the Coosa, Tallapoosa, Cahaba, and Alabama* (1995) and *Putting Loafing Streams to Work: The Building of Lay, Mitchell, Martin, and Jordan Dams, 1910–1929* (1997). He writes regularly for the state's newspapers and is a frequent lecturer on the history of the Alabama Constitution.

BRADLEY MOODY is Associate Professor of Political Science and Public Administration at Auburn University Montgomery. He held the position of Distinguished Teaching Professor at Auburn University Montgomery from 1997 to 2000 and received the Auburn University Montgomery Alumni Association's Faculty Service Award in 1984 for his teaching and service contributions. His primary teaching and research interests are in the areas of state and local politics, managing public organizations, and the American presidency.

ANNE PERMALOFF is Professor of Political Science and Public Administration and Distinguished Research Professor at Auburn University Montgomery. She is coauthor of *Political Power in Alabama: The More Things Change*... (1995, named an Outstanding Academic Book by *Choice*) and *Big Mules and Branchheads: James E. Folsom and Political Power in Alabama* (1985). Her more than thirty-five academic articles cover computer applications in political science, public budgeting, Alabama politics, and public policy. She is active in civic work and is a regular contributor to the state's commentary pages.

ROBERT MARTIN SCHAEFER is the Chair of the Department of Social and Behavioral Sciences and Associate Professor of Political Science at the University of Mobile. He is coeditor of *American Political Rhetoric* (4th ed., 2001) and author of a forthcoming book on Walker Percy. He is President of the Alabama Political Science Association (2000–2001) and also President of Society Mobile–La Habana.

WILLIAM H. STEWART is Professor Emeritus of Political Science at the University of Alabama and the former Chairman of the Department of Political Science. He is among the most prolific researchers on government and politics in Alabama. He is the coauthor of *Alabama Government and Politics* (1988) and the author of *The Alabama State Constitution* (1994). He is widely quoted by political reporters, and he writes a weekly history column for his hometown newspaper in Hartselle, Alabama.

JOE A. SUMNERS is Director of the Economic Development Institute at Auburn University. He helped plan and organize the 1995 Symposium on the Alabama Constitution and edited the Symposium's *Proceedings*. He is author of *Governing Alabama: The People's Choice*, an issues book used in Alabama high schools. His essay "The 1901 Alabama Constitution: Alabama's Anchor" appeared in *Alabama Issues 1998*. He holds a doctorate in political science from the University of Georgia and has written articles that have appeared in the *American Political Science Review* and *Evaluation and Program Planning*.

G. ALAN TARR is Professor of Political Science at Rutgers University, Camden Campus. He is a specialist in constitutional law and the judicial process and also teaches courses in the history of political theory. He is a Director of the Council for State Constitutional Studies, the editor of a major reference series on American state constitutions, and the author of numerous books and articles on constitutionalism. He has been a consultant on the development of subnational constitutions in Russia and South Africa.

BAILEY THOMSON is Associate Professor of Journalism at the University of Alabama and coordinator of his department's graduate studies. In addition to his scholarly work on the history of journalism, he writes frequently for the state's newspapers on constitutional reform. His editorial series "Dixie's Broken Heart," which appeared in the *Mobile Register,* won a Distinguished Writing Award from the American Association of Newspaper Editors and was featured in *Best Newspaper Writing of 1999,* published by the Poynter Institute.

HOWARD P. WALTHALL, SR., is Professor of Law at Samford University's Cumberland School of Law in Birmingham. He is director of Cumberland's State Constitutional Law Project. Currently, he is coauthor of a forthcoming book titled *Alabama's Supreme Court and Legal Institutions: A History.*

SAMUEL L. WEBB is Associate Professor of History at the University of Alabama at Birmingham. His primary interests are in southern political history and in the constitutional and legal history of the nation. He is the coeditor of *Alabama Governors: A Political History of the State* (2001) and the author of *Two-Party Politics in the One-Party South: Alabama's Hill Country, 1874–1920* (1997).

JAMES W. WILLIAMS, JR., has served as Executive Director of the Public Affairs Research Council of Alabama since its inception in 1988. In that position, he speaks and writes frequently about public policy issues. Before coming to Alabama in 1988, he worked for sixteen years in privately supported governmental research agencies located in Texas and Michigan. He is past president and current secretary of the Governmental Research Association of the United States, a professional organization of individuals in the governmental research field.